HIGH COURT CASE SUMMARIES™

PROPERTY

Keyed to Dukeminier, Krier, Alexander, Schill, and Strahilevitz's Casebook on Property, 8th Edition

WEST
ACADEMIC
PUBLISHING

© West, a Thomson business, 2002, 2007
© 2011 Thomson Reuters
© 2015 LEG, Inc. d/b/a West Academic
    444 Cedar Street, Suite 700
    St. Paul, MN 55101
    1-877-888-1330

West, West Academic Publishing, and West Academic are trademarks of West Publishing Corporation, used under license.

Printed in the United States of America

ISBN: 978-1-63459-589-6

Table of Contents

_____

Alphabetical Table of Cases

CHAPTER ONE

First Possession: Acquisition of Property by Discovery, Capture, and Creation

Johnson v. M'Intosh

Instant Facts: M'Intosh (D) acquired title to land under grant from the United States; Johnson (P) acquired title to the same land by purchase from the Painkeshaw Indians.

Black Letter Rule: Discovery of land in America by a European power gives absolute title subject only to the Indian right of occupancy.

Pierson v. Post

Instant Facts: While Post (P) was pursuing a fox, Pierson (D) killed the fox and took possession it.

Black Letter Rule: A hunter must either trap or mortally wound a wild animal in order to acquire title to it.

Ghen v. Rich

Instant Facts: Ghen (P) shot and killed a whale, which sank to the bottom of the sea. Three days later, Ellis found the whale on the shore and sold it to Rich (D).

Black Letter Rule: Title to a wild animal is acquired when a hunter apprehends the beast in accordance with custom.

Keeble v. Hickeringill

Instant Facts: When Keeble (P) lured wildfowl to his land with decoys, Hickeringill (D) frightened the wildfowl away by firing a gun.

Black Letter Rule: A person may not maliciously prevent another from capturing wild animals in the pursuit of his trade.

International News Service v. Associated Press

Instant Facts: International News Service (D) copied news that Associated Press (P) gathered.

Black Letter Rule: Where a company has expended resources in creating news and information, the creator can exclude others from copying it until its commercial value as news has passed away.

Feist Publications, Inc. v. Rural Telephone Service Co.

Instant Facts: A publisher of white pages and yellow pages that was not in the telephone business copied the subscriber information in the telephone service provider's directory for use in its own publications, and the telephone company sued for copyright infringement.

Black Letter Rule: The names, towns, and telephone numbers listed in a run-of-the-mill alphabetical telephone directory are not protected by copyright.

Harper & Row Publishers, Inc. v. Nation Enterprises

Instant Facts: Time magazine contracted with Harper & Row (P) to publish an article about President Gerald Ford's memoirs, which Harper & Row was soon going to publish in their entirety, but The Nation magazine got a copy of the manuscript and published verbatim excerpts in advance of Time's story; after Time refused to pay the contract price to Harper & Row (P), the publishing company sued The Nation (D) for copyright infringement.

Black Letter Rule: The prepublication use of verbatim excerpts from an as-yet unpublished work does not constitute fair use.

Diamond v. Chakrabarty

Instant Facts: Chakrabarty (P) invented a bacterium that broke down crude oil and could be used to remediate oil spills; he applied for patents for the process and the bacterium, and the latter was initially denied, but the appellate court reversed the denial.

Black Letter Rule: The language employed in the Patent Act is given broad application, such that a micro-organism that is the product of human ingenuity, as opposed to nature, is patentable.

White v. Samsung Electronics America, Inc.

Instant Facts: Samsung (D) printed advertisements containing a robot wearing a blond wig and a dress while turning letters on a set resembling the "Wheel of Fortune" game show set, and Vanna White (P) sued for privacy violations.

Black Letter Rule: The common law right of privacy prohibits the appropriation of one's identity, regardless of the means employed.

Moore v. Regents of the University of California

Instant Facts: The Regents (D) removed Moore's (P) spleen and retained it for research purposes. As a result of this research, the Regents (D) established a cell line from Moore's (P) cells and obtained a patent for it.

Black Letter Rule: A doctor has a duty to disclose the extent of his research and economic interests in a patient's body parts. Human body parts are not property such that they may be converted.

Pocono Springs Civic Association, Inc. v. MacKenzie

Instant Facts: The owners of a vacant lot in a housing development attempted to abandon the lot in order to avoid having to pay association fees.

Black Letter Rule: A covenant running with the land cannot be terminated by abandonment when the owner still holds title in fee simple absolute.

Hawkins v. Mahoney

Instant Facts: After Hawkins (P) escaped, the prison got rid of all of his personal property, even though at the time he had already been apprehended and returned to the prison, and has asked for his property back.

Black Letter Rule: The presumption or inference of intent to abandon one's property, based solely on the acts of the owner, is a rebuttable presumption.

Eyerman v. Mercantile Trust Co.

Instant Facts: Neighbors of a deceased woman sought the court's help in preventing the demolition of the decedent's home, despite a provision in the dead woman's will asking that the home be razed and the empty lot sold.

Black Letter Rule: The taking of property by inheritance or a will is not an absolute right, but is one created by the laws of the state, and the state may foreclose that right or make it conditional, within constitutional limits.

Johnson v. M'Intosh

(Successor to Indian Title) v. (Successor to United States Title)

21 U.S. (8 Wheat) 543 (1823)

COURT DECLARES THAT CONQUEST HAS VESTED TITLE IN THE UNITED STATES THAT IS SUPERIOR TO THE TITLE OF THE INDIANS

■ **INSTANT FACTS** M'Intosh (D) acquired title to land under grant from the United States; Johnson (P) acquired title to the same land by purchase from the Painkeshaw Indians.

■ **BLACK LETTER RULE** Discovery of land in America by a European power gives absolute title subject only to the Indian right of occupancy.

■ **PROCEDURAL BASIS**

Appeal from judgment in action to eject.

■ **FACTS**

Johnson (P) purchased land from the Chiefs of the Piankeshaw Indians. The Chiefs were duly vested by the tribe to represent those rights that the Indians had. M'Intosh (D) acquired title to this same piece of land by grant from the United States. The United States obtained this land by grant from Virginia.

■ **ISSUE**

Is title by grant from a discovering nation superior to title obtained by purchase from those that the nation conquered?

■ **DECISION AND RATIONALE**

(Marshall, J.) Yes. Upon the discovery of America, the nations of Europe agreed that discovery would vest title in the discovering nation against all other powers of Europe. The discoverer governed its relations with the natives as it deemed fit. In the establishment of these relations, the Indians were given the right to occupancy. However, their right to absolute title was divested and taken by the discoverer. This principle, that title vests in the European nation that discovers the land, was especially recognized by England. As early as 1496 the King of England commissioned an explorer to take title to all land discovered by the explorer, except land previously discovered by Christian people. After the revolution, title to all land passed from Great Britain to the colonies. As mentioned, this title was absolute subject only to the Indian right of occupancy. The colonies affirmed the principle that title traced to a discovery is superior to Indian title. Virginia, for example, declared the "exclusive right of pre-emption from the Indians." The land which is at controversy in this case was granted from Virginia to the United States. The United States has also affirmed the principle that title traced to a discovery is superior to Indian title. The title which discovery has given is as follows: Discovery gives an exclusive right to extinguish an Indian right of occupancy either by purchase or by conquest. This court will not decide whether it is just to expel the Indians. "Conquest gives a title which the courts of the conqueror cannot deny, whatever the private and speculative opinions of individuals may be." Usually the principles of human relations dictate that conquered peoples be allowed to assimilate with the conqueror. However, since the Indians were fierce savages, they could not be assimilated. In consequence, the Indians were driven out by the sword. Those that were not warlike retained the right to occupancy. However they did not have the right to grant land. Consequently, the Piankeshaw Indians did not have the right to sell the land to Johnson (P). Judgment affirmed.

Analysis:

Conquest is the taking of land by force. In actuality, this is how the Europeans came to own much of the Americas. Though this doctrine may disturb many, it has very relevant doctrinal underpinnings. The reasoning comes from John Locke's labor theory. According to this theory, when a man mixes his labor with a parcel of land, by cultivating it for example, he owns that piece of land. The Europeans owned the land because they worked it. Whether the reasoning is faulty or not, the idea is important. One of the goals of property law is to encourage the efficient and productive use of land. This principle appears, for example, in the law of adverse possession, nuisance, and eminent domain.

■ **CASE VOCABULARY**

ABSOLUTE TITLE: Perfect title; unencumbered title.

CEDE: To transfer, usually from one government to another.

CONVEY: To transfer realty to another person.

CONVEYANCE: The transfer of land from one person to another.

EJECTMENT: An action to recover the possession of land.

OCCUPANCE: Same as possession.

PATENT: A grant of public property by the United States.

REGAL GOVERNMENT: The state.

SOVEREIGN: A state which has supreme authority.

VEST: To give a right to.

Pierson v. Post

(Killer of Fox) v. (Pursuer of Fox)

3 Cai. R. 175, 2 Am.Dec. 264 (1805)

COURT DECLARES THAT A HUNTER MUST EITHER TRAP OR MORTALLY WOUND A WILD ANIMAL BEFORE HE ACQUIRES TITLE TO IT

■ **INSTANT FACTS** While Post (P) was pursuing a fox, Pierson (D) killed the fox and took possession it.

■ **BLACK LETTER RULE** A hunter must either trap or mortally wound a wild animal in order to acquire title to it.

render its escape virtually impossible

takes place on public land

■ **PROCEDURAL BASIS**

Writ of Certiorari after judgment in action for damages for trespass on the case.

■ **FACTS**

Post (P) discovered a fox on wild and uninhabited land. In an attempt to capture the fox Post (P) began to hunt and pursue the fox with his dogs. Even though Pierson (D) knew that Post (P) was hunting the fox, he killed the fox and took possession of it. Post (P) contends that he acquired title to the fox because he was the first to hunt it. Pierson (D) maintains that he acquired title to the fox because he killed the fox.

■ **ISSUE**

Does mere pursuit of a wild animal vest title in the pursuer?

Issue: How does one acquire ownership in wild animals?

■ **DECISION AND RATIONALE**

(Tompkins, J.) No. Since a fox is a wild animal, a property right can be acquired in it only if the hunter "occupies" it. Some authorities feel that a hunter can occupy a wild animal only if he traps it. Other authorities feel that a hunter can occupy a wild animal if he mortally wounds it and remains in pursuit. This is because a hunter in pursuit of a mortally wounded animal has effectively captured the animal. But all authorities agree that mere pursuit of a wild animal is insufficient to vest title in the hunter. This is to prevent litigation. If mere pursuit were to vest title, it would be very difficult to determine who was the first to pursue. Since Post (P) was in mere pursuit of the fox, he acquired no title to it. Judgment reversed.

P. 20 By so mortally maiming it or entrapping it as to render its escape a virtual impossibility

■ **DISSENT**

(Livingston, J.) Since foxes are a public nuisance, the killing of foxes is in the public interest. Therefore, the rule that this court should adopt would encourage the destruction of these animals. The following rule accomplishes this: A pursuer acquires title to a wild animal if he is in reach of the animal or if he has a reasonable prospect of capturing the animal. Since it is nearly certain that Post (P) would have captured the fox, the judgment below should be affirmed.

Analysis:

There are two justifications advanced for the rule that capture is required to vest title. First, this rule advances society's goal of capturing wild animals (the desire to make "efficient use" of property). Society rewards the captor only because this rule fosters competition. More competition means more hunters. More hunters results in the more efficient capturing of wild animals. The second reason for this rule is that it is easy to administer. While it is easy to determine who has captured a wild animal, it would be very difficult to determine who was the first to pursue a wild animal. Alternatively, one may use the principle of first in time to understand this case: "He who first occupies a wild animal owns it." Of course, the fight is over whether one must be the first to chase a wild animal or the first to capture it. The majority rules that one must be the first to capture it. Interestingly, the majority went against the established custom, which recognized hot pursuit as vesting a right of ownership in the pursuer.

■ **CASE VOCABULARY**

BODILY SEISIN: Actual physical possession of some body, *e.g.*, a wild animal.

CERTIORARI: A writ issued by a superior court ordering an inferior court to produce a record of a case tried in the inferior court; the writ is a process by which the superior court may review the proceedings below.

CONSTRUCTIVE POSSESSION: Dominion and control over an object, though not physical possession.

FERAE NATURAE: A wild animal.

HOSTEM HUMANI GENERIS: Enemies of the human race.

INSTITUTE: A textbook containing principles of law.

PANDECTS: A compilation of Roman law, consisting of the chief ideas of the most authoritative jurists.

PURSUER: One who attempts to capture property.

RATIONE SOLI: Because of the land; in the context of title to animals this refers to ownership because of the presence of the wild animal on the claimant's land.

[handwritten notes:] first in first time, first in right in first in time but first in time to chase or first to capture in time majority says first in time to capture

[handwritten notes:] B/C on public property, public land rule of capture applies

Ghen v. Rich

(Hunter) v. (Finder)

8 F. 159 (D. Mass. 1881)

COURT DECLARES THAT TITLE TO A WILD ANIMAL IS ACQUIRED WHEN THE HUNTER APPREHENDS THE BEAST IN ACCORD WITH CUSTOM

■ **INSTANT FACTS** Ghen (P) shot and killed a whale, which sank to the bottom of the sea. Three days later, Ellis found the whale on the shore and sold it to Rich (D).

■ **BLACK LETTER RULE** Title to a wild animal is acquired when a hunter apprehends the beast in accordance with custom.

[handwritten: Is this at odds with Pierson?]

[handwritten: Custom here is more efficient than the general rule that wild animals must be captured]

[handwritten: can I apprehend an animal w/o trapping or mortally wounding it?]

■ **PROCEDURAL BASIS**

Suit in trial court for damages for conversion of property.

■ **FACTS**

Ghen (P) shot and killed a whale in Cape Cod, which sank to the bottom of the sea. Three days later Ellis found the whale on the shore and sold it to Rich (D). In killing the whale, Ghen (P) followed the local custom of Cape Cod. The custom is as follows: Fishermen kill the whales with bomb-lances. Each fisherman's lance leaves a unique brand so that the killer of the whale can be known. When the whales are killed, they sink to the bottom, but rise again to the surface in two to three days. The whales then float out to sea or float ashore. When a whale floats ashore, the finder usually sends word to the killer. The killer retrieves the whale and usually pays a small fee to the finder. This business and custom is practiced by few people since it requires great skill, experience, and capital. Ghen (P) contends that title may be acquired when the hunter apprehends a beast in accordance with custom. Rich (D) contends that custom does not govern the acquisition of title.

■ **ISSUE**

Is title to a wild animal acquired when a hunter apprehends the beast in accordance with custom?

■ **DECISION AND RATIONALE**

(Nelson, J.) Yes. Other cases have held that title may be acquired by a hunter if he apprehends the beast in accordance with custom. This is because a custom usually embraces an entire industry. When a custom embraces an entire industry, there is no need for the court to fashion a judge-made rule. Rather, the custom is good enough. Custom is compelling in this case for several reasons: the custom affects few people; it has been relied upon for many years; it requires the hunter to perform all that is possible given the circumstances of whale hunting in Cape Cod; it gives a reasonable fee to the finder; without this custom, this industry would die, since no person would engage in the industry if his labor could be appropriated by a chance finder. Since Ghen (P) captured the whale in accordance with the custom of Cape Cod, title has vested in him. Judgment for Plaintiff.

[handwritten: So even though Ellis found the whale, Ghen was the one who shot + killed the whale + did this in accordance with custom]

[handwritten: this could also coincide with Pierson where trapping/ mortally wounding gives title]

[handwritten: YES!]

Analysis:

One of the ways to understand this case is to recall one of the goals of property law. Property law should promote the efficient capture of wild animals. The custom of a local hunting trade is often more efficient than the general rule that wild animals must be captured, because a hunting custom has been refined to fit the particular needs of that trade. In this case, for example, it is more efficient to award the whale to the killer, even though he does not immediately capture it, because the killer ship can go off and look for other whales without waiting for the dead whale to rise to the surface. In *Pierson v. Post* it was custom to award the wild fox to the man first in hot pursuit. In that case, however, the custom did not promote the efficient capture of wild animals, or at least the majority did not think that the custom promoted this goal. Thus, custom did not prevail.

So this actually coincides w/ the majority in Pierson, even though Pierson goes against a custom and Ghen upholds the custom

■ CASE VOCABULARY

APPROPRIATION: The act of making a particular thing one's own.

DECEIT: A misrepresentation of the truth so as to induce another person to act in a particular manner.

FRAUD: A misrepresentation of the truth so as to induce another person to act in a particular manner.

LIBEL: In maritime law, the equivalent of a lawsuit.

LIBELLANT: In maritime law, the equivalent of a plaintiff.

MARITIME LAW: That system of law which pertains to the sea and commerce thereon.

RESPONDENT: Defendant

STATUTE OF LIMITATIONS: The time period that a person must possess an object before he takes title to it.

USAGE: A local custom which is so well-established that all are presumed to act with reference thereto.

Keeble v. Hickeringill

(Hunter) v. (Duck Frightener)

(1707) 11 East 574, 103 Eng.Rep. 1127; 11 Mod. 74, 130 (as Keble v. Hickringill); 3 Salk. 9 (as Keeble v. Hickeringhall)

COURT DECLARES THAT AN INDIVIDUAL MAY NOT MALICIOUSLY PREVENT ANOTHER FROM CAPTURING WILD ANIMALS IN PURSUIT OF HIS TRADE

■ **INSTANT FACTS** When Keeble (P) lured wildfowl to his land with decoys, Hickeringill (D) frightened the wildfowl away by firing a gun.

■ **BLACK LETTER RULE** A person may not maliciously prevent another from capturing wild animals in the pursuit of his trade.

■ **PROCEDURAL BASIS**

Appeal from judgment in action for damages for interfering with the capture of wild animals.

■ **FACTS**

↗ private property

Keeble (P) owned a pond. Keeble lawfully (P) placed decoys and other equipment near the pond to lure and catch wildfowl. Keeble (P) hunted the wild animals in pursuit of his trade. With the purpose of frightening away the wildfowl, Hickeringill (D) fired a gun three times near the pond. The wildfowl were permanently frightened away.

■ **ISSUE**

May a landowner, in pursuit of his trade, lawfully capture wildfowl free of the malicious interference of another?

■ **DECISION AND RATIONALE**

(Holt, J.) Yes. There are two public policy reasons why a landowner may, in pursuit of his trade, lawfully capture wildfowl free of the malicious interference of another. First, every man should be able to enjoy the use of his land as he sees fit so long as the use is lawful. Second, the capture of wildfowl in pursuit of a trade is profitable; it creates wealth for the tradesman, for employees, and for the nation at large. There are cases where an individual may interfere with another in the pursuit of his trade. For example, if Hickeringill (D) had lured the wildfowl away from Keeble's (P) land by setting up decoys on his own land, there would be no action. This is because Hickeringill (D) also has the right to enjoy his land as he sees fit. But Hickeringill (D) did not lure the wildfowl away by placing decoys on his own land. He maliciously frightened the wildfowl away by firing a gun. Therefore, he is liable for damages. Judgment affirmed.

Analysis:

The doctrine of ratione soli asserts that an owner of land owns the wild animals on that land. Note, however, that this rule may discourage the efficient capturing of wild animals if the owner refuses to capture them. On the other hand, it discourages trespassing. Were it not for this rule individuals may be tempted to trespass on another's land to be the first to capture a wild a This doctrine had little influence on the Court's decision, however. The doctrine is nevertl

---

important because it serves to protect a landowner's constructive right to possession as against a trespasser. As an interesting side note, at least one court faced with a dispute over ownership of oil and gas used the rules set forth in the wild animal cases to resolve the dispute, likening fugitive natural resources like oil and gas to wild animals. This approach has been strongly criticized, though, and has not been followed. The capture rule has been identified as similar to the first in time, first in right rule of prior appropriation in western water law.

■ **CASE VOCABULARY**

ACTION UPON THE CASE: A general term for a lawsuit.

FIRST IN TIME: The principle that he who first takes possession to unclaimed property takes title.

LAWFUL: Authorized by the law; sanctioned by the law.

MALICIOUS: Having evil motives.

THITHER: Toward a particular place.

VIVARY: A place for keeping wild animals.

International News Service v. Associated Press

(Copier) v. (Creator)

248 U.S. 215, 39 S.Ct. 68 (1918)

U.S. SUPREME COURT DECLARES THAT NEWLY PRINTED NEWS IS PROTECTED FROM COPYING

■ **INSTANT FACTS** International News Service (D) copied news that Associated Press (P) gathered.

■ **BLACK LETTER RULE** Where a company has expended resources in creating news and information, the creator can exclude others from copying it until its commercial value as news has passed away.

■ **PROCEDURAL BASIS**

Appeal from judgment in action for injunction to prevent the copying of news.

■ **FACTS**

The Associated Press (P) gathered news from several member newspapers. This collection of news was then made available to all of the members of Associated Press (P). International News Service (D) copied news from one of the papers and published it.

■ **ISSUE**

Is there a property interest in freshly printed news that allows the creator to prevent others from copying it?

■ **DECISION AND RATIONALE**

Yes. Since Associated Press (P) has invested time and resources into the creation of the news, it can prevent others from copying the news until the commercial value of the news has passed away. If the court allowed the copying of fresh news, no news service could manage to stay in business.

Analysis:

This case can be viewed in two possible ways. First, we can understand the case as attempting to encourage the creation of property. In this case, AP (P) created a collection of news. This property can be viewed as intangible, that is, as intellectual property. So the court enjoined INS (D) from copying AP's (P) collection of news to encourage the creation of such news. Without such protection, the court reasoned, such collected news would not be created. Another way to view this case is to see it not as protecting intangible, intellectual property, but as protecting tangible property. In this view, the court is protecting the chattels (the words) themselves, not merely protecting the intellectual concept from being copied. This view is consistent with Cheney Brothers v. Doris Silk Corp. In that case, Doris Silk (D) was not appropriating the actual clothes but merely the intellectual idea. Since Cheney Brothers (P) had not patented the idea, they were not protected. Had Doris Silk (D) physically taken the chattels, as INS (D) had done in this case, it would have been held liable.

■ CASE VOCABULARY

APPROPRIATING: To take for oneself.

MISAPPROPRIATION: The improper taking of another's property for the sole purpose of capitalizing on the good name of the property owner.

PIRATING: The illegal reprinting or stealing of copyrighted material.

UNFAIR COMPETITION: Dishonest rivalry in commerce; the misappropriation for commercial gain of another's property.

Feist Publications, Inc. v. Rural Telephone Service Co.

(Publisher) v. (Telephone Company)

499 U.S. 340 (1991)

COMPILATIONS OF FACTS MUST BE SOMEWHAT ORIGINAL, OR CREATIVELY SELECTED OR ARRANGED, TO BE COPYRIGHTABLE

■ **INSTANT FACTS** A publisher of white pages and yellow pages that was not in the telephone business copied the subscriber information in the telephone service provider's directory for use in its own publications, and the telephone company sued for copyright infringement.

■ **BLACK LETTER RULE** The names, towns, and telephone numbers listed in a run-of-the-mill alphabetical telephone directory are not protected by copyright.

■ **PROCEDURAL BASIS**

Supreme Court review of a federal appellate court decision in the plaintiff's favor.

■ **FACTS**

Rural Telephone Service (P) provided telephone service to several Kansas communities. Rural (P) was required by state regulation to publish an annual directory consisting of both white pages and yellow pages. The white pages listed each subscriber's names, town, and phone number; the yellow pages listed the businesses in the community and included revenue-generating display advertising. Feist (D) was a publishing company that published telephone directories covering a broader geographic area. Feist (D) competed directly with Rural (P) for advertisers. Feist (D) was not a phone company, so it did not have direct access to subscribers' telephone numbers the way Rural (P) did. Feist (P) was able to enter into licensing agreements with the service providers for the other communities covered by its publications, but Rural (P) refused to allow Feist (D) access to its listings. Litigation ensued, and the district court held that Rural's (D) refusal was based on the unlawful purpose of extending its monopoly in the telephone business. Feist (D) then used Rural's (P) listings without Rural's (P) consent. Rural (P) had planted several fake listings in its phone books, so it knew Feist (P) was copying its listings. Rural (P) sued for copyright infringement, and the district court granted summary judgment in its favor. The Tenth Circuit affirmed, and the Supreme Court granted certiorari.

■ **ISSUE**

Did the copyright held by Rural (P) in its directory protect the names, towns, and telephone numbers copied by Feist (D)?

■ **DECISION AND RATIONALE**

(O'Connor, J.) No. The names, towns, and telephone numbers listed in a run-of-the-mill alphabetical telephone directory are not protected by copyright. Facts are not generally copyrightable, although compilations of facts may be. To qualify for copyright protection, the work must be original to the author. Even a slight amount of creativity will suffice. The distinction between facts and compilations is one between creation and discovery: the first person to find and report a fact has not created the fact; he or she has merely discovered its existence. Factual compilations, on the other hand, may possess the requisite originality. Even a directory that contains no protectable written expression, only facts, qualifies for copyright protection if it

---

features an original selection or arrangement. But even if a work is copyrighted, not every detail or component within it is entitled to protection. A subsequent compiler is free to use the facts included in another's publication to aid in preparing a competing work, as long as the competing work does not feature the same selection and arrangement. Copyright assures protection of original expression, but encourages others to build freely on the ideas and information contained in another's work. Thus, in the present context, only the compiler's selection and arrangement may be protected. The raw facts may be copied at will. The "sweat of the brow" doctrine used to protect compilers' hard work, but that doctrine has been rejected.

To establish copyright infringement, two elements must be proven: (1) ownership of a valid copyright; and (2) copying of constituent elements of the work that are original. The question here is whether Rural (P) has proved the second element. The raw data, consisting of names, towns, and phone numbers, was clearly not original, but the question remains whether Rural selected, coordinated, or arranged these uncopyrightable facts in an original way. Originality is not a rigorous standard, but it is not entirely meaningless either. Rural (P) fails to meet this very low threshold. Its selection, coordination, and arrangement of facts was entirely typical and devoid of even a trace of creativity, resulting in a garden-variety directory that listed subscribers alphabetically by surname. Reversed.

Analysis:

In this unanimous opinion delivered by Justice O'Connor, the Court held that the names, towns, and telephone numbers copied by Feist (D) were not original to Rural (P) and therefore were not protected by the valid copyright in Rural's (P) combined white and yellow pages directory. The Court reasoned that Rural's (P) white pages did not satisfy the minimum constitutional standards for copyright protection, because the information they included lacked the requisite originality. Rural (P) had not selected, coordinated, or arranged the uncopyrightable facts in any original way. The Court concluded that, "[b]ecause Rural's [(P)] white pages lack the requisite originality, Feist's [(D)] use of the listings cannot constitute infringement."

■ CASE VOCABULARY

COPYRIGHT: Statutory protection of work such as a literary work, musical composition, or film or other audiovisual creation giving the creator (or the holder of the copyright) the right to regulate the publication, reproduction, distribution, performance, or use of the copyrighted material for a certain period of time. It is an incorporeal right (*i.e.*, a right to something intangible as opposed to tangible, such as a right to land).

Harper & Row Publishers, Inc. v. Nation Enterprises

(Book Publisher) v. (Magazine Publisher)

471 U.S. 539 (1985)

THE RIGHT OF FIRST PUBLICATION IS SUBJECT TO THE RIGHT OF FAIR USE, BUT THERE WAS NO FAIR USE HERE

NEWS 9

Tragedy struck today as the Supreme Court ruled that news organizations can't use the "fair use" doctrine to steal.

stus.com

■ **INSTANT FACTS** Time magazine contracted with Harper & Row (P) to publish an article about President Gerald Ford's memoirs, which Harper & Row was soon going to publish in their entirety, but The Nation magazine got a copy of the manuscript and published verbatim excerpts in advance of Time's story; after Time refused to pay the contract price to Harper & Row (P), the publishing company sued The Nation (D) for copyright infringement.

■ **BLACK LETTER RULE** The prepublication use of verbatim excerpts from an as-yet unpublished work does not constitute fair use.

■ **PROCEDURAL BASIS**

Supreme Court review of an appellate decision reversing the trial court judgment in the plaintiff's favor.

■ **FACTS**

In February 1977, shortly after leaving the White House, President Ford contracted with Harper & Row (P) to publish his memoirs. Two years later, when the memoirs were almost complete, prepublication rights were granted to Time magazine for $25,000, half of which was payable up front. Several weeks before the Time article was to be released, an article based on Ford's memoirs appeared in The Nation (D). The Nation's (D) editor had received a purloined copy of the manuscript from an unidentified source and quickly put together a compilation of quotes, facts, and paraphrases so that the manuscript could be returned before anyone discovered it was missing. Time magazine canceled its article and refused to pay the second half-payment to Harper & Row (P). Harper & Row (P) sued The Nation (D) for copyright infringement and won at trial, but the court of appeals reversed, holding that the story constituted a fair use. The Supreme Court granted certiorari.

■ **ISSUE**

Did The Nation's (D) publication of an article based on Ford's memoirs, before they were published, constitute a fair use?

■ **DECISION AND RATIONALE**

(O'Connor, J.) No. The prepublication use of verbatim excerpts from an as-yet unpublished work does not constitute fair use. Fair use is the privilege of persons other than the owner of a copyright to use the copyrighted material in a reasonable manner without the owner's consent. The fair use doctrine is set out in the Copyright Act, which embodies the common law. The Copyright Act also recognizes the right of first publication. Only one person can be the first publisher, and the law recognizes that a copyright owner has the right to control the first public distribution of an authorized copy. The right of first publication is expressly subject to the fair use doctrine. The unpublished nature of a work is a key, but not necessarily determinative, factor tending to negate a defense of fair use in such cases. Although the scope of fair use is wider when the information conveyed relates to matters of public concern, the doctrine cannot be so expanded as to destroy any expectation of copyright protection in the work of a public figure. Given the protections already afforded by the First Amendment, we see no need to expand the doctrine of fair use to create a public figure exception to copyright protection.

The four factors especially relevant to a determination of whether a use was fair are: (1) the purpose and character of the use; (2) the nature of the copyrighted work; (3) the substantiality of the portion used in relation to the work as a whole; and (4) the effect on the potential market for or value of the copyrighted work. Although publishing the news is an important purpose, that is only one factor. Moreover, the fact that the publication in this case, though "newsy," was for commercial gain weighs against a finding of fair use. The Nation (D) intended to "scoop" the other publications. Fair use presupposes good faith and fair dealing, which are questionable in this case. As to the second element, the law generally recognizes a greater need to publish facts as opposed to fiction, but The Nation (D) exceeded what was necessary to publish just the facts here. Thirdly, the editor admitted to lifting the most powerful verbatim quotes because they qualitatively embodied Ford's distinctive expression; this was not, as the magazine would have us believe, an infinitesimal amount of Ford's original language. But the fourth factor is the single most important element of fair use. Time's refusal to publish its story and pay the contract price were direct results of the infringement. A fair use doctrine that allows extensive prepublication of direct quotations from an unpublished manuscript would pose a substantial danger to the marketability of the work. We conclude that The Nation's (D) use of the verbatim excerpts from the unpublished manuscript was not a fair use. Reversed and remanded.

Analysis:

The Court was not quite as cohesive here as it was in the *Rural Telephone* case. In this six-three opinion, the Court held that The Nation's use of verbatim excerpts from President Ford's unpublished manuscript was not a fair use. As Justice O'Connor wrote, "[u]nder ordinary circumstances, the author's right to control the first public appearance of his undisseminated expression will outweigh a claim of fair use." In his dissent, Justice Brennan argued that the Court was advancing the protection of the copyright owner's economic interest "through an exceedingly narrow definition of the scope of fair use."

Diamond v. Chakrabarty

(Commissioner of Patents and Trademarks) v. (Patentee)

447 U.S. 303 (1980)

GENETICALLY ENGINEERED BACTERIA ARE ENTITLED TO PATENT PROTECTION, WHEREAS BACTERIA EXISTING IN NATURE ARE NOT

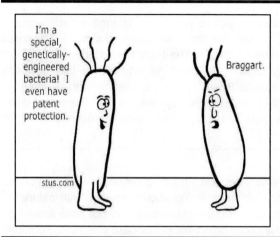

■ **INSTANT FACTS** Chakrabarty (P) invented a bacterium that broke down crude oil and could be used to remediate oil spills; he applied for patents for the process and the bacterium, and the latter was initially denied, but the appellate court reversed the denial.

■ **BLACK LETTER RULE** The language employed in the Patent Act is given broad application, such that a micro-organism that is the product of human ingenuity, as opposed to nature, is patentable.

■ **PROCEDURAL BASIS**

Supreme Court review of a patent court of appeals decision in the patentee's favor.

■ **FACTS**

Chakrabarty (P) invented a genetically engineered bacterium that was capable of breaking down crude oil and therefore valuable in treating oil spills. He applied for a patent for the process and the bacterium itself, and the latter was rejected and the grounds that bacteria are products of nature. The Court of Customs and Patent Appeals reversed, and the case went to the Supreme Court.

■ **ISSUE**

Was the patentee entitled to a patent on the genetically engineered bacterium?

■ **DECISION AND RATIONALE**

(Burger, C.J.) Yes. The language employed in the Patent Act is given broad application, such that a micro-organism that is the product of human ingenuity, as opposed to nature, is patentable. The statute provides that whoever invents or discovers any new and useful process, machine, manufacture, or composition of matter, or any new and useful improvement thereof, may obtain a patent on it. "Manufacture" has been interpreted as the production of articles for use from raw or prepared materials by giving the materials new forms, qualities, properties, or combinations, by hand or machinery. "Composition of matter" expansively includes all compositions of two or more substances and all composite articles, whether they result from chemical union or mechanical mixture, or are gases, fluids, powders, or solids. These interpretations show that Congress intended that patent laws have a broad scope. Judged in this light, the micro-organism is worthy of patent protection. It is a product of human ingenuity. The applicant has produced a new bacterium that is not found in nature. His discovery is not of nature's handiwork, but his own.

The Plant Patent Act does not change this result. Congress recognized in that act that there is a difference between products of nature and human-made inventions. The patentee's bacterium falls into the latter category. Congress does not need to specifically recognize that micro-organisms can be patentable subject matter in order for that to be true. Once Congress has spoken, it is up to the courts to construe the language that Congress has employed. The subject-matter provisions of patent law have been cast in broad terms to promote the progress of science and the useful arts. We are not dissuaded by the Commissioner's argument that research endeavors such as those of the patentee's present a grave risk. The dangers of genetic research are not before us, but are rather a matter of legislative concern. Affirmed.

■ DISSENT

(Brennan, J.) We must be careful to not extend patent protection beyond what Congress intended. When there is an absence of legislative direction, the courts should let Congress speak. In this case, however, there is no legislative vacuum. The Plant Patent Act and the Plant Variety Protection Act both evidence a congressional limitation on patentability that excludes bacteria. Moreover, the Patent Act does not include living organisms, whether human-made or not. It is the role of Congress, not this Court, to broaden or narrow the reach of the patent laws, especially where, as here, the composition sought to be patented implicates matters of public concern.

Analysis:

The dissent's concern relates to the controversy over and ethical questions raised by genetic engineering. Some people thought that any genetic engineering was "tampering with nature" or "messing with God's work." Were it not for that concern, the dissenters may not have looked so hard for justification for their conclusion that the micro-organism in this case was not patentable. Plant patent laws do not adequately address questions of bacteria patents.

■ CASE VOCABULARY

PATENT: A grant issued by the government to an inventor, giving him or her the exclusive right to make, use, or sell the invention for a specified number of years, constituting a legitimate monopoly.

White v. Samsung Electronics America, Inc.

(Game Show Hostess) v. *(Electronics Manufacturer)*

989 F.2d 1512 (9th Cir. 1993), cert. denied, 508 U.S. 951 (1993)

NOT ALL AGREE THAT USING A "VANNA WHITE ROBOT" IN ADVERTISEMENTS VIOLATED WHITE'S RIGHT TO PRIVACY

Vanna White is a joke, but nevertheless we can't parody her for profit.

stus.com

■ **INSTANT FACTS** Samsung (D) printed advertisements containing a robot wearing a blond wig and a dress while turning letters on a set resembling the "Wheel of Fortune" game show set, and Vanna White (P) sued for privacy violations.

■ **BLACK LETTER RULE** The common law right of privacy prohibits the appropriation of one's identity, regardless of the means employed.

■ **PROCEDURAL BASIS**

Dissenting opinion on denial of rehearing after the court of appeals reversed summary judgment in the defendant's favor.

■ **FACTS**

Vanna White (P), hostess of "Wheel of Fortune," markets her identity to advertisers for profit. Samsung Electronics America, Inc. (D), through an advertising firm, published a print advertisement in which a robot wearing a blond wig and dress was placed before a letter board similar to that used on the "Wheel of Fortune" set. The robot was deliberately designed to resemble White (P) to promote the defendant's videocassette recorders in a humorous manner. White (P) never consented to the advertisement and sued Samsung (D) in federal court, alleging violations of her right of publicity. The district court granted summary judgment to the defendant, and White (P) appealed. On appeal the Ninth Circuit reversed, holding that questions of fact existed that precluded summary judgment. Thereafter, the appellate court denied a petition for rehearing, and Judge Kozinski dissented.

■ **ISSUE**

Did the Ninth Circuit Court of Appeals err in refusing to reconsider its decision that the right of publicity protects a celebrity's identity, even though the celebrity's name or likeness has not been appropriated?

■ **DECISION AND RATIONALE**

Not provided.

■ **DISSENT**

(Kozinski, J.) Yes. The protection offered by the majority threatens to quell creativity and innovation by privatizing the public image of individuals. While copyright and trademark laws protect the fruits of one's labor, without which innovation and cultural advancement would be hindered, overprotection of such rights endangers these same virtues. Innovation and advancement become difficult prospects when the building blocks upon which such advancement is based are protected by intellectual property laws.

The federal district court judge reasonably held that because Samsung (D) did not use White's (P) name, likeness, voice, or signature, it did not violate her right of publicity. The court of appeals, however, reasoned that if the advertisement *reminds* people of White (P), allowing it could "eviscerate" her rights. What the majority is doing, however, goes beyond protecting White's (P) rights, and actually expands them. By refusing to recognize a parody exception to the right of publicity, the panel directly contradicts the Copyright Act. Copyright law specifically gives the world at large the right to make fair use parodies—parodies that do not borrow too much of the original. But the majority's decision decimates this federal scheme. Like it or not, we are the Court of Appeals for the Hollywood Circuit, and we must recognize a right to mock, for profit as well as fun, the cultural icons of our time.

Analysis:

The *White* holding was controversial because it protected more than a person's name, voice, and physical likeness, and extended protection to other indicia of a person's identity. The court did not provide any definitive guidance as to what indicia are sufficient to recover under a right of publicity. In *White*, the court concluded that Vanna White (P) was the only individual to whom the advertisement at issue could refer, but the opinion does not indicate how the case would differ if the indicia were not as pointed.

■ CASE VOCABULARY

COPYRIGHT: The right to copy; specifically, a property right in an original work of authorship (including literary, musical, dramatic, choreographic, pictorial, graphic, sculptural, and architectural works; motion pictures and other audiovisual works; and sound recordings) fixed in any tangible medium of expression, giving the holder the exclusive right to reproduce, adapt, distribute, perform, and display the work; the body of law relating to such works. Copyright law is governed by the Copyright Act of 1976.

FAIR USE: A reasonable and limited use of a copyrighted work without the author's permission, such as quoting from a book in a book review or using parts of it in a parody. Fair use is a defense to an infringement claim, depending on the following statutory factors: (1) the purpose and character of the use, (2) the nature of the copyrighted work, (3) the amount of the work used, and (4) the economic impact of the use.

PARODY: A transformative use of a well-known work for purposes of satirizing, ridiculing, critiquing, or commenting on the original work, as opposed to merely alluding to the original to draw attention to the later work. In constitutional law, a parody is protected as free speech. In copyright law, a work must meet the definition of a parody and be a fair use of the copyrighted material, or else it may constitute infringement.

RIGHT OF PRIVACY: The right to personal autonomy. The U.S. Constitution does not explicitly provide for a right of privacy or for a general right of personal autonomy, but the Supreme Court has repeatedly ruled that a right of personal autonomy is implied in the "zones of privacy" created by specific constitutional guarantees. The right of privacy includes the right of a person and the person's property to be free from unwarranted public scrutiny

RIGHT OF PUBLICITY: The right to control the use of one's own name, picture, or likeness and to prevent another from using it for commercial benefit without one's consent.

Moore v. Regents of the University of California

(Spleen Source) v. *(Spleen Exploiter)*

51 Cal.3d 120, 793 P.2d 479, 271 Cal.Rptr. 146 (1990); cert. denied, 499 U.S. 936, 111 S.Ct. 1388

COURT DECLARES THAT EXCISED BODY PARTS ARE NOT ONE'S OWN PROPERTY

■ **INSTANT FACTS** The Regents (D) removed Moore's (P) spleen and retained it for research purposes. As a result of this research, the Regents (D) established a cell line from Moore's (P) cells and obtained a patent for it.

■ **BLACK LETTER RULE** A doctor has a duty to disclose the extent of his research and economic interests in a patient's body parts. Human body parts are not property such that they may be converted.

■ **PROCEDURAL BASIS**

Appeal from an order by the appellate court reversing a demurrer to a complaint for damages for conversion.

■ **FACTS**

After undergoing tests, Moore (P) was told by the Regents (D) that he had hairy-cell leukemia and that his spleen should be removed. The Regents (D) did not tell Moore (P) that his cells were unique and that access to them was of great scientific value. After the splenectomy, Moore (P) underwent some seven years of follow-up tests that he was led to believe were important to his treatment. During these tests blood and tissue were removed from Moore (P). Additionally, the Regents (D) retained Moore's (P) spleen for research without his knowledge or consent. Eventually, he was informed that his bodily substances were being used for research, but he was never informed of the Regent's (D) commercial interest in them. Subsequently, the Regents (D) created a cell line from Moore's (P) cells, received a patent for it, and commercially marketed these items for a great deal of money. Moore (P) sues for tortious conversion of his body parts.

■ **ISSUE**

(1) Does a doctor have a duty to disclose the extent of his research and economic interests in a patient's body parts? (2) Are human body parts property such that they may be converted?

■ **DECISION AND RATIONALE**

(Panelli, J.) (1) Yes. (2) No. A doctor must disclose the extent of his research and economic interest in a patient's body parts. This is so that a patient's interests are not compromised for the sake of the doctor's interests. The existing law of conversion does not give Moore (P) a cause of action. To establish a conversion Moore (P) must show either interference with his ownership or his right of possession. Since Moore (P) did not retain possession of his body parts after their removal, he must show an ownership interest in them. There are three reasons why we conclude that Moore (P) did not retain an ownership interest. First, there is no case law to support the contention that a person retains an ownership interest in excised body parts. This lack of authority is not surprising, since the law of property interests in human organs, dead bodies, fetuses, etc., is unique. The law of property interests in human organs, etc., has been crafted to meet policy goals rather than to comport with normal property law. The second reason why Moore (P) did not retain a property interest in his body parts is as follows: California statutes limit a patient's control over excised body parts. Health & Safety Code § 7054.4 restricts the use of excised parts and requires their ultimate destruction. This so severely restricts the enjoyment of body parts that it is hard to call them property that can be owned. Finally, the patent cannot possibly be Moore's (P) property. This is because the patent is simply (factually and legally) a different object than the organs. Moore (P) argues, along with the appeals court, that nonetheless an ownership interest should be found. He relies on cases that find a proprietary interest in one's likeness or photograph. The analogy is inappropriate, however, because one's likeness is unique, whereas the patent and the cell line creates lymphokines which are the same in every human. Pushing yet farther, the court of appeals concluded that there must be an ownership interest to protect the privacy and dignity of the patient. But this is unnecessary since the duty to disclose protects these interests. Having decided that existing conversion law does not support Moore's (P) claim, we next consider whether conversion law should be expanded. We conclude that conversion liability should not be extended for three reasons. The first reason comes from a weighing of policy considerations. On the one hand is the patient's right to make an informed decision. On the other hand is the fact that conversion is a strict liability tort. To allow an action for conversion to be extended to cases like this would expose innocent researchers (who may have unwittingly obtained the body parts) to liability. This would make companies unlikely to invest in such research and slow scientific progress. Since the duty to disclose adequately protects a patient's right to informed consent, the social policy of fostering scientific progress requires that conversion liability not be extended. The second reason why conversion liability should not be extended is because the problems involved in this area are better suited to the legislature. Finally, the duty of the doctor to disclose his research and economic interests in the patient's body parts adequately protects the patient's right to determine the fate of his body parts. If he does not like what the doctor proposes to do with his body parts, he may seek another doctor. Since Moore's (P) claim for conversion of his body parts is not supported by existing law, he cannot maintain a claim. Order of the appellate court reversed.

■ **CONCURRENCE**

(Arabian, J.) I concur in the majority's opinion. I write separately to emphasize that the human body is sacred and that it should not be treated as property which can be bartered in a free market.

■ **CONCURRENCE AND DISSENT**

(Broussard, J.) I concur in the majority's opinion with respect to a doctor's duty to disclose. However, I dissent from the view that Moore (P) has no cause of action for conversion. If a plaintiff consents to the removal of his organ for research purposes, I agree that he has no cause of action. However, if a plaintiff is misled and thereby deprived of the opportunity to determine the disposition of his body parts after removal, he has a cause of action. This cause of action is the traditional common law action of conversion. This is because the Uniform Anatomical Gift Act [a donor has the authority to make a gift of his body parts upon his death] supports the notion that a patient retains a property interest in excised body parts. Moreover, the Uniform Anatomical Gift Act gives this property interest (the right to designate the use of the excised body part) to patients and not to doctors. The tort of conversion protects a plaintiff from interference with his right to designate the use of his property. Since the Regents (D) have deprived Moore (P) of the opportunity to determine the disposition of his body parts, they are converters. Finally, I think that the majority's and Justice Mosk's reasoning that it is immoral to create a market place for human body parts is flawed. It appears to me that the majority has created a marketplace for body parts. It has merely barred Moore (P) and other plaintiffs from participating in the markets, while it has given such a right to the Regents (D) and other defendants.

■ **DISSENT**

(Mosk, J.) It is true that there are many restrictions on the use of property. However, what remains after these restrictions is still property. As such, Moore (P) had at least as much right to dispose of his body parts as the Regents (D) did. Therefore, Moore (P) has stated a claim for conversion. I also disagree with the majority's reasoning in deciding whether to extend the tort of conversion for two reasons. First, I feel that the specter of slavery and the like haunts our biotechnology industry. This specter comes to light whenever scientists claim the right to exploit a person's body for profit. Second, I feel that it is unfair for the Regents (D) to take all of the gain from Moore's (P) body parts, while Moore (P) gets nothing. Yet by failing to recognize a tort of conversion, the majority gives a windfall to the Regents (D). Moore (P) and the Regents (D) should be allowed to bargain for the right to his organs. When the majority suggests that patients like Moore (P) cannot sell organs, it is wrong. Contrary to the suggestions of the majority, The Uniform Anatomical Gift Act [whether an individual may sell excised body parts or not] allows individuals to sell body parts. They may simply not sell body parts for use after they die. Since the Act recognizes a right to sell body parts, there should be an action for conversion. Also, the duty of a doctor to disclose is no protection for the plaintiff because it may be difficult to prove the elements of this cause of action. Moreover, the duty to disclose only protects the patient's right to refuse to sell. It does not grant him the right to sell. Finally, the duty to disclose gives Moore (P) an action against his doctor. It does not reach a second class of defendants: research laboratories. These may well be the true exploiters.

Analysis:

Notice that Moore (P) argued that his case was similar to those in which courts have recognized a property interest in one's own name and likeness, known as the "right of publicity" cases. The Court here quickly dispensed with this argument, concluding that body parts, like the spleen at issue here, are not unique to each individual, but rather are common to all humans. Additionally, note the discussion of the "bundle of rights," sometimes referred to as the "bundle of sticks." Under the law, property is not so much about things but rather about rights over things: the right to use, to possess, to exclude, and to transfer/sell. At its barest, property law is all about these four rights and who has them. Thus, in this case, the discussion turns, at least in part, on who has the right to sell or gift the spleen, or excised body parts in general. This bundle of rights concept is an underlying concept throughout property law.

■ **CASE VOCABULARY**

BUNDLE OF RIGHTS: A collection of rights which taken together characterize property ownership.

CONSENSUAL PEDIGREE: The history of consent.

CONVERSION: The taking of the right of ownership to property from another.

DECEIT: An intentional distortion of the truth.

DELIBERATIVE FORUM: A place where ideas are debated, such as a legislature.

DEMURRER: An answer by a defendant alleging that a plaintiff has alleged nothing that entitles him to a remedy.

FIDUCIARY DUTY: The duty to act in the interest of another.

FRAUD: An intentional distortion of the truth.

INTENTIONAL INFLICTION OF EMOTIONAL DISTRESS: Purposely causing another to be emotionally distressed.

INTER ALIA: Among other things.

NEGLIGENT MISREPRESENTATION: Not taking care, as a reasonable person would, to represent the facts accurately.

PATENT: A grant of a privilege.

POST MORTEM: After death.

RIGHT OF POSSESSION: The right to occupy land.

STRICT LIABILITY TORT: A cause of action where the defendant must pay for damages whether or not he was negligent or at fault.

SUI GENERIS: Unique; one-of-a-kind.

Pocono Springs Civic Association, Inc. v. MacKenzie

(Homeowner's Association) v. (Landowners)

446 Pa.Super. 445, 667 A.2d 233 (1995)

COVENANT CONTINUES TO RUN WITH LAND DESPITE INTENT TO ABANDON

■ **INSTANT FACTS** The owners of a vacant lot in a housing development attempted to abandon the lot in order to avoid having to pay association fees.

■ **BLACK LETTER RULE** A covenant running with the land cannot be terminated by abandonment when the owner still holds title in fee simple absolute.

■ **PROCEDURAL BASIS**

Appeal of order granting summary judgment for plaintiffs in action to recover unpaid dues.

■ **FACTS**

Joseph and Doris MacKenzie (D) had owned a vacant lot in a housing development since 1969. Tired of paying association fees on the vacant land, the MacKenzies (D) decided to sell their lot in 1987. However, they were unable to find a buyer because the property was not suitable for an on-lot sewage system. The MacKenzies (D) then made several attempts to abandon their property and avoid further association fees. First, the MacKenzies (D) attempted unsuccessfully to turn the lot over to the Pocono Springs Civic Association, Inc. (the "Association") (P). They then ceased paying property taxes. Although the Tax Claim Bureau offered the property for sale, there were no takers. Finally, the MacKenzies (D) mailed a notarized statement to "all interested parties" expressing their desire to abandon the lot, and the MacKenzies (D) ceased paying the association fees. The Association (P) sued the MacKenzies (D) for payment. At trial, the MacKenzies (D) defended on grounds that they had abandoned the lot. The trial court held that the abandonment defense was invalid and granted summary judgment in favor of the Association (P). The MacKenzies (D) appeal.

■ **ISSUE**

Can property be considered "abandoned" even though the owner still possesses perfect title?

■ **DECISION AND RATIONALE**

(Rowley, J.) No. Property cannot be considered "abandoned" when the owner still possesses perfect title. Pursuant to Pennsylvania law, abandoned property is that to which an owner has voluntarily relinquished all right, title, claim and possession with the intention of terminating his ownership, but without vesting it in any other person and with the intention of not reclaiming further possession or resuming ownership. The MacKenzies (D) have not relinquished their rights or title to their lot. They remain owners of real property in fee simple. Neither title nor deed has been sold or transferred. Thus, based upon our definition of "abandonment," the MacKenzies' (D) defense must fail. Despite their intent to the contrary, they have not abandoned their property. Affirmed.

Analysis:

Just what does it take for poor Mr. and Mrs. MacKenzie (D) to unload this burdensome piece of land? They tried to sell it, to give it away, and to have it foreclosed upon. They sent a letter to their neighbors expressing their intent to abandon. They never lived on the land, and probably had not set foot on it in years. Nevertheless, they were required to continue paying association fees simply because no one else wanted the land. The opinion quotes the definition of "abandonment," stating that "perfect title . . . cannot be abandoned," and then later notes that "real property cannot be abandoned." Then what kind of property *can* be abandoned? Personal property only? Under the modern Restatement (Third) of Property, Servitudes § 7.12, the result would be different; covenants to pay maintenance fees terminate after a reasonable time.

■ **CASE VOCABULARY**

PERFECT TITLE: Title representing absolute right of possession, as in a fee simple absolute, which is valid beyond all reasonable doubt.

Hawkins v. Mahoney

(Prisoner) v. (Warden)

990 P.2d 776 (Mont. 1999)

A PRISON ESCAPEE DOES NOT GIVE UP ALL RIGHTS TO HIS PERSONAL PROPERTY

They recaptured me. But I recaptured my personal property.

■ **INSTANT FACTS** After Hawkins (P) escaped, the prison got rid of all of his personal property, even though at the time he had already been apprehended and returned to the prison, and has asked for his property back.

■ **BLACK LETTER RULE** The presumption or inference of intent to abandon one's property, based solely on the acts of the owner, is a rebuttable presumption.

■ **PROCEDURAL BASIS**

State appellate court review of a trial court decision against the plaintiff prisoner.

■ **FACTS**

Hawkins (P) escaped from prison in July 1997. Immediately after his escape, prison officials packed up his belongings in boxes labeled with his name, sealed the boxes with security tape, and placed them in the prison storage room. Two days later, Hawkins (P) was apprehended and returned to prison. Hawkins (P) was found guilty of escape and put in disciplinary segregation. He requested the return of his personal belongings several times over the next thirty days. Finally, in September, Hawkins (P) was escorted to the storage room and allowed to remove his legal papers from the box, but he was advised that prison protocol was to sell or destroy the property of an escapee immediately after escape. Sometime thereafter, prison officials destroyed or sold Hawkins' (P) remaining personal property, valued at $2,290. Hawkins sued the prison officials and the state, arguing that they destroyed his personal property without due process of law. The court held that Hawkins (P) had abandoned his property when he escaped, and that the abandonment gave the defendants a complete defense to any claim that depended on Hawkins' (P) ownership of the property.

■ **ISSUE**

Was Hawkins' (P) escape irrefutable proof of abandonment of his personal property?

■ **DECISION AND RATIONALE**

(Trieweiler, J.) No. The presumption or inference of intent to abandon one's property, based solely on the acts of the owner, is a rebuttable presumption. The case relied on by the trial court, *Herron v. Whiteside*, is distinguishable. In *Herron*, the prison employees and inmates ransacked Herron's cell after he escaped and appropriated his property for themselves. In this case, the prison officials securely stored Hawkins' (P) property, but they did not dispose of it immediately after his escape as the rules required. Moreover, in *Herron*, the court held that the intent to abandon can be inferred from a prisoner's escape. It is true that abandonment requires a showing of intent, and that the intent may be inferred by the acts of the owner.

However, we do not believe that escape gives rise to an irrebuttable presumption, at least prior to the time when someone else takes possession of the property with the intent to acquire ownership. At no point after Hawkins' (P) escape, and before his request for the return of his property, did the Montana State Prison reduce Hawkins' (P) property to their possession with the intent to acquire title to, or ownership of, it. Upon Hawkins' (P) return to prison and request for his property prior to it being claimed by anyone else, he effectively rebutted the presumption that he intended to abandon his property and regained his status as the owner as against all others. The district court erred when it ruled that Hawkins (P) had abandoned his property and had no right to request its return. Reversed and remanded.

Analysis:

On remand, Hawkins (P) alleged that the defendants' actions constituted conversion of his personal property. Both sides moved for summary judgment. The prison argued that the property policy in effect at the time of Hawkins' (P) escape was determinative of Hawkins' (P) claim. The policy provided that an escaped prisoner's property would be considered contraband and would be confiscated and destroyed or sold at auction, so it was within its rights in acting accordingly. The trial court agreed and granted the defendants' motion, and in 2004 the state supreme court affirmed.

■ **CASE VOCABULARY**

ABANDONMENT: Knowing relinquishment of one's right or claim to property without passing rights to another and with no intention to reclaim possession.

Eyerman v. Mercantile Trust Co.

(Decedent's Neighbor) v. (Executor)

524 S.W.2d 210 (Mo. Ct. App. 1975)

THE COURT CAN STEP IN TO STOP A DIRECTIVE IN A WILL IF ENFORCING IT WOULD VIOLATE PUBLIC POLICY

■ **INSTANT FACTS** Neighbors of a deceased woman sought the court's help in preventing the demolition of the decedent's home, despite a provision in the dead woman's will asking that the home be razed and the empty lot sold.

■ **BLACK LETTER RULE** The taking of property by inheritance or a will is not an absolute right, but is one created by the laws of the state, and the state may foreclose that right or make it conditional, within constitutional limits.

■ **PROCEDURAL BASIS**

State appellate court review of a lower court decision in the estate's favor.

■ **FACTS**

Johnston owned distinctive property in the Kingsbury Place development in St. Louis. Her will provided that after she died, her home would be razed and the land would be sold, with the proceeds going into the residue of her estate. Neighboring property owners objected and moved for an injunction to prevent the demolition, based on certain covenants that ran with the land in the development. A temporary restraining order was granted, but at trial it was dissolved and all issues were resolved against the plaintiffs. They appealed.

■ **ISSUE**

Were the plaintiffs entitled to an injunction to prevent the destruction of a landmark house in their neighborhood?

■ **DECISION AND RATIONALE**

(Rendlen, J.) Yes. The taking of property by inheritance or a will is not an absolute right, but is one created by the laws of the state, and the state may foreclose that right or make it conditional, within constitutional limits. One has more control over the use of his property while he is alive than he can force on someone else after his death. For instance, a man may not have to cultivate his land, even if the public would benefit from it, but if he attempts to compel his successor to act in the same way against the public good, the law will step in. Although public policy evades precise definition, senseless destruction of property serving no good purpose is held in disfavor. The estate does not stand to gain anything if the will's provisions are enforced. The land is worth about $5,000, but after the demolition costs are paid only $650 would remain for the estate's residue. The house, if left standing, is worth $40,000. Moreover, razing the home would depreciate adjoining property values by $10,000. It would cost nearly $200,000 to build a house of comparable size and architectural quality. The house is an historical landmark, and to remove it would be like giving the neighborhood a missing front tooth. No good can come of the destruction of this home. In fact, to allow an executor to exercise the power to enforce a provision in a will that stems from the apparent whim and caprice of the testatrix contravenes public policy. Reversed.

■ DISSENT

(Clemens, J.) The court pretends to know what the testatrix's motives were. We have no idea what reasons were behind her decision to request, in her will, that her home be razed after her death. And no grounds exist for finding that the razing is contrary to public policy. The covenants recognize that Kingsbury Place will have vacant lots from time to time—in fact, there already is one. There is no reason to believe that another vacant lot will require a greater police presence or otherwise damage the neighborhood. The neighbors are not entitled to injunctive relief based on imagined possibilities. It is not the function of the judiciary to *create* public policy. Prejudice to the public interest must clearly appear before a court is warranted in pronouncing a transaction void on public policy grounds. It requires judicial imagination to hold that the mere presence of a second vacant lot violates public policy in this case. As much as our aesthetic sympathies may lie with the neighbors, those sympathies should not interfere with our legal judgment. Johnston had the right during her lifetime to have her house razed, and nothing precludes her executor from doing the same upon her death.

Analysis:

In finding a possible public policy violation, the court emphasized the potential loss in value of neighboring property, the designation of the surrounding area as a landmark, and the need for dwelling units in the city. Although the court found these factors relevant, they are not the type that would generally justify direct contravention of a testatrix's unambiguous intent. The dissent opined that a testatrix's intent should be given effect in the absence of a clear public injury, and that there was no danger of such an injury in this case.

■ CASE VOCABULARY

COVENANT: A written agreement; a promise or obligation contained in an instrument under seal, such as a deed. The term is often used in relation to land, such as a "covenant for quiet enjoyment," which is a promise by the conveyor of land that he will protect the buyer against lawful claims made on the land. A "covenant of seisin" is a promise made by a grantor of property that he lawfully possesses the property and has the right to convey it. Covenants are classified in many ways. "Covenants in gross" are those that do not run with the land (*i.e.*, they do not pass to succeeding owners). "Covenants running with the land" do pass to succeeding owners. "Covenants against encumbrances" are promises made by the grantor stating that an estate has no burdens on it, such as claims or liens. Covenants are usually express, but may be implied from the agreement.

EXECUTOR: Person appointed by a testator to carry out the directives of his will. This may be done expressly or by implication. A woman so appointed is an executrix. When a person is appointed by the court to administer a decedent's estate, he or she is called an administrator or administratrix.

TESTATRIX: A woman who dies having left a will or testament.

CHAPTER TWO

Subsequent Possession: Acquisition of Property by Find, Adverse Possession, and Gift

Armory v. Delamirie

Instant Facts: Armory (P) found a jewel and took it to Delamirie's (D) jewelry shop. Delamirie (D) refused to return the jewel.

Black Letter Rule: The finder of lost property has a title superior to all but the true owner.

Hannah v. Peel

Instant Facts: Hannah (P) found a brooch on Peel's (D) property. Peel (D) never lived on this parcel of property.

Black Letter Rule: If the owner of property has never occupied his land, the finder of property on this land has a superior title against the land owner.

McAvoy v. Medina

Instant Facts: A customer of the shop owner placed his wallet on the counter, but neglected to remove it. McAvoy (P) found the wallet.

Black Letter Rule: A finder has no title to property that is mislaid.

Van Valkenburgh v. Lutz

Instant Facts: The Lutzes (D) occupied the Van Valkenburgh's (P) land by building a one-bedroom shack on it, by cultivating a garden on it, and by storing rubbish on it. In another action to establish a right of way across the land, the Lutzes (D) admitted that the land belonged to the Van Valkenburghs (P).

Black Letter Rule: In order to acquire title by adverse possession, possession must be actual, it must be under claim of title, and the land must either enclosed or sufficiently improved.

Mannillo v. Gorski

Instant Facts: A property owner sought to enjoin the alleged trespass of an adjoining landowner whose pathway encroached 15 inches and who claimed title to the strip by adverse possession.

Black Letter Rule: Possession need not be knowingly and intentionally hostile, but it must be notorious enough to give the true owner actual or constructive notice of the encroachment.

Howard v. Kunto

Instant Facts: Three adjacent landowners each held deeds that did not coincide with the actual legal descriptions of the physical properties.

Black Letter Rule: Tacking on successive possessions of property is permitted for purposes of establishing adverse possession if the successive owners are in privity.

O'Keeffe v. Snyder

Instant Facts: Three of O'Keeffe's paintings were stolen from an art gallery. The thefts were not reported to anyone.

Black Letter Rule: The statute of limitations is tolled if the owner of stolen chattel makes diligent efforts to locate and recover the lost chattel.

Newman v. Bost

Instant Facts: After giving the keys to much of the furniture in the house to Newman (P), the decedent pointed to the furniture and said to Newman (P) that he was giving it all to her. In one of the pieces of furniture was a life insurance policy.

Black Letter Rule: Symbolic delivery of a gift is not effective. Constructive delivery is allowed only when it is impractical to deliver actual possession.

Gruen v. Gruen

Instant Facts: The elder Gruen gave Gruen (P) a painting but reserved a life estate for himself. Gruen (P) has never had possession of the painting.

Black Letter Rule: A party may give a future interest in chattels as a gift while reserving a life estate in himself.

Armory v. Delamirie

(Finder) v. (Subsequent Possessor)

1 Strange 505 (1722)

[handwritten: follows rule]

COURT DECLARES THAT THE FINDER OF LOST PROPERTY HAS A TITLE SUPERIOR TO ALL BUT THE TRUE OWNER

■ **INSTANT FACTS** Armory (P) found a jewel and took it to Delamirie's (D) jewelry shop. Delamirie (D) refused to return the jewel.

■ **BLACK LETTER RULE** The finder of lost property has a title superior to all but the true owner.

[handwritten right margin: → finder → not true owner, so Armory has title, so Delamirie must return the jewel to Armory]

■ **PROCEDURAL BASIS**

Appeal from judgment in action to recover property found by plaintiff.

■ **FACTS**

Armory (P) found a jewel and took it to Delamirie's (D) jewelry shop to have it appraised. Delamirie's (D) apprentice removed the stones. Delamirie (D) offered three half pence to Armory (P) for the jewel. Armory (P) refused this offer and demanded the jewels to be returned to him. Delamirie (D) refused to return the stones. Armory (P) sues.

■ **ISSUE**

Does the finder of lost property have a title superior to all but the true owner?

■ **DECISION AND RATIONALE**

Yes. A finder of property does not acquire an absolute title; the true owner has absolute title. However, the finder does acquire a title superior to the rest of the world. Since Armory (P) found the jewel, and since Delamirie (D) is not the true owner, Armory (P) has a superior title. Judgment affirmed.

Analysis:

The rule announced in this case is called the prior possessor rule. It achieves multiple social goals: (1) It protects an owner who cannot prove that he is the true owner. (2) It protects individuals who entrust goods to others. Entrusting goods to others promotes social welfare. For example, an individual may entrust his clothes to the laundry without worrying that he may not get them back. Since he is the prior possessor, he will prevail over the laundry. (3) It protects the expectations of prior possessors, who expect to prevail. (4) It promotes peaceable possession. If prior possessors did not prevail, individuals might begin to steal property, hoping that the law would protect them.

■ **CASE VOCABULARY**

TROVER: A suit to recover the value of the plaintiff's chattel that the defendant has converted.

Hannah v. Peel

(Finder) v. (Property Owner)

[1945] K.B. 509 (1945)

more or an exception/ nuance to rule

COURT DECLARES THAT A PROPERTY OWNER DOES NOT NECESSARILY HAVE TITLE TO ALL THAT IS FOUND ON HIS PROPERTY

■ **INSTANT FACTS** Hannah (P) found a brooch on Peel's (D) property. Peel (D) never lived on this parcel of property.

■ **BLACK LETTER RULE** If the owner of property has never occupied his land, the finder of property on this land has a superior title against the land owner.

[handwritten notes in right margin:] old rule: lost property goes to the finder instead of landowner. seems more ok like an exception/ modification to general rule

[handwritten notes below box:] seems at odds w/ rule on p. 12 SHG ?, which is asserting new rule that superior title goes to the landowner, not the finder, and only yields to item's true owner

↳ but here, the landowner/ owner never took possession

[right margin:] never assumed dominiun+ control

■ PROCEDURAL BASIS

Action to recover money found by plaintiff.

■ FACTS

In 1938 Peel (D) purchased a home. He never lived in this home. In July of 1940 Peel's (D) home was requisitioned by the government. In August of 1940 Hannah (P) was stationed at this home of Peel's (D). While stationed there, Hannah (P) found a brooch in a room being used for a sick bay. The room was in a remote place of the house. At this point, Peel (D) had no knowledge of the brooch. Hannah (P) gave the brooch to the police. Two years later, since the true owner was not found, the police awarded the brooch to Peel (D). Hannah (P) sues for damages or replevy. Hannah (P) contends that he has superior title, since he is the finder. Peel (D) contends that he has title, since he owned the land where the brooch was found.

■ ISSUE

If a landowner has never lived on a parcel of land, does a finder of property on that land have superior title to the landowner?

■ DECISION AND RATIONALE

[left margin handwritten:] applying old rule

(Birkett, J.) Yes. The case authority gives support to the contentions of both parties. There are three principle cases in this area. First, *Bridges v. Hawkesworth.* In that case, a bag of money was left in a shop. The bag was left in that area of the shop accessible to the general public. The principle issue in that case was whether superior title lay in the finder or in the shop owner. The court applied the old rule: superior title goes to finder. The court ruled this way because the shop owner never possessed the bag and because the place where the bag was found was open to the public. In *South Staffordshire Water Co. v. Sharman,* a servant found two rings on the landowner's land while working for the landowner. The issue in that case was whether superior title lay in the finder or the landowner. They applied a new rule: superior title goes to the landowner. The court ruled this way because the finder worked for the landowner. By employing the servant, the landowner was exercising control over that part of the land where the rings were found. In *Elwes v. Briggs Gas Co.,* a prehistoric boat was found in land that was leased to the defendant. The issue was whether the boat belonged to the lessor or lessees. The court ruled that the boat belonged to the lessor. From these cases the following is evident: 1) A landowner possesses everything attached to or under his land and 2) a landowner does not

[right margin handwritten:] old rule – superior title goes to finder, no finder

peel rule – superior title goes to landowner

necessarily possess that which is unattached to his land. In this case, since the brooch was not attached to the land, neither *Bridges v. Hawkesworth* or *South Staffordshire Water Co. v. Sharman* governs. This court chooses to follow *Bridges v. Hawkesworth* in this case. It is noted that this result rewards Hannah (P) for meritorious conduct, such as giving the brooch to the police. Judgment for Plaintiff.

old rule — superior title goes to finder

Analysis:

Lost property goes to the finder. This "prior possessor rule" protects owners who cannot prove title, it encourages the entrusting of goods to others, it protects the expectations of possessors, and it promotes peaceable possession. One exception to the rule is that if an employee finds a lost article on the employer's premises, the property goes to the owner. One reason for this is the view that the employee is acting on behalf of the employer. There is a criticism of this exception, however. It discourages finders from reporting found articles. If they do not report the lost article, they keep it. If they do report it, they lose it. Reporting lost articles is a social goal, because it helps return lost property to the true owner. Another exception is that lost property found under the soil or embedded in the soil belongs to the landowner. The reason for this rule is that owners of land expect that they own not just the surface, but all that lies underneath it. It also discourages trespassers from coming onto land in search of treasure.

■ CASE VOCABULARY

CHATTELS: Personal property, as distinct from real property, or land

DEMISE: To transfer property from one to another. The conveyance of an estate in property from one person to another.

FREEHOLD: An estate in land that entitles one to current possession, sale, etc.

FREEHOLDER: Owner of land.

LOCUS IN QUO: The area under consideration.

PARCEL: An item of personal property; also used to mean a plot or area of land.

WRIT: A judicial order to perform some act.

Items found in private places go to landowner unless homeowner never took possession of the item

p. 11 SH 6 public
law of finders rewards possessors of found items, subject to two modifications; (Armory) ↗ general rule
1) prior possessors defeat subsequent possessors UNLESS, prior possessor never took possession (Hannah) → true title an exception to rule homeowner
2) rightful owner defeats the possessor

McAvoy v. Medina

(Finder) v. (Shop Owner)

93 Mass. (11 Allen) 548 (1866)

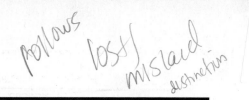
(handwritten: Follows lost/mislaid distinction)

COURT RULES THAT A "FINDER" DOES NOT HAVE TITLE TO MISLAID PROPERTY

■ **INSTANT FACTS** A customer of the shop owner placed his wallet on the counter, but neglected to remove it. McAvoy (P) found the wallet.

■ **BLACK LETTER RULE** A finder has no title to property that is mislaid.

(handwritten: pull SHG lost vs. mislaid)

(handwritten: lost item = accidentally parted with → goes to finder; mislaid item = intentionally place, but unintentionally left behind → turn to management who holds in trust for true owner)

■ **PROCEDURAL BASIS**

Appeal from judgment in action to recover money found by plaintiff.

■ **FACTS**

A customer of a shop placed his wallet on the counter but neglected to remove it; the customer had mislaid his wallet. McAvoy (P) found the wallet and gave it to the shop owner Medina (D) to keep until the true owner should claim it. If the true owner did not claim it, McAvoy (P) requested that Medina (D) advertise the lost money. The true owner was never found and Medina (D) refused to turn the money over to McAvoy (P).

■ **ISSUE**

Does the finder of mislaid property have title to that property?

(handwritten: McAvoy is the finder of mislaid — not lost property — so he did not gain title)

■ **DECISION AND RATIONALE**

(Dewey, J.) No. The ordinary rule is that a finder of lost property has title superior to all the world except the true owner. Here, however, the property was mislaid, not lost. When property is mislaid in a shop, the shop owner has a duty to safeguard the property until the true owner returns. Therefore, a finder can never gain title to mislaid property. *Bridges v. Hawkesworth* is distinguishable. In that case, the property was not voluntarily placed somewhere and then forgotten. Rather, in that case, the property was lost. In this case, since the property was not lost but mislaid, McAvoy (P) can claim no title. Judgment affirmed.

Analysis:

Lost property goes to the finder, but mislaid property goes to the shop owner. One way to understand this rule is to look to one of the goals of property law, to promote the return of lost property to its true owner. If property is mislaid, the true owner will likely retrace his steps and return to the shop where he mislaid it. Thus, the rule that places mislaid property in the hand of the shop owner will more efficiently return mislaid property to the true owner. There are two criticisms to this rule. First, it is difficult to determine whether property has been mislaid or lost. For example, a wallet found on the floor could easily have fallen through a person's pocket and been lost, but it also could have been mislaid on a counter and knocked to the floor by another customer. The second criticism is that individuals retrace their steps for both lost and mislaid property.

(handwritten: finder has title to lost, but not mislaid property)

Van Valkenburgh v. Lutz

(Title Holder) v. (Adverse Possessor)

304 N.Y. 95, 106 N.E.2d 28 (1952)

COURT MAKES IT DIFFICULT TO OBTAIN LAND BY ADVERSE POSSESSION: THE POSSESSOR MUST ACTUALLY BE ON THE LAND, HE MUST BELIEVE THAT IT IS HIS, AND HE MUST ENCLOSE IT OR SUBSTANTIALLY IMPROVE IT

not to seems apply anymore?

no longer applies

old elements of adverse possession?

Mary + William Lutz

■ **INSTANT FACTS** The Lutzes (D) occupied the Van Valkenburgh's (P) land by building a one-bedroom shack on it, by cultivating a garden on it, and by storing rubbish on it. In another action to establish a right of way across the land, the Lutzes (D) admitted that the land belonged to the Van Valkenburghs (P).

still applies

■ **BLACK LETTER RULE** In order to acquire title by adverse possession, possession must be actual, it must be under claim of title, and the land must be either enclosed or sufficiently improved.

1 2 3

■ **FACTS**

no longer applies   no longer applies

In 1912 the Lutzes (D) bought lots 14 and 15 in a large subdivision. Instead of climbing a steep grade to get to their lot, the Lutzes (D) crossed lots 19–22, which they did not own, to get to their lot. With regard to lots 19–22, the Lutzes (D) cleared it, built a one-bedroom shack on it, and grew vegetables on it. The vegetables were sold. In 1937 the Van Valkenburghs (P) purchased a lot near the Lutzes (D). In 1947, the Van Valkenburghs (P) purchased lots 19–22, the lots that the Lutzes (D) had been using. Soon after, the Van Valkenburghs (P) sent a letter to the Lutzes (D) informing them that they, the Van Valkenburghs (P), now owned the property. The letter also requested that the Lutzes (D) remove their property from the land. The Lutzes (D) removed only part of their property, but claimed a prescriptive right of way across the land. Later, the Van Valkenburghs (P) erected a fence across the land, preventing the Lutzes (D) from crossing the land. The Lutzes (D) sued the Van Valkenburghs (P), admitting that the Van Valkenburghs (P) owned the land, but claiming a right of way across the land. The Lutzes (D) prevailed on this issue. The Van Valkenburghs (P) sue here to gain possession of the lots. The Lutzes (D) contend that they acquired title to the lots by adverse possession.

*C – continuous
O – open, notorious
A – actual
H – hostile*

■ **ISSUE**

(1) Must possession be actual in order to acquire title by adverse possession? (2) Where a person claims title not founded upon a written instrument, must a person either protect land by a substantial enclosure or cultivate or improve land to be deemed to be in possession? (3) Must land be possessed under a claim of title to acquire it by adverse possession?

■ **DECISION AND RATIONALE**

No adverse possession for the Lutzes

(Dye, J.) Yes. Yes. Yes. New York Civil Practice Act § 39 [requirements to acquire title by possession] clearly states that land must be actually possessed. This requirement is not met here for two reasons: 1) The garden occupied only a small portion of lots 19–22, and 2) the Lutzes' garage encroached on the land by only a few inches. New York Civil Practice Act § 40 [requirements to acquire title by adverse possession] clearly states that where a person claims title not founded upon a written instrument, he must show that the land was protected by a substantial enclosure or that he cultivated or improved the land. This requirement is not met here. Concededly, the land was not enclosed. The land was not sufficiently improved for two reasons: 1) The shack was too small; 2) The garden was insubstantial; and 3) placing rubbish on the land is not an improvement. New York Civil Practice Act § 39 clearly states that land must be possessed under claim of title. Since Lutz (D) testified that he knew that the land belonged to the Van Valkenburghs (P) in this action and in the prior action by Lutz (P) to establish a right of way, he fails to prove the "claim of title" element of the adverse possession statute. (Judgment reversed)

■ DISSENT

There is substantial evidence to indicate that the land was substantially improved. Second, the land need not be completely occupied. It need be occupied only to the extent necessary to put the true owner on notice. There was enough evidence to support this element. Finally, in order to satisfy the "claim of right" element of the statute, it is not necessary that the Lutzes (D) believed that the property was theirs. It is sufficient only that they intended to acquire and use the land as their own. The fact that the Lutzes (D) admitted that they did not have title is only evidence of whether or not they intended to acquire and use the land as their own. This is true because this admission was made after the statute had run.

Analysis:

Acquisition of title by adverse possession requires actual possession and (sometimes) improvement of the land. The majority felt that the Lutzes (D) did not satisfy these requirements. The dissent takes the view that actual possession means only possession that will put the owner on notice. Another goal of property law is to encourage honesty. This is one way to explain why the majority requires that an adverse possessor acquire title only under "claim of right." If a possessor honestly believes that property is his, he may be eligible to receive title to it.

■ CASE VOCABULARY

DISSEIZED: To dispossess.

DIVEST: To take a right of ownership away from.

EASEMENT: The right to use land.

EASEMENT BY ADVERSE POSSESSION: The right to use the property of another acquired under the doctrine of adverse possession.

ORAL DISCLAIMER: Oral repudiation of ownership.

PRESCRIPTIVE RIGHT: An easement obtained by adverse possession.

VEST: To give a present right to ownership.

Mannillo v. Gorski

(Landowner) v. (Encroacher)

54 N.J. 378, 255 A.2d 258 (1969)

COURT ABANDONS HOSTILITY REQUIREMENT BUT REQUIRES OPEN AND NOTORIOUS ADVERSE POSSESSION IN BORDER DISPUTE

- ■ **INSTANT FACTS** A property owner sought to enjoin the alleged trespass of an adjoining landowner whose pathway encroached 15 inches and who claimed title to the strip by adverse possession.

- ■ **BLACK LETTER RULE** Possession need not be knowingly and intentionally hostile, but it must be notorious enough to give the true owner actual or constructive notice of the encroachment.

■ FACTS

Mannillo (P) and Gorski (D) owned adjacent lots. For a period of over 20 years, steps and a concrete walk leading from Gorski's (D) house encroached upon Mannillo's (P) land some 15 inches. As a result, Mannillo (P) filed a complaint seeking to enjoin Gorski's (D) alleged trespass. Gorski (D) counterclaimed for a declaratory judgment to the effect that Gorski (D) had gained title to the 15-inch strip of land by adverse possession. Mannillo (P) contended that Gorski (D) did not gain title by adverse possession because her taking was not of the requisite hostile nature. According to Mannillo (P), encroachment must be accompanied by an intention to invade the rights of another. Gorski (D) was not aware that the steps and path encroached onto Mannillo's lot, but rather operated under the mistaken belief that she owned the land. The trial court accepted Mannillo's (P) argument and entered judgment for Mannillo (P). Gorski (D) appealed.

■ ISSUE

(1) Must possession be accompanied by a knowing intentional hostility for adverse possession? (2) Does a minor border encroachment satisfy the "open and notorious" requirement for adverse possession?

■ DECISION AND RATIONALE

(Haneman, J.) (1) No. Possession need not be accompanied by a knowing intentional hostility for adverse possession. Entry and continuance of possession under the mistaken belief that the possessor has title to the lands involved may exhibit the requisite hostile possession to sustain the obtaining of title by adverse possession. If knowing intentional hostility were required, as the Maine doctrine suggests, we would be rewarding the possessor who entered with a premeditated and predesigned hostility and we would be punishing the honest, mistaken entrant. Rather, we choose to follow the Connecticut doctrine and hold that mistake does not negate the hostility requirement. The key to adverse possession is the true owner's neglect to recover possession of his land, which does not hinge on whether the adverse entry is caused by mistake or intent. (2) No. A minor border encroachment does not satisfy the "open and notorious" requirement for adverse possession. Generally when possession of land is clear enough to be immediately visible, the true owner may be presumed to have knowledge of the adverse occupancy. However, a border dispute such as the instant action does not create a clear situation of adverse occupancy. Indeed, the only way that Mannillo (P) could have determined that Gorski (D) was encroaching was to have a survey performed. Landowners should not be required to bear the expense of a survey every time the adjacent landowner makes some improvement. Thus, we hold that no presumption of knowledge arises from a minor encroachment along a common boundary. Only where the true owner has actual knowledge of the encroachment may it be said that the possession is open and notorious. Nevertheless, we realize that this may impose an undue hardship on the adverse possessor who mistakenly encroaches on his neighbor's property while making an improvement. Equity may require that the court force the true owner to convey the land upon payment of the fair value by the adverse possessor. We remand this case for a determination of whether Mannillo (P) had actual knowledge of the encroachment and, if not, whether Mannillo (P) should be required to convey the strip of land to Gorski (D).

Analysis:

According to this court, adverse possession requires entry and possession for some requisite period of time that is exclusive, continuous, uninterrupted, visible, and notorious. The court abandons the requirement that the possession be openly and knowingly hostile. On one hand, the court's adoption of the Connecticut doctrine makes sense, because it does not award an intentional wrongdoer over an honest, mistaken entrant. In another light, however, the Maine doctrine makes more sense. The Maine doctrine rewards only the person who actually desires to take possession of land. If a person mistakenly erects a fence beyond his boundary with no intention to claim title if he later finds out that he is encroaching on his neighbor's land, why should this person be rewarded? With regard to the "open and notorious" requirement, the court states a simple but important concept. Possession must be of such a degree that the true owner has actual knowledge, or should have knowledge, of the intrusion. Minor border encroachments are often insufficient to provide actual knowledge, and the court justly holds that they do not provide constructive knowledge either. Finally, note the court's discussion of its equitable powers: if the encroacher does not meet the requirements for adverse possession, he can nevertheless have a court force the true owner to sell the land if the court determines that this is the most equitable result.

■ CASE VOCABULARY

DICHOTOMY: Division into two contradictory parts.

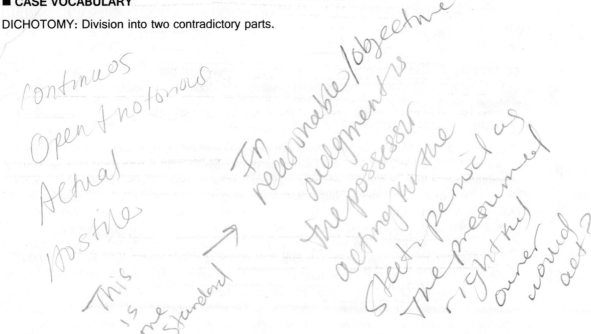

Howard v. Kunto

(Landowner) v. (Landowner)

477 P.2d 210 (Wash. Ct. App. 1970)

CONTINUOUS SEASONAL OCCUPANCY BY SUCCESSIVE OWNERS ESTABLISHES ADVERSE POSSESSION

■ **INSTANT FACTS** Three adjacent landowners each held deeds that did not coincide with the actual legal descriptions of the physical properties.

■ **BLACK LETTER RULE** Tacking on successive possessions of property is permitted for purposes of establishing adverse possession if the successive owners are in privity.

■ **PROCEDURAL BASIS**

On appeal to review a trial court decision for the plaintiff.

■ **FACTS**

Dating back to 1932, a fifty-foot tract of land bordering the Hood Canal in Washington and the summerhouse upon it had passed through several owners, until Kunto (P) took possession by deed in 1959. In each transaction, the same legal description was used on the deed and surveys were conducted on the property. The Moyers occupied the parcel of land immediately east of Kunto's (D) land. Howard (P) owned land easterly adjacent to the Moyers' property. In 1960, Howard (P) sought to convey a one-half interest in his property to the Yearlys. Upon commissioning a survey of his property, Howard learned that the legal description on his deed did not coincide with his property and that he was in fact the record owner of the Moyers' property. Likewise, the Moyers were the record owners of the property owned by Kunto (D), who owned the property immediately to the west of the land upon which his house was constructed. After making this discovery, Howard (P) agreed with Moyer to convey record title of his property—that which Moyer previously believed to belong to him—in exchange for Moyer's interest in the Kunto (D) property. Because neither Moyer nor any of his predecessors in interest had ever asserted ownership of the Kunto (D) property, he agreed to the conveyance. Thereafter, Howard (P) and Yearly filed an action to quiet title. When considering Kunto's (D) claim that he had acquired title to the property by adverse possession, the trial court concluded that Kunto had not continuously possessed the property because it was used only for summer occupancy, and that he was not permitted to "tack" his predecessors' occupancy of the property to establish the ten-year statutory period required for adverse possession. Kunto (D) appealed.

■ **ISSUE**

May a person who holds record title to tract A under the mistaken belief that he has title to tract B (immediately contiguous to tract A), and who subsequently occupies tract B, for the purpose of establishing title to tract B by adverse possession, use the periods of possession of tract B by his immediate predecessors, who also had record title to tract A, even when everyone's possession was limited to summer occupancy?

■ DECISION AND RATIONALE

(Pearson, J.) Yes. "To constitute adverse possession, there must be actual possession which is uninterrupted, open and notorious, hostile and exclusive, and under a claim of right made in good faith for the statutory period." Uninterrupted possession does not require constant year-round occupancy, but rather such control over the property as ordinarily marks the conduct of owners in general in holding, managing, and caring for property of a similar nature and condition. Accordingly, occupancy of the summerhouse during summer months over the ten-year statutory period sufficiently establishes adverse possession. Kunto (D), however, has not personally occupied the property for the required ten-year period. Accordingly, to establish continuity for the statutory period, tacking of Kunto's (D) predecessors' possession must be allowed. In the ordinary situation in which one seeks more property than is described in a deed, "a purchaser may tack the adverse use of its predecessor in interest to that of his own where the land was intended to be included in the deed between them, but was mistakenly omitted from the description." Such tacking is permitted because the current possessor is in privity of estate with each successive possessor by operation of the deed running between them. The notion of privity ensures that continuous trespassers, seeking ownership of property without a valid claim of right, will not defeat the property interests of true owners. In reality, however, privity is a judicial recognition of a reasonable connection between successive occupants who have a good faith claim of right. Whether they seek more property than represented in their deed or a different parcel altogether, their successive interests are in privity, and tacking is permissible to establish adverse possession. Because Kunto (D) and his successors continuously occupied the parcel for more than the statutory period, he is entitled to quiet title to the disputed property. Reversed.

Analysis:

As the court indicates, the facts of this case are quite unusual. In the ordinary adverse possession situation, a landowner seeks to gain ownership over more property than his deed reflects. Often, a landowner will, for instance, erect a fence around his boundary that actually crosses his property line into a neighbor's land. Over time, that encroachment upon the neighbor's land grants the landowner ownership of the neighbor's land within the fence perimeter, assuming all elements of adverse possession have been satisfied.

■ CASE VOCABULARY

ADVERSE POSSESSION: A method of acquiring title to real property by possession for a statutory period under certain conditions, especially a nonpermissive use of the land with a claim of right when that use is continuous, exclusive, hostile, open, and notorious.

CONTINUOUS-ADVERSE-USE PRINCIPLE: The rule that the uninterrupted use of land—along with the other elements of adverse possession—will result in a successful claim for adverse possession.

PRIVITY: The connection or relationship between two parties, each having a legally recognized interest in the same subject matter (such as a transaction, proceeding, or piece of property); mutuality of interest.

RECORD OWNER: A property owner in whose name the title appears in the public records.

TACKING: The joining of consecutive periods of possession by different persons to treat the periods as one continuous period; especially, the adding of one's own period of land possession to that of a prior possessor to establish continuous adverse possession for the statutory period.

O'Keeffe v. Snyder

(Title Holder) v. (Adverse Possessor)

83 N.J. 478, 416 A.2d 862 (1980)

[handwritten: she likes this case]
[handwritten: statute of limitations]

COURT MAKES IT MORE DIFFICULT TO OBTAIN TITLE TO PERSONAL PROPERTY BY ADVERSE POSSESSION: IF THE OWNER USES DILIGENCE TO LOCATE AND RECOVER THE PROPERTY, THE STATUTE IS TOLLED

[handwritten right margin: tolling statute of limitations means it has been legally suspended]

■ **INSTANT FACTS** Three of O'Keeffe's paintings were stolen from an art gallery. The thefts were not reported to anyone.

■ **BLACK LETTER RULE** The statute of limitations is tolled if the owner of stolen chattel makes diligent efforts to locate and recover the lost chattel.

■ **PROCEDURAL BASIS**

Appeal from an order by the appellate court reversing an order of summary judgment for defendant in action to replevy chattels.

■ **FACTS**

In 1946 three paintings by O'Keeffe (P) were stolen from an art gallery operated by her husband, Stieglitz. O'Keeffe (P) suspected that Estrick may have stolen the paintings. However, she did not confront him about it; neither did she report the theft to the police. O'Keeffe explains that she did not pursue her efforts to find the paintings because she was settling her deceased husband's estate. Finally, in 1972 O'Keeffe (P) authorized Bry to report the theft to the Art Dealers Association of America, which maintains a registry of stolen paintings. It is not clear whether such a registry existed in 1946. In 1976 O'Keeffe (P) discovered that Frank had sold her paintings to Snyder (D). Frank acquired the paintings from his father. Frank does not know how his father acquired the paintings, but he recalls seeing them in his father's house as early as 1941. This is inconsistent with O'Keeffe's allegation of theft. For the purposes of this appeal, Snyder (D) concedes that the paintings are stolen. Frank claims continuous possession for over 30 years through his father and claims title by adverse possession.

[handwritten right margin: Also about tacking]

[handwritten right margin: when the registry exists is important. If registry existed from 1946 on, she was remiss in not reporting it]

■ **ISSUE**

If possession of chattels is obtained by theft, and the true owner makes diligent efforts to locate and recover the chattels, is the statute of limitations for adverse possession tolled?

■ **DECISION AND RATIONALE**

(Pollock, J.) Yes. In no circumstances can a thief transfer good title. However, if Frank acquired a voidable title from his father, who may have been a thief, Frank has the power to transfer good title to a good faith purchaser under the U. C. C. If Snyder (D) was not a good faith purchaser, or if Frank did not have a voidable title, Snyder (D) may still acquire title by adverse possession. However, in certain situations, the statute of limitations is tolled to avoid harsh results. Unlike land that is adversely possessed, the owner of chattels may not know that her property has been stolen, or she may not know who the adverse possessor is. This is especially true with stolen art, which is often concealed. O'Keeffe (P) contends that nothing short of public display should suffice to put the true owner on notice. However, this rule is harsh to good faith

[handwritten bottom: replevin - cause of action for recovery of a stolen item]

purchasers who wish to display art in the privacy of their homes. The following compromise, called the discovery rule, balances these interests. Upon discovery of theft the statute of limitations is tolled if the true owner of the chattels makes diligent efforts, under the circumstances, to locate and recover the chattels. Depending upon the circumstances, this may include reporting the theft to the police or registering the lost chattels with a registry so as to notify potential buyers that it may be stolen. Reversed and remanded for a finding of whether O'Keeffe (P) used diligence in discovering who had the lost paintings.

Analysis:

The policy goals motivating the doctrine of adverse possession include: (1) after a long time, titles should be settled; and (2) the efficient use of land should be encouraged. In this case, we see the converse of these principles. A true owner who is not at fault in failing to recover his property should not be divested of title, based on simple notions of justice. Notice, however, that this rule may harm a good faith purchaser who had the bad luck to buy stolen property. The court does not give this concern much weight. It reasons that a purchaser may always learn whether property is stolen or not. In practice, however, a good faith buyer may not be so fortunate.

■ CASE VOCABULARY

CONVERSION: To take property from another.

DISCOVERY RULE: The rules by which one may obtain title to chattels by adverse possession. It provides that the statute of limitations does not run if the true owner uses diligence to discover the possessor of his property.

IMPLEAD: To bring a third party into a lawsuit on the ground that such third party is liable to the defendant.

INTERROGATORY: A formal set of questions propounded to a party designed to elicit the facts.

LEGATEES: A person who takes property under a will.

PLENARY HEARING: A complete hearing of a case to fully determine the facts.

REPLEVIN: An action to regain possession.

REPLEVY: To take or get back by a right for replevin.

SUMMARY JUDGMENT: Judgment rendered in a case based only on consideration of the law, where there is no dispute of the facts.

VOIDABLE TITLE: Title which remains valid until the true owner asserts ownership.

Newman v. Bost

(Donee) v. (Administrator of Donor's Estate)

122 N.C. 524, 29 S.E. 848 (1898)

COURT MAKES IT MORE DIFFICULT TO GIVE GIFTS: SYMBOLIC DELIVERY IS NOT ALLOWED

[handwritten: constructive]

[handwritten: Must be manual/actual unless impossible to do so?]

■ **INSTANT FACTS** After giving the keys to much of the furniture in the house to Newman (P), the decedent pointed to the furniture and said to Newman (P) that he was giving it all to her. In one of the pieces of furniture was a life insurance policy.

■ **BLACK LETTER RULE** Symbolic delivery of a gift is not effective. Constructive delivery is allowed only when it is impractical to deliver actual possession.

[handwritten: ☆]

■ PROCEDURAL BASIS

Appeal from judgment in action for damages for conversion.

■ FACTS

After decedent was stricken ill, he gave to Newman (P) all that was in his home. He did this as follows: In the presence of Houston, he had Newman (P) summoned. He asked Newman (P) to give him his keys. Decedent then handed the keys to Newman (P), saying that he wanted her to have everything in his house. He then pointed to specific pieces of furniture including a locked bureau. Among the keys given to Newman (P) was a key that unlocked his bureau. This was the only key to the bureau. In this bureau was a life insurance policy covering the life of the decedent. Bost (D), administrator of decedent's estate, sold all of the property in the decedent's home. Newman (P) sues for the value of the life insurance policy as well as for the value of the other goods in the home.

[handwritten margin: manual not practicable then constructive or symbolic]

■ ISSUE

Is symbolic delivery sufficient to make a gift good? Is constructive delivery sufficient when delivery of actual possession is impractical?

[handwritten: No] [handwritten: yes] [handwritten: handing over a means of obtaining possession & control]

■ DECISION AND RATIONALE

(Furches, J.) No. Yes. First, in order to make a valid gift, the donor must intend to make the gift. In this case it is not clear whether the decedent intended to give only the bureau that he pointed to or its contents or both. Thus, the life insurance, which was in the bureau, was not a good gift. Second, in order to make a valid gift, the donor must deliver actual possession. This rigid rule was made for a time when few could read. As time passed, written conveyances became acceptable, as the statute of frauds and wills makes clear. Accordingly, when actual delivery is impractical, constructive delivery will suffice. However, we are still mindful of fraud so we do not allow symbolic delivery. Constructive delivery is the handing over of the means of obtaining possession and control. An example is the handing over of keys to a car. Regarding the life insurance, actual delivery of possession is not impractical. The decedent could have easily had someone else get the life insurance policy and hand it over to Newman (P). Thus, there can be no constructive delivery. Since there was neither actual or constructive delivery, there was no gift of the life insurance policy. However, since the furniture in the house to which

[handwritten margin left: What does decedent want her to have? Did that include the life insurance policy?]

[handwritten margin right: But she does get bedroom furnishings]

[handwritten bottom: Court says like insurance policy not included]

Newman (P) had the keys was heavy and impractical to deliver, the handing over of the keys was good constructive delivery. Also, the furniture in Newman's (P) own bedroom was actually delivered to her, since she exercised control over it. The other furnishings in the house, to which Newman (P) did not have keys, were not constructively or actually delivered. Affirmed in part, reversed in part, and remanded for a new trial.

Analysis:

In this case there are two competing policy goals in operation. The first goal is to protect owners of property from being defrauded. The second goal is to promote the free alienability of property. This court has reconciled these competing goals with a compromise. Symbolic delivery will not be allowed, and constructive delivery will be allowed only if actual delivery is impractical under the circumstances. This compromise between the desire to make property freely alienable and the desire to protect the owner from being defrauded also appears in the law of concurrent interests.

■ CASE VOCABULARY

ADMINISTRATOR: A person appointed by a testator to carry out the directions in his will.

DONATIO CAUSA MORTIS: A gift made when death is impending.

ESTATE: The accumulated property and legal rights of a deceased person.

EXPRESS: Made clear, usually by verbal or written communication, as contrasted with implied.

GIFT CAUSA MORTIS: A gift made when death is impending.

GIFT INTER VIVOS: A gift made while alive and healthy.

IN EXTREMIS: Near death.

INTESTATE: One who has died without a will; the estate of one who has died without a will.

ISSUE: The children of a testator

STATUTE OF WILLS: The statute enacted in England which allowed persons to dispose of their property at death as they desired.

TESTATOR: One who has made a will.

lots of social class issues involved

Gruen v. Gruen

(Donee) v. (Possessor)

68 N.Y.2d 48, 496 N.E.2d 869, 505 N.Y.S.2d 849 (1986)

COURT MAKES IT EASIER TO GIVE GIFTS: A PARTY MAY GIVE A REMAINDER TO ANOTHER WHILE RESERVING A LIFE ESTATE IN HIMSELF

■ **INSTANT FACTS** The elder Gruen gave Gruen (P) a painting but reserved a life estate for himself. Gruen (P) has never had possession of the painting.

■ **BLACK LETTER RULE** A party may give a future interest in chattels as a gift while reserving a life estate in himself.

■ **PROCEDURAL BASIS**

Appeal from an order of the appellate division reversing a judgment in an action for delivery of chattels.

■ **FACTS**

Gruen's (P) father wrote a letter to him giving him a painting for his birthday. However, the elder Gruen reserved a life estate for himself, The original letter was destroyed on the instructions of the elder Gruen. The elder Gruen felt this was necessary for tax reasons. However, he did send a second letter to Gruen (P) giving him the painting, though not mentioning that he reserved a life estate in himself. Seventeen years later, the elder Gruen died. Gruen (D), the defendant's stepmother, now has possession of the painting and refuses to deliver it to Gruen (P). Gruen (D) contends that the purported gift is invalid because title vests only after the death of Gruen. That is, she contends that the gift was testamentary and did not satisfy the formalities of a will. Alternatively, Gruen (D) contends that a donor may not make a valid gift of a chattel while reserving a life estate in himself because possession is not delivered.

■ **ISSUE**

May a valid inter vivos gift be made where the donor reserves a life estate in the chattel and the donee has never taken possession?

■ **DECISION AND RATIONALE**

(Simons, J.) Yes. An inter vivos gift requires that the donor intend to make a present transfer of title. If the intention is to make a transfer of title only after death, the gift is invalid unless made by a will. Gruen (D) errs in maintaining that the elder Gruen intended to make a transfer of title only at his death. On the contrary, he intended to make a present transfer of a future interest. Title to this future interest, which is a remainder, vested at the time of the gift. It is irrelevant that possession is not taken until some time in the future. As to Gruen's (D) contention that the gift was invalid because possession was not delivered, we note that the rule that possession must be delivered to consummate a gift is flexible. This is a better statement of the rule: The delivery that is required is that delivery that is best under the circumstances. In this case, since Gruen (P) had only a remainder, it was impossible to deliver such an interest until the elder Gruen had died. Moreover, it would be silly to have the elder Gruen deliver possession merely to take it back so that he could enjoy his life estate. Judgment affirmed.

Analysis:

One of the principle goals of property law is to promote the alienability of property. This goal is of such importance that the court in *Gruen v. Gruen* allowed the elder Gruen to make a gift of a future interest, even though it was not possible to deliver possession of this interest, and even though the possibility of fraud was great. The possibility of fraud is generally great in the area of future interests because a person may easily claim that he was given a gift, but that he was not given possession because he was given a future interest. The tension between the possibility of fraud and the desire to make property freely alienable appears throughout the law of estates and concurrent interests.

■ CASE VOCABULARY

CONSTRUCTIVE DELIVERY: Delivery of the means by which property may be possessed.

DECEASED: Dead person.

DELIVERY: To give over possession.

DISPOSITIVE: Of such a nature or quality as to by itself determine the outcome of a case.

IRREVOCABLE: Incapable of being taken back.

LIFE ESTATE: A possessory estate in property that has one's life as the measure of duration.

REMAINDER INTEREST: An interest in property that is not currently possessory, but will become possessory in the future.

RESERVE: To keep for oneself rather than conveying to another.

ROYALTIES: Proceeds from the earnings of property or business.

SYMBOLIC DELIVERY: Delivery in the eyes of the law; the performing of some act that represents delivery, such as executing a writing.

TESTAMENTARY: Pertaining to a will.

VEST: To give a present right to ownership.

WILL: An instrument by which one disposes of his property and legal rights upon his death.

CHAPTER THREE

Possessory Estates

White v. Brown

Instant Facts: Jessie Lide died leaving a will stating "I wish Evelyn White (P) to have my home to live in and not to be sold. . . . My house is not to be sold."

Black Letter Rule: Unless a contrary intention appears by the terms of the will and its context, a will conveys a testator's entire interest.

Baker v. Weedon

Instant Facts: John Weedon left a life estate to Weedon (P) and a remainder to the Bakers (D). Weedon (D) wishes to sale the land now to reap its value; Baker (P) wishes to retain ownership of the land to allow its value to increase.

Black Letter Rule: A trial court shall order a judicial sale only if it is in the best interest of both the freehold tenant and the holder of the future interest.

Mahrenholz v. County Board of School Trustees

Instant Facts: The Huttons conveyed land to the School Board (D) "to be used for school purposes only." Subsequently, the school used the land for storage.

Black Letter Rule: Language such as "to be used for school purposes only" creates a fee simple determinable.

Mountain Brow Lodge No. 82, Independent Order of Odd Fellows v. Toscano

Instant Facts: A deed provided that a lot shall revert back to the grantor if the grantee, a lodge (P), either failed to use the lot or attempted to sell it.

Black Letter Rule: The use of land may be restricted in a conveyance.

Ink v. City of Canton

Instant Facts: The descendants of Harry Ink conveyed to The City of Canton (P) land to be used for park purposes only. Subsequently, the state of Ohio instituted eminent domain proceedings against the land.

Black Letter Rule: The proceeds from an eminent domain proceeding are to be divided between the holder of the fee simple on condition subsequent and the holder of the reverter.

White v. Brown

(Heir) v. (Heir)

559 S.W.2d 938 (Tenn. 1977)

COURTS PRESUME THAT A CONVEYANCE OF REAL PROPERTY IN A WILL WAS INTENDED TO CONVEY A FEE SIMPLE ESTATE, UNLESS CONTRARY INTENT IS DEMONSTRATED

■ **INSTANT FACTS** Jessie Lide died leaving a will stating "I wish Evelyn White (P) to have my home to live in and not to be sold. . . . My house is not to be sold."

■ **BLACK LETTER RULE** Unless a contrary intention appears by the terms of the will and its context, a will conveys a testator's entire interest.

■ **PROCEDURAL BASIS**

Appeal from judgment in action to construct a will.

■ **FACTS**

White (P), along with her husband and daughter, lived in Jessie Lide's house for 25 years. When Jessie Lide died, she left a holographic will which read in part: "I wish Evelyn White (P) to have my home to live in and not to be sold. . . . My house is not to be sold." White (P) contends that the will conveyed a fee simple interest in the house. Brown (D) contends that the will merely conveyed a life estate to White (P). The trial court ruled that the will, on its face, unambiguously conveyed a life estate. Since the trial court found that the will was facially unambiguous, it did not consider extrinsic evidence.

■ **ISSUE**

Unless a contrary intention appears by the terms of the will and its context, does a will convey a testator's entire interest?

■ **DECISION AND RATIONALE**

(Brock, J.) Yes. At common law, there was a presumption that a testator conveyed only a life estate. However, the legislature has enacted a rule of construction which reverses this presumption: A will shall convey all the real estate belonging to the testator unless a contrary intention appears by the terms of the will and its context. Several cases demonstrate the strength of the presumption that a testator conveys his entire interest. In *Green v. Young,* testatrix left her property to her husband "to be used by him for his support and comfort during his life." Yet, the will was held to pass a fee simple to the husband. In *Williams v. Williams,* the testator devised real property to his children "for and during their natural lives." Yet, the will was held to pass a fee simple. Therefore, it is clear that if the only language in Lide's will was that the home was for White (P) to "live in", a fee simple would pass. However, the language "not to be sold" complicates matters. We must look to the context to determine if Lide intended to convey only a life estate. Where there is ambiguity, we construe a will to dispose of the testator's entire estate, which would be a fee simple in this case. In this case, it appears that Lide attempted to pass a fee simple to White (P) and further attempted to restrain her from alienating the property. This attempt to restrict alienation is clear: "My house is not to be sold."

A restraint on alienation is void as against public policy, leaving White (P) with a fee simple. Judgment reversed.

■ **DISSENT**

(Harbison, J.) Lide's will is not ambiguous. It is clear that she intended to pass only a life estate: ". . . to have my home to live in and not to be sold." *Green v. Young* is distinguishable because in that case the testatrix bequeathed all of her real and personal property to her husband, so it is reasonable to presume that a fee simple was intended. Here, Lide bequeathed to White (P) only real property. *Williams v. Williams* is not applicable because it contains other clauses which indicate a clear intent to pass a fee simple: the children of the testator "were to have all the residue of my estate." In this case, the testatrix knew how to convey all her property. She demonstrated this when she left all her personal property to her niece. As to White (P), she merely wished that she "live in" her home; she intended to convey a life estate.

Analysis:

The law promotes the free alienability of property, so it seems odd, in a country founded on the economic principles of "freedom of contract," that the law would (or could) restrict the conditions that people can put on the transfer of their own property. However, remember the historical background in which property laws developed. Under the laws of England at the time of the American Revolution, property could perpetually be bound up in the hands of a single family. The only way to free the property was to go through complicated and expensive legal proceedings, which resulted in the creation of a landed aristocracy—a system the Founders were loathe to replicate here in the United States.

■ **CASE VOCABULARY**

ALIENATION OF PROPERTY: The principle that the owner of a piece of property should be able to sell or use the land as he or she sees fit, without limitation by the former owner.

ESTATE: The extent or nature of one's interest in property. Also, the sum total of all of one's property at death.

FEE SIMPLE: The largest estate in land that one may own.

INTESTATE: To die without a will.

LIFE ESTATE: An estate that lasts either for the life of the owner or the life of another person.

REMAINDER: The future interest that becomes possessory after the expiration of some intervening estate.

RESTRAINT ON ALIENATION: A restriction on the sale or conveyance of property.

Baker v. Weedon

(Remaindermen) v. (Life Tenant)

262 So.2d 641, 57 A.L.R.3d 1183 (Miss. 1972)

IN ORDERING A SALE OF LAND, COURTS MUST BALANCE THE INTERESTS OF THOSE WHO HAVE A PRESENT INTEREST AND THOSE WITH A FUTURE INTEREST

■ **INSTANT FACTS** John Weedon left a life estate to Weedon (P) and a remainder to the Bakers (D). Weedon (D) wishes to sale the land now to reap its value; Baker (P) wishes to retain ownership of the land to allow its value to increase.

■ **BLACK LETTER RULE** A trial court shall order a judicial sale only if it is in the best interest of both the freehold tenant and the holder of the future interest.

■ **PROCEDURAL BASIS**

Interlocutory appeal from ruling of the trial court ordering the sale of land.

■ **FACTS**

John Weedon's first marriage to Lula Edwards resulted in two children, Florence Weedon Baker and Delette Weedon Jones. Florence Weedon Baker mothered three children, Henry Baker (P), Sarah Baker Lyman (P) and Louise Virginia Baker Heck (P). These children were the plaintiffs in the trial court and are the appellants here. After a second marriage, John Weedon finally married Anna Plaxico (D), 38 years his junior. Anna (D) and John had no children together. Anna Plaxico, now Anna Plaxico Weedon (D), was the defendant in the trial court and the appellee here. In his will, John Weedon left to Anna Plaxico a life estate and left to his grandchildren a contingent remainder: "I give to . . . Anna Plaxico Weedon (D) all of my property . . . during her life . . . and in the event she dies without issue then . . . I give . . . all of my property to my grandchildren." John Weedon died in 1932. Anna (D) ceased to farm the land in 1955 due to her age and began to rent to property. It is undisputed that this rental income and Anna's (D) other income is insufficient to support her. In 1964, just as the commercial value of the land was increasing rapidly, the state sought a right-of-way through the property. At trial, the property was worth $168,500. However, the property's estimated value in four years is placed at $336,000. Although Anna (D) now lives in a new home, she is in economic distress and prays that the land be sold so that she can reap her share of the property value. The Bakers (P) wish to allow the property to increase in value before it is sold. The trial court ordered the land sold because it felt that the land was being wasted. The Bakers (P) appeal.

■ **ISSUE**

Shall a trial court order a judicial sale only if it is in the best interest of all parties?

■ **DECISION AND RATIONALE**

(Patterson, J.) Yes. Trial courts have jurisdiction to order the sale of land for the prevention of waste if the facts so merit. However, the trial court can order a sale only if it is in the best interest of all the parties. This rule has the necessary flexibility to meet unique situations and to yield equitable solutions. In this case, though it is true that a sale would benefit Weedon (D), it would bring great financial loss to the Bakers (P). Thus, a judicial sale is not in the best interest of all parties. We suggest, however, that a sale of part of the land may be equitable under the circumstances. Ordered reversed.

Analysis:

The law prefers that property be alienable because it maximizes the value of land. When land is divided into present and future interests, however, the land is often worth more to the freehold tenant if it is not sold and more to the future tenant if it is sold. Thus, the law must make a choice. Several rules have developed in an attempt to maximize the value and equities to both the freehold tenant and the future tenant. Note, however, that no solution will make all parties happy. In order to avoid the problems created by a legal life estate followed by a remainder, a grantor can create a trust. In a trust, a trustee holds the legal fee simple to the property. The trustee must manage the fee simple for the benefit of all parties. He may allow the life tenant into possession or he may pay income from the fee simple to the life tenant, but in any case, he must do what is equitable for both the life tenant and the future tenant. Since the trustee holds the legal fee simple, he may sell the fee simple if it is in the best interests of both parties. Thus, a trust is far more flexible than a legal life estate followed by a remainder.

■ CASE VOCABULARY

ECONOMIC WASTE: To allow land to depreciate in value; to not put land to its best and most valuable use.

FUTURE INTEREST: An interest in land that is not currently possessory.

INHERITANCE: Property which descends to another upon the death of someone.

REMAINDERMEN: Those persons who have an interest in property that will not become possessory until some intervening estate has expired.

TRUST: A legal entity created by one person for the benefit of another; usually, the trustee has legal title to the property, and the beneficiary is entitled to the income from the trust.

Mahrenholz v. County Board of School Trustees

(Holder of Future Interest) v. (Holder of Defeasible Fee Simple)

93 Ill.App.3d 366, 417 N.E.2d 138 (1981)

COURT DISTINGUISHES BETWEEN LANGUAGE WHICH CREATES A FEE SIMPLE DETERMINABLE AND FEE SIMPLE ON CONDITION SUBSEQUENT

- **INSTANT FACTS** The Huttons conveyed land to the School Board (D) "to be used for school purposes only." Subsequently, the school used the land for storage.

- **BLACK LETTER RULE** Language such as "to be used for school purposes only" creates a fee simple determinable.

■ PROCEDURAL BASIS

Appeal from demurrer in action to quiet title.

■ FACTS

In 1941 the Huttons conveyed property to the Trustees of School District No.1. The deed stated: "This land to be used for school purposes only; otherwise to revert to grantors herein." Also in 1941 the Huttons conveyed their reversionary interest in this property to Jacqmain. In 1959, Jacqmain conveyed this reversionary interest to Mahrenholz (P). When Mr. and Mrs. Hutton died, their only legal heir was Harry Hutton. In 1977 Harry Hutton conveyed any possibility of reverter or right of entry that he may have had in the land to Mahrenholz (P). Later in 1977 Hutton disclaimed any interest he had in the land to the School Board (D). The property that the Huttons conveyed to the school was used for classes until 1973. Since then, the school has used the property for storage. Mahrenholz (P) contends that the deed conveying the land to the school board created a determinable fee simple followed by a possibility of reverter. The school board (D) contends that the deed created a fee simple followed by right of entry.

■ ISSUE

Does language such as "to be used for school purposes only" create a fee simple determinable?

■ DECISION AND RATIONALE

(Jones, J.) Yes. First, since neither a right of entry nor a possibility of reverter can be transferred by will or inter vivos conveyance, Mahrenholz (P) could not have acquired the land from Jacqmain. Thus, we must determine what interest, if any, Mahrenholz (P) acquired from Harry Hutton. To determine whether a fee simple on condition subsequent or a fee simple determinable was created, we need to examine the words in the deed. Words such as "so long as the land is used for school purposes" or "while it was used for school purposes" or "until the land ceased to be used for school purposes" create a fee simple determinable. Words such as "on the condition that the land be used for school purposes" or "provided that the land be used for school purposes" create a fee simple subject to condition subsequent. Upon examination of the language in the deed, it appears that the Huttons conveyed a fee simple determinable. The phrase "for school purpose only" suggest that Huttons wanted to give the land only as long as it was needed and no longer. The second phrase, "otherwise to revert to grantors," seems to trigger an automatic return of the property to the Huttons. Thus, the grant indicates a fee simple determinable. There are many cases where similar language was held to create a fee simple determinable. For example, in *U.S. v. 1119.15 Acres of Land,* "when said land cease to be used for school purposes it is to revert to the above grantor" was held to create a fee simple determinable. *Latham v. Illinois Central Railroad Co.* is distinguishable because in that case land was granted to the grantee "their successors and assigns *forever* . . . in case of non-use of said land for the above purposes, title shall revert back to grantors." In contrast, Hutton did not grant land forever, but only so long as it was used for school purposes. In *McElvain v. Dorris,* the grantor granted land "to be used for mill purposes, and if not for mill purposes the title reverts back to the former owner." The court held that this created a fee simple on condition subsequent. This case in not applicable for two reasons: (1) It is not clear whether the court held that this language created a fee simple on condition subsequent or whether it was referring to an earlier provision in the deed; (2) the court's holding may simply reflect the parties' agreement as to what the provision meant. A more appropriate case is *North v. Graham.* There, "said land . . . to revert to the party of the first whenever it ceases to be used . . ." was held to create a fee simple determinable. Therefore, the 1941 deed from the Huttons to the School Board (D) created a fee simple determinable. Reversed.

Analysis:

The case illustrates how significantly different legal outcomes can turn on the wording of a deed. If a deed is construed to create a fee simple determinable, the title *automatically* reverts to the grantor or his successor in interest if the condition subsequent is broken. If a deed is construed to create a fee simple on condition subsequent, the title reverts to the grantor or his successor only if he retakes the land. If he fails to retake the land, the grantee may acquire fee simple absolute by adverse possession or abandonment.

■ CASE VOCABULARY

DEFEASIBLE FEE SIMPLE: A fee simple estate in land which can be divested if a pre-determined condition subsequent actually occurs.

FEE SIMPLE DETERMINABLE: A fee simple which is divested from the owner and reverts back to the grantor upon the occurrence of a pre-determined condition subsequent.

FEE SIMPLE SUBJECT TO CONDITION SUBSEQUENT: A defeasible fee which gives the grantor the right to re-take the land from the grantee if a pre-specified condition subsequent actually occurs.

INTER VIVOS CONVEYANCE: A conveyance made while the grantor is alive.

POSSIBILITY OF REVERTER: The future interest that corresponds to the fee simple determinable. If the pre-specified condition subsequent occurs, the property automatically reverts to the grantor (who is the holder of the possibility of reverter).

Mountain Brow Lodge No. 82, Independent Order of Odd Fellows v. Toscano

(Holder of Fee) v. (Possible Holder of Future Interest)

257 Cal.App.2d 22, 64 Cal.Rptr. 816 (1967)

[handwritten: She likes this case]

A CONDITION WHICH PROHIBITS THE SALE OF LAND IS A RESTRAINT ON WHO MAY USE THE LAND AND IS VOID UNLESS A FEE SIMPLE SUBJECT TO CONDITION SUBSEQUENT IS INTENDED

■ **INSTANT FACTS** A deed provided that a lot shall revert back to the grantor if the grantee, a lodge (P), either failed to use the lot or attempted to sell it.

■ **BLACK LETTER RULE** The use of land may be restricted in a conveyance.

■ **PROCEDURAL BASIS**

Appeal from final judgment in action to quiet title.

■ **FACTS**

[handwritten: Grantor] *[handwritten: Grantee]*

Toscano, an active member of the Mountain Brow Lodge (P), deeded property to the Lodge (P). The deed state that the land was conveyed in consideration of "love and affection." The deed provided that the lot shall revert back to Toscano if the Lodge (P) either failed to use the lot or attempted to sell or transfer it. The Lodge (P) contends that this language is a restraint on who may use the land. As such, the Lodge (P) contends, it is a restraint on alienation and is void. Toscano's heirs (D) contend that the language creates a fee simple subject to a condition subsequent.

■ **ISSUE**

[handwritten: void provision]

May the use of land be restricted in a conveyance?

■ **DECISION AND RATIONALE**

[handwritten: not allowed] *[handwritten: not void, created a fee simple subject to condition subsequent]*

(Gargano, J.) Yes. Clearly, a condition which prohibits the sale of land is a restraint on who may use the land and as such is void. The remaining question, then, is whether the condition which requires that the Lodge (P) use the land created a defeasible fee or whether it is a void restraint on alienation. Considering that Toscano (D) was an active member of the lodge and that he conveyed it in "loving consideration," the clause which reads "the land is restricted for the *use* of the second party" meant that the land be used for Lodge purposes. It did not mean or intend to restrict alienation. Thus, this clause created a fee simple subject to condition subsequent. Even though a restraint on how land may be used can possibly be a restraint on who may use the land, such restraints are still allowed in California. Restraints on the use of land are also allowed in other jurisdictions. Judgment declaring the restriction on the sale of land reversed. Judgment declaring the restriction on the use of land affirmed.

[handwritten: allowed] *[handwritten: who vs. how]*

■ **DISSENT**

(Stone, J.) The clause which requires that the Lodge (P) use the land is a restraint on alienation because it effectively prohibits the sale to another person.

[handwritten: Can't restrict who - the user, but can restrict how - the purpose]

Analysis:

In this case, the court struggles to accommodate another principle of property law: The owner of property should be able to use his land as he desires, and he should be able to restrict the use of his land in a conveyance. As the dissent points out, these two goals often come into conflict. When the goals do come into conflict, courts will often weigh the two policy goals and choose that which yields the most equitable result.

■ CASE VOCABULARY

HABENDUM CLAUSE: That portion of a deed which describes the restrictions or limitations that go along with the property being conveyed.

See notes

the court wants to encourage gifts to charity

Ink v. City of Canton

(Holder of Reverter) v. (Holder of Fee Simple Determinable)

4 Ohio St.2d 51, 212 N.E.2d 574 (1965)

COURT RULES THAT PROCEEDS FROM EMINENT DOMAIN PROCEEDING ARE TO BE DIVIDED BETWEEN THE HOLDER OF THE FEE SIMPLE DETERMINABLE AND THE HOLDER OF THE REVERTER

■ **INSTANT FACTS** The descendants of Harry Ink conveyed to The City of Canton (P) land to be used for park purposes only. Subsequently, the state of Ohio instituted eminent domain proceedings against the land.

■ **BLACK LETTER RULE** The proceeds from an eminent domain proceeding are to be divided between the holder of the fee simple on condition subsequent and the holder of the reverter.

■ **PROCEDURAL BASIS**

Appeal from judgment in action for declaratory judgment.

■ **FACTS**

In 1936, the descendants of Harry Ink (P) conveyed land to the City of Canton (D). The land was for use as a park and for no other use. The City of Canton (D) used the land as restricted until 1961 when the state of Ohio condemned it using its power of eminent domain. The state paid $130,822 into an account to be paid to those with interests in the land. Ink (P) claims the right to retake the premises (and take the entire $130,822) since the land is no longer being used as a park. The City of Canton (D) claims that it gets the entire sum since it has not voluntarily elected to stop using the land for a park.

■ **ISSUE**

Should the proceeds from an eminent domain proceeding be divided between the holder of the fee simple on condition subsequent and the holder of the reverter?

■ **DECISION AND RATIONALE**

Yes. Where property is conveyed with a use restriction, it would seem reasonable that the land revert to the grantor when eminent domain proceedings prevent that use. This rule seems harsh to the grantee. On the other hand, the great weight of authority holds that there is no reverter when eminent domain proceedings prevent the land from being used as restricted. There are two justifications given for this. First, it is said that the grantor's interest is too remote to value. However, valuation of a reverter is often possible. Second, it is said that the grantee should be excused from using the land as required since the law (eminent domain) has made performance impossible. No reasoning is offered for this justification. To the contrary, this rule seems unfair for two reasons. First, the grantor's reverter is destroyed. Second, the grantee gets more than the original grant: He is given land without a use restriction. Originally, he was only · given land with a use restriction. Where are grantee has paid for a fee simple on condition subsequent, we feel that the following division of the eminent domain proceeds seems logical: The grantee should be entitled to value of the land with a use restriction. The grantor should be entitled to the value of the land with no restriction *less* the value of the land with a use restriction. The grantor should get this because this is what he refrained from conveying to the grantee. In this case, The City of Canton (D) paid nothing for the fee. Also, The City of Canton (D) has a fiduciary duty to use the land for a park. Thus, the rule stated above as applied to this case yields the following result: The City of Canton (D) gets the value of the land with a use restriction. Ink (P) gets the value of the land with no restriction *less* the value of the land with a use restriction. If The City of Canton (D) fails to use its proceeds for park purposes, this money shall revert to Ink (P).

Analysis:

In *Baker v. Weedon,* the issue was whether to sell the land and divide the proceeds between the owner of the freehold and the holder of the future interest. The solution crafted by the court was that the land be sold if it was in the best interests of both parties. Here, the issue is not whether to sell the land, but how to divide the proceeds. Again, the court simply does what is fair: Divide the proceeds in proportion to the interests held by the respective parties.

■ CASE VOCABULARY

EMINENT DOMAIN: The right of a state to take private property for public use (the state, however, must pay for the property).

CHAPTER FOUR

Future Interests

Broadway National Bank v. Adams

Instant Facts: Adams (D) owed money to the Bank (P), which the Bank (P) sought to collect by requiring direct payment to it of trust income payable to Adams (D).

Black Letter Rule: A creditor of a trust beneficiary is not entitled to payment of the trust income by assignment by the beneficiary, or otherwise directly from the trustee, if the terms of the trust prohibit such action.

The Symphony Space, Inc. v. Pergola Properties, Inc.

Instant Facts: A property owner filed a declaratory judgment action when the holder of a buy-back option notified the owner of its intent to buy back the property covered by the agreement.

Black Letter Rule: There is no exception to the Rule Against Perpetuities for commercial option agreements.

Broadway National Bank v. Adams

(Creditor) v. (Debtor/Trust Beneficiary)

133 Mass. 170 (1882)

THE BANK'S ACCESS TO TRUST FUNDS WAS RESTRICTED BY THE LANGUAGE OF THE TRUST INSTRUMENT

■ **INSTANT FACTS** Adams (D) owed money to the Bank (P), which the Bank (P) sought to collect by requiring direct payment to it of trust income payable to Adams (D).

■ **BLACK LETTER RULE** A creditor of a trust beneficiary is not entitled to payment of the trust income by assignment by the beneficiary, or otherwise directly from the trustee, if the terms of the trust prohibit such action.

■ **PROCEDURAL BASIS**

Original bill in equity in the state supreme court.

■ **FACTS**

Adams (D) was the beneficiary under a spendthrift trust established by his brother's will, pursuant to which Adams was to be paid the income from the trust fund, during his lifetime, semiannually by payment to him personally, "free from the interference or control of his creditors." It was the trustor's stated intent "that the use of said income shall not be anticipated by assignment." Adams (D) owed the Bank (P) a debt, which the Bank (P) sought to collect by seeking a court order requiring payment of the trust income to the Bank (P) directly. The court refused to direct such payments.

■ **ISSUE**

May a creditor reach the trust income payable to a beneficiary debtor where the terms of the trust provide that the income is not alienable by anticipation, nor subject to taking for the beneficiary's debts?

■ **DECISION AND RATIONALE**

(Morton, C.J.) No. A creditor of a trust beneficiary is not entitled to payment of the trust income by assignment by the beneficiary, or otherwise directly from the trustee, if the terms of the trust prohibit such action. Adams's (D) brother was the absolute owner of his property prior to his death and could dispose of it by gift to Adams (P) with whatever legal restrictions he saw fit. His intent, as expressed in the provision of the will establishing the trust, was clear. That intent was not to give Adams (D) an absolute right to accrued trust income with the power to assign it, but rather to give Adams (D) the right to semiannual payments that became his absolute property only after payment to him. The intent of the creator of the trust must be honored if the terms of the trust do not violate public policy, which they did not here. Under the circumstances, the trust fund income may not be reached by the Bank (P) before it is paid to Adams (D).

Analysis:

The Bank (P) argued that trust terms such as those before the court violated public policy because they could defraud a beneficiary's creditors by investing the beneficiary with apparent

---

wealth, thereby inducing creditors to improvidently give the beneficiary credit. The court made short work of that contention, observing that creditors can readily ascertain the terms and restrictions of such trusts, because wills are a matter of public record. Once a will is reviewed, there would be no basis for relying on a life estate created by a trust if the terms clearly provided that the estate so created was not liable for the beneficiary's debts.

■ CASE VOCABULARY

SPENDTHRIFT TRUST: A trust that prohibits the beneficiary's interest from being assigned and also prevents a creditor from attaching that interest; a trust by the terms of which a valid restraint is imposed on the voluntary or involuntary transfer of the beneficiary's interest.

The Symphony Space, Inc. v. Pergola Properties, Inc.

(Property Owner) v. (Holder of Buy-Back Option)

88 N.Y.2d 466, 669 N.E.2d 799, 646 N.Y.S.2d 641 (1996)

THE RULE AGAINST PERPETUITIES APPLIES TO BUY-BACK OPTION AGREEMENTS

■ **INSTANT FACTS** A property owner filed a declaratory judgment action when the holder of a buy-back option notified the owner of its intent to buy back the property covered by the agreement.

■ **BLACK LETTER RULE** There is no exception to the Rule Against Perpetuities for commercial option agreements.

■ **PROCEDURAL BASIS**

Appeal to the Court of Appeals of New York (New York's highest court) of two lower court decisions refusing to exempt commercial option agreements from the purview of New York's version of the Rule against Perpetuities.

■ **FACTS**

In 1978, Broadwest Realty Corp. sold a two-story building in Manhattan to Symphony Space, Inc. (P), a non-profit entity devoted to the arts. The sale price of the building, which contained both a theater and office space, was $10,010, well below the property's market value. The deal included a lease-back provision under which Broadwest leased the office-space portion of the building from Symphony (P) for $1 per year. It also included a 25-year mortgage with Broadwest serving as mortgagee, and, finally, for an additional sum of $10, Broadwest was granted the option to repurchase the building "at any time after July 1, 1979, so long as the Notice of Election specifies that the Closing is to occur during any of the calendar years 1987, 1993, 1998, and 2003." The deal was advantageous to both sides for tax reasons. In 1981, three years after the initiation of the sale/lease-back, Broadwest sold and assigned its interest in the lease, option agreement, and mortgage to another party for $4.8 million. That party then transferred its newly-acquired interest to Pergola Properties, Inc., and four other entities (D's) as tenants in common. Because the value of the property had increased significantly since the original deal had been signed, Pergola (D) decided to exercise the option to buy back the premises. Hoping to keep ownership of the building, Symphony (P) filed a declaratory judgment action arguing that the option agreement that it originally entered into with Broadwest was void under New York's version of the Rule against Perpetuities. The trial and intermediate appellate courts agreed with Symphony (P), and Pergola (D) appealed to New York's highest court.

■ **ISSUE**

Are options to purchase commercial property exempt from the Rule against Perpetuities and its prohibition of remote vesting?

■ **DECISION AND RATIONALE**

(Kaye, C.J.) No. New York has recognized the Rule against Perpetuities since 1830. As with the common law rule, the purpose of our version is (1) to limit control of title to real property by dead landowners who seek to reach into future generations; and (2) to "ensure the productive use and development of property by its current beneficial owners by simplifying ownership,

---

facilitating exchange and freeing property from . . . impediments to alienabilty." *Metropolitan Transp. Auth. v. Bruken Realty Corp.* Our current statutory version of the rule, found in EPTL 9–1.1, contains two subsections important for today's action. First, subsection (a) voids any estate in which the conveying instrument suspends the absolute power of alienation for longer than lives in being at the creation of the estate plus twenty-one years. Second, subsection (b) prohibits remote vesting by invalidating any interest not certain to vest within the specified time period. In addition to these statutory formulas, New York also retains the common law rule against unreasonable restraints on alienation. It is against this background that we consider the validity of the option agreement in the present case. Pergola (D) proffers three grounds for upholding the option: the statutory prohibition against remote vesting does not apply to commercial options; the option here cannot be exercised beyond the statutory period; and this Court should adopt the "wait and see" doctrine. We will consider each in turn. Under the common law, options to purchase land are subject to the rule against remote vesting. Under New York law, the same is true even when options to purchase are part of an arms-length commercial transaction and not a family disposition of land. In reaching the conclusion that EPTL 9–1.1(b) applies to commercial option agreements, this court has placed emphasis on the fact that the legislature specifically intended to incorporate the American common-law rules governing perpetuities into the New York statute. Furthermore, because the common law prohibition against remote vesting applies to both commercial and noncommercial options, it likewise follows that the legislature intended EPTL 9–1.1(b) to apply to commercial purchase options as well. Consequently, any creation of a general exception to EPTL 9–1.1(b) for all commercial purchase options would remove an entire class of contingent future interests that the legislature intended the statute to cover. Such a statutory change would require legislative action. Pergola (D) cites *Metropolitan Transp. Auth. v. Bruken Realty Corp.* in support of its position. However, *Bruken* applies only to preemptive rights, and because preemptive rights only minimally affect alienability of land, they are treated differently from option agreements. In the present case, the option agreement creates precisely the sort of control over future disposition of the property that we have previously associated with purchase options and that the common law rule against remote vesting seeks to prevent. The option grants its holder absolute power to purchase the property at the holder's whim and at a token price. The property owner is thus discouraged from investing in improvements to the property. Furthermore, the option's existence significantly impedes the owner's ability to sell the property, thereby rendering it practically inalienable. If the option is exercisable beyond the statutory perpetuities period, refusing to enforce it would thus further the purpose and rationale underlying the statutory prohibition against remote vesting. Pergola (D) alternatively claims that the agreement does not permit exercise of the option after expiration of the statutory perpetuities period, meaning there is no conflict with the Rule against Perpetuities. Where the parties to a transaction are corporations and no measuring lives are stated in the instruments, the perpetuities period is simply 21 years. The agreement at issue here allows the option holder to exercise the option "at any time during any Exercise Period" set forth in the agreement. Moreover, the agreement provides that the option may be exercised "at any time after July 1, 1979," so long as the closing date is scheduled during 1987, 1993, 1998, or 2003. Even factoring in the requisite notice, the option could potentially be exercised as late as July 2003—more than 24 years after its creation. Pergola's (D) contention that the agreement does not permit exercise of the option beyond the 21-year period is thus contradicted by the plain language of the instrument. Nor can New York's "saving statute," which creates a presumption that a grantor intended to create a valid estate, be invoked to shorten the duration of the exercise period under the agreement. While the saving statute obligates reviewing courts to avoid constructions that frustrate the parties' intended purposes, it does not authorize courts to rewrite instruments that unequivocally allow interests to vest outside the perpetuities period. The rules of construction of EPTL 9–1.3 apply only if a contrary intention does not appear in the instrument. The unambiguous language of the agreement here expresses the parties' intent that the option be exercisable at any time during a 24-year period. Thus, the instrument does not permit a construction that the parties intended the option to last only 21 years. For this reason, the saving statute is inapplicable. Pergola (D) next urges that we adopt the "wait and see" doctrine, which holds that an interest is valid if it actually vests during the perpetuities period, irrespective of what might have happened. The option here would survive under the "wait and see" approach since it was exercised in 1987, well within the 21-year limitation. This court, however, has long refused to "wait and see" whether a perpetuities violation in fact occurs. The very language of EPTL 9–1.1, moreover, precludes us from adopting that approach. Under the statute, an interest is invalid "unless it must vest, if at all, not later than twenty-one years after one or more lives in being." Because the option here could have vested after expiration of the 21-year perpetuities period, it offends the rule. We therefore conclude that the option agreement is invalid. Finally, Pergola (D) argues that, if the option fails, the contract of sale conveying the property from Broadwest to Symphony (P) should be rescinded due to the mutual mistake of the parties. Such a rescission is inappropriate. A contract entered into under mutual mistake of fact is generally subject to rescission. However, the mistake here is one of law, and rescission is therefore not required. The Rule against Perpetuities reflects the public policy of the State. Granting the relief requested by Pergola (D) would thus be contrary to public policy since it would compel performance of contracts violative of the rule. Affirmed.

Analysis:

Symphony is an instructive case because it provides a good example of how the common law Rule against Perpetuities works to limit a prior owner's control of property. Additionally, it provides the reader with some introduction to a current alternative version or reading of the common law rule that is gaining some acceptance in American law. One of the more difficult subjects studied in law school, the Rule against Perpetuities holds that "[n]o interest is good unless it must vest, if at all, not later than twenty-one years after some life in being at the creation of the interest." *John C. Gray, The Rule Against Perpetuities.* To put it another way, if a future interest such as a contingent remainder (the Rule does not apply to reversions, possibilities of reverter, and rights of entry) is not absolutely certain to vest within a life in being at the time of the creation of the instrument plus twenty-one years, it is void. In determining whether an interest is void under the Rule, one must first identify the measuring life, or the "life in being." The measuring life can be anyone alive at the time of the creation of the future interest, though it generally is found to belong to someone who has the power to control the time at which the future interest will vest. Thus, the measuring life may be that of a prior life tenant, the party who is to take the contingent interest, any person who has the ability to affect the identity of that taker, or anyone who has the power to affect a condition precedent attached to the interest. Once the measuring life is determined, an interest's validity is ascertained by looking to whether the interest must vest within the perpetuities period, which, again, is the life in being plus twenty-one years. If the interest is not certain to vest within that period of time, the interest is deemed void and is stricken from the grant. *Symphony* is also instructive because it provides the reader with an introduction to one of the current alternative theories to the common law Rule against Perpetuities—the wait-and-see doctrine. Under the wait-and-see doctrine, a court will not automatically strike down a future interest simply because it might vest outside the perpetuities period, but will instead wait to see whether it actually vests outside the period. New York did not adopt the less-restrictive alternative in *Symphony,* but other jurisdictions have.

■ **CASE VOCABULARY**

BUY-BACK OPTION AGREEMENT: A commercial agreement which gives one party a right to purchase property from its current owner but carries with it no obligation to do so.

PREEMPTIVE RIGHTS: The right to purchase something before it is sold to someone else (a right of first refusal).

RULE AGAINST PERPETUITIES: Common law rule which holds that no contingent interest will be permitted unless that interest must vest, if at all, within a certain period of time determined by a life in being at the creation of the contingent interest plus twenty-one years.

WAIT AND SEE DOCTRINE: Alternative to the stringent application of the Rule against Perpetuities under which contingent interests are only voided when they do not actually vest during the perpetuities period—the possibility that a contingent interest might vest outside the period is irrelevant.

CHAPTER FIVE

Co-Ownership and Marital Interests

Riddle v. Harmon

Instant Facts: Mrs. Riddle did not want her husband to get their land automatically when she died, so she tried to sever the joint tenancy without him.

Black Letter Rule: A joint tenant can unilaterally sever a joint tenancy without the use of an intermediating third party by conveying his or her property interest to himself or herself.

Harms v. Sprague

Instant Facts: As a favor to Sprague, John mortgaged his and William's land, without telling William, and later devised everything to Sprague when he died.

Black Letter Rule: A mortgage does not sever a joint tenancy, and the surviving joint tenant takes the interest of a deceased joint tenant without being encumbered by the mortgage.

Delfino v. Vealencis

Instant Facts: The Delfinos owned 99/144 of the property and wanted a residential development, while Vealencis owned 45/144 and wanted to keep her garbage business on it.

Black Letter Rule: A partition by sale should only be ordered if the physical attributes of the land in question are such that a partition is impracticable or inequitable, and the interests of the owners would be promoted by a partition by sale.

Spiller v. Mackereth

Instant Facts: After another tenant vacated their building, Spiller used it as a warehouse, and Mackereth demanded he pay rent or vacate half of the building.

Black Letter Rule: In the absence of an agreement to pay rent, a cotenant in possession is not liable to his or her cotenants for the value of his or her use and occupation of the property unless there is ouster of a cotenant.

Swartzbaugh v. Sampson

Instant Facts: Mr. Swartzbaugh leased part of some land for a boxing pavilion, but Mrs. Swartzbaugh, the joint tenant, never signed the lease and wants to cancel it.

Black Letter Rule: A joint tenant, during the existence of a joint estate, has the right to convey or mortgage his or her interest in the property, even if the other joint tenant objects.

Sawada v. Endo

Instant Facts: Kokichi and Ume Endo conveyed their property to their sons the same day that Kokichi got into an auto accident that injured the Sawadas.

Black Letter Rule: An estate by the entirety is not subject to the claims of creditors of only one of the spouses because neither spouse acting alone can transfer his or her interest.

In re Marriage of Graham

Instant Facts: Flight attendant supports husband through business school, covering seventy percent of their expenses, and after he graduates they get a divorce.

Black Letter Rule: An educational degree is not property, and therefore is not subject to division upon divorce.

Elkus v. Elkus

Instant Facts: Beginning opera singer marries a voice coach, and after her career skyrockets while he coaches her during marriage, he wants his share upon divorce.

Black Letter Rule: An increase in the value of one spouse's career, when it is the result of the efforts of the other spouse, constitutes marital property and is thus subject to equitable distribution.

Varnum v. Brien

Instant Facts: Six same sex couples sought marriage licenses from the county recorder, who refused to issue the licenses based on a state statute that provided that only a marriage between a male and a female is valid.

Black Letter Rule: A statute restricting civil marriage to a man and a woman violates the equal protection clause of the Iowa constitution.

Riddle v. Harmon

(Husband) v. (Wife's Executrix)

102 Cal.App.3d 524, 162 Cal.Rptr. 530 (1980)

CALIFORNIA APPELLATE COURT HOLDS THAT A JOINT TENANT MAY SEVER A JOINT TENANCY BY CONVEYING HIS OR HER INTEREST IN THE PROPERTY TO HIMSELF OR HERSELF WITHOUT THE USE OF A THIRD PERSON "STRAWMAN"

■ **INSTANT FACTS** Mrs. Riddle did not want her husband to get their land automatically when she died, so she tried to sever the joint tenancy without him.

■ **BLACK LETTER RULE** A joint tenant can unilaterally sever a joint tenancy without the use of an intermediating third party by conveying his or her property interest to himself or herself.

■ **PROCEDURAL BASIS**

Appeal from summary judgment to quiet title.

■ **FACTS**

Mr. (P) and Mrs. Riddle, husband and wife, purchased some real estate and took title as joint tenants. Several months before she died, Mrs. Riddle had an attorney plan her estate. This attorney told her that her property was held in joint tenancy and thus, upon her death, it would pass to her husband (P). After learning this, Mrs. Riddle wished to sever the joint tenancy so she could pass on her interest in the land by the use of a will. Her attorney prepared a deed which allowed Mrs. Riddle to grant an undivided one-half interest in the property to herself. This document also explicitly stated that its purpose was to "terminate those joint tenancies formerly existing" between Mr. and Mrs. Riddle. Mrs. Riddle's attorney also prepared a will disposing of her interest in the property. Both the grant deed and will were executed on December 8, 1975. Mrs. Riddle died on December 28, 1975. The trial court denied her plan to sever the joint tenancy and quieted title to the property to her husband. Harmon (D), executrix of Mrs. Riddle's will, appeals from that judgment.

■ **ISSUE**

Can a joint tenant unilaterally sever a joint tenancy without the use of an intermediary by conveying his or her interest to himself or herself?

■ **DECISION AND RATIONALE**

(Poche, J.) Yes. One joint tenant may unilaterally sever a joint tenancy without the use of an intermediary device. In *Clark v. Carter* (1968) 265 Cal.App.2d 291, 70 Cal.Rptr. 923 [transfer of property requires two parties, a grantor and grantee] a similar wife's actions of conveying her interest to herself were found to be insufficient to sever a joint tenancy. This idea of requiring two separate parties to transfer property was rooted in the English common law ceremony of livery of seisin. In this ceremony, the feoffor (grantor) would hand a symbol of the land, whether a branch or some of the earth, to the feoffee (grantee), and then relinquish possession of the land. Of course, one could not hand oneself a clod of dirt; two parties were needed. Here, however, the archaic rule that one cannot convey an interest in property to oneself is discarded. The rationale of the *Clark* case is rejected because the use of clods of earth as the means of transferring title has been replaced with grant deeds and title companies. Many attorneys have created several methods to get around the *Clark* case and its rule that one cannot be both grantor and grantee simultaneously. Examples of such means can be found in *Burke v. Stevens* (1968) 264 Cal.App.2d 30, 70 Cal.Rptr. 87 [permitted wife's use of associate of her attorney as third party in property transfer used to sever joint tenancy] and *Reiss v. Reiss* (1941) 45 Cal.App.2d 740, 114 P.2d 718 [wife severed joint tenancy by transferring interest to son as trustee of a trust for her use and benefit]. Mrs. Riddle could have terminated the joint tenancy through any number of means. Judgment reversed.

Analysis:

In essence, the court used the reasoning of the state legislature regarding the creation of a joint tenancy and flipped it around. The California legislature stated in Civil Code § 683 that a joint tenancy could be created not only by two or more persons receiving a title from another person, but also, among other means, by "the transfer from a sole owner to himself and others." As the state deemed a strawman unnecessary to the creation of a joint tenancy, the court extended that loosened requirement to the termination of a joint tenancy as well.

■ CASE VOCABULARY

FEOFFEE: The person to whom a fee, or interest in land, is conveyed; the grantee.

FEOFFMENT: The granting of an interest in land under English common law.

FEOFFOR: The person who conveys a fee to another person; the grantor.

JUS ACCRESCENDI: The right of the surviving joint tenant or tenants to take the whole estate upon the death of one or more of the other joint tenants; the right of survivorship.

LIVERY OF SEISIN: Element of the common law ceremony of feoffment by which a feoffor would hand over a symbol of the land being conveyed, such as a lump of the soil or a branch, to the feoffee as a means of transferring possession of the land.

STRAWMAN: A third party who receives property from a joint tenant with the intent to convey the property right back to the joint tenant with the purpose of helping to sever the joint tenancy.

fee = interest in land

Harms v. Sprague

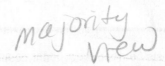

(Surviving Brother) v. *(Dead Brother's Executor)*

105 Ill.2d 215, 473 N.E.2d 930 (1984)

ILLINOIS SUPREME COURT HOLDS THAT A MORTGAGE GRANTED BY ONE JOINT TENANT DOES NOT SEVER THE JOINT TENANCY AND DOES NOT SURVIVE THE DEATH OF THE MORTGAGOR AS A LIEN ON THE PROPERTY

■ **INSTANT FACTS** As a favor to Sprague, John mortgaged his and William's land, without telling William, and later devised everything to Sprague when he died.

■ **BLACK LETTER RULE** A mortgage does not sever a joint tenancy, and the surviving joint tenant takes the interest of a deceased joint tenant without being encumbered by the mortgage.

■ **PROCEDURAL BASIS**

Appeal from complaint to quiet title and for declaratory judgment.

■ **FACTS**

William Harms (P) and his brother, John Harms, took title to real estate on June 26, 1973, as joint tenants, with full rights of survivorship (first property). Years later, in a separate transaction, Charles Sprague (D) wished to purchase other property (second property) from the Simmonses (D) for $25,000, but had to sign a promissory note for $7,000. On June 12, 1981, John Harms and Sprague (D) executed a promissory note for $7,000 payable to the Simmonses (D). The note states that it was to be paid from the proceeds of the sale of John Harms' interest in the first property, but no later than six months from the date the note was signed. The last of five monthly interest payments on the note was recorded November 6, 1981, John Harms also executed a mortgage, in favor of the Simmonses (D), on his undivided one-half interest in the (first property) joint tenancy property to secure payment of the note. William Harms (P) (co-tenant in the first property) was unaware of the mortgage. John Harms died on December 10, 1981, and devised his entire estate to Sprague (D). The mortgage from John Harms to the Simmonses was recorded on December 29, 1981. The trial court held that the mortgage severed the joint tenancy and survived John Harms' death. The appellate court reversed and found the property unencumbered by the mortgage.

■ **ISSUE**

(1) Is a joint tenancy severed when one joint tenant mortgages his or her interest in the property? (2) Does such a mortgage become a lien on the property after the death of the mortgagor?

■ **DECISION AND RATIONALE**

(Moran, J.) (1) No. A lien on a joint tenant's interest in property will not effectuate a severance of the joint tenancy, absent the conveyance by deed following the repayment of a mortgage debt. This rule is reflected in *Peoples Trust and Savings Bank v. Haas* (1927) 328 Ill. 468 [judgment lien secured against one joint tenant did not sever joint tenancy], and *Van Antwerp v. Horan* (1945) 390 Ill. 449 [levy upon interest of a debtor joint tenant does not destroy unity of interest and does not sever joint tenancy]. In a mortgage situation, the title of the mortgagee (lender) really only exists between the mortgagee and mortgagor (borrower), so no title transfer occurs between them. Thus, a mortgage is, in essence, a lien, and a lien on the mortgagor's interest in property does not sever the joint tenancy. Because the mortgage did not sever the joint tenancy, the inherent right of survivorship still exists. William Harms' (P's) right of survivorship became operative upon the death of his brother. (2) No. A surviving joint tenant acquires the share of the deceased joint tenant through the conveyance which granted the joint tenancy in the first place. The property right of the deceased joint tenant, John Harms, was extinguished at the moment of his death. At that moment, the lien of the mortgage ceased to exist as well. Judgment affirmed.

Analysis:

Not all jurisdictions follow this logic. Some courts hold that a surviving joint tenant would have to take on the deceased joint tenant's interest subject to any mortgage against it. This position would be fair to the mortgagee, who would otherwise lose the financial security in the transaction.

■ CASE VOCABULARY

LIEN: A claim secured by property for payment of a debt.

MORTGAGE: An interest in land which provides security for the payment of a debt, such as a loan, or the performance of a specific duty.

MORTGAGEE: Person that loans money to another in exchange for that person's title to the land being used as the security for the loan; the person who "receives" the mortgage.

MORTGAGOR: Person who gives legal title or a lien to a mortgagee in order to secure a mortgage loan; the borrower, or debtor, in a mortgage transaction.

PROMISSORY NOTE: A written promise to pay a specific sum of money at a given time, or on demand, to a specific person.

REDEMPTION: The right to repurchase land and free it from the foreclosure of a mortgage.

TITLE THEORY: Theory of mortgage law that states that until a mortgage is satisfied, or foreclosed, a mortgagor retains the right to possession of the property and legal title to the property belongs to the mortgagee.

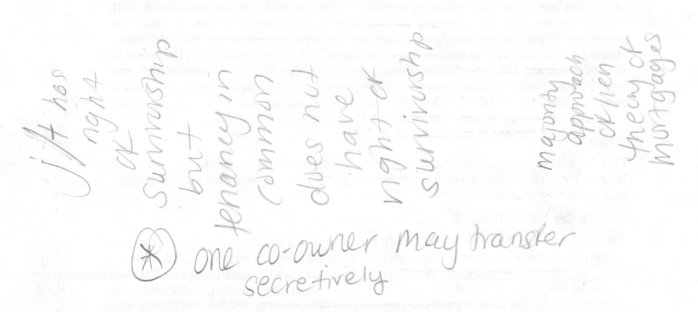

jt has right of survivorship but tenancy in common does not have right of survivorship

majority approach of lien theory of mortgages

⊛ one co-owner may transfer secretively

Delfino v. Vealencis

(Building Developers) v. (Garbage Lady)

181 Conn. 533, 436 A.2d 27 (1980)

CONNECTICUT SUPREME COURT HOLDS THAT WHERE THE HOME AND GARBAGE BUSINESS OF A TENANT IN COMMON ARE LOCATED ON CONCURRENTLY OWNED PROPERTY, A PARTITION BY SALE CANNOT BE ORDERED AS IT WOULD NOT BE IN THE BEST INTERESTS OF ALL PARTIES INVOLVED

■ **INSTANT FACTS** The Delfinos owned 99/144 of the property and wanted a residential development, while Vealencis owned 45/144 and wanted to keep her garbage business on it.

■ **BLACK LETTER RULE** A partition by sale should only be ordered if the physical attributes of the land in question are such that a partition is impracticable or inequitable, and the interests of the owners would be promoted by a partition by sale.

■ **PROCEDURAL BASIS**

Appeal from hearing in action seeking a partition of property by sale.

■ **FACTS**

Angelo and William Delfino (Ps) and Helen Vealencis (D) own real property as tenants in common. The property is a rectangular 20.5 acre parcel of land with Vealencis' (D's) house on the extreme western end of it. The Delfinos (Ps) own an undivided 99/144 interest in the land, and Vealencis (D) owns a 45/144 interest. They (Ps and D) are the sole owners of the property. Vealencis (D) also runs a garbage removal business on a portion of the land. None of the people involved is in actual possession of the remainder of the property. The Delfinos (Ps) want to develop the property into forty-five residential lots. In 1978, the Delfinos (Ps) brought an action in the trial court seeking a partition [dividing of the lands resulting in individual ownership of the interests of each joint tenant] of the property by sale. They (Ps) also wanted the proceeds of the sale divided according to their (P's) and Vealencis' (D's) respective interests. Vealencis (D) moved for a judgment of in-kind partition [physical division of the property into separate tracts]. After a hearing, the trial court concluded that a partition in kind would result in "material injury" to both the Delfinos (Ps) and Vealencis (D). The court then ordered the property to be sold at auction by a committee and that the proceeds be paid into the court and redistributed to the tenants. Vealencis (D) appealed.

■ **ISSUE**

Can a partition by sale be ordered when a physical partition is possible, and a partition by sale would protect the interests of the owner of a larger share of the property over the owner of the other share?

■ **DECISION AND RATIONALE**

(Healey, J.) No. Under Connecticut General Statutes § 52-500 [statute governing sale of real or personal property owned by two or more persons] a court is not required to order a physical partition even in cases of extreme hardship. A partition by sale, however, should only be ordered when the physical attributes of the land make a partition in kind impracticable or inequitable, and when the interests of all the owners, not just one, would better be promoted by such a sale. Here, the property is essentially rectangular, and Vealencis' (D) dwelling is located on the extreme western side of it. There are only two competing ownership interests, the Delfinos' (P) and Vealencis' (D) shares, as well. These facts demonstrate that a physical partition of the property into two separate tracts is clearly practicable here. Moreover, the lower court's failed to consider that a partition by sale would force Vealencis (D) to surrender her home and business, both of which were located on the property. Vealencis (D) had been in actual and exclusive possession of the property for some time. Though Vealencis' (D) business might possibly cause difficulty for the Delfinos (Ps) in their attempt to develop residential lots, the interests of all the tenants in common must be considered. The potential economic gain of one tenant or group of tenants alone cannot justify a partition by sale. The trial court erred in ordering a partition by sale. Judgment set aside and case remanded.

Analysis:

Although courts usually say that partition in kind is preferred, more often than not it is the opposite that occurs. The present trend has been to order sale in partition in a great majority of cases. This is usually done in deference to the wishes of all parties involved, or because the courts believe that sale of the property is actually the fairest means of ending any conflict between them.

■ CASE VOCABULARY

PARTITION BY SALE: A court-ordered division of land held by joint tenants or tenants in common by which the land is sold and the proceeds are divided among the tenants according to the size of their interests in the land.

PARTITION IN KIND: A court-ordered, physical division of land held by joint tenants or tenants in common by which each tenant's interest is converted into a parcel taken from the whole, and each tenant then takes exclusive possession of their share of the land.

Spiller v. Mackereth

(Warehouse Occupant) v. (Other Tenant)

334 So.2d 859 (Ala. 1976)

ALABAMA SUPREME COURT HOLDS THAT WHERE NO AGREEMENT EXISTS BETWEEN COTENANT TO PAY RENT, A COTENANT IN POSSESSION IS NOT LIABLE FOR RENT TO OTHER COTENANT UNLESS OUSTER IS ESTABLISHED

■ **INSTANT FACTS** After another tenant vacated their building, Spiller used it as a warehouse, and Mackereth demanded he pay rent or vacate half of the building.

■ **BLACK LETTER RULE** In the absence of an agreement to pay rent, a cotenant in possession is not liable to his or her cotenants for the value of his or her use and occupation of the property unless there is ouster of a cotenant.

■ **PROCEDURAL BASIS**

Appeal from action awarding rent to nonpossessing cotenant.

■ **FACTS**

John Spiller (P) and Hettie Mackereth (D) owned a building as tenants in common. A lessee, Auto-Rite, was renting the building but later vacated, and when moving out Auto-Rite removed the locks. Spiller (P) began using it as a warehouse and acquired new locks to secure the merchandise he (P) stored inside. Mackereth (D) then wrote a letter dated November 15, 1973 demanding that Spiller (P) either vacate half the building or pay half the rental value. When Spiller (P) did neither, Mackereth (D) brought suit. The trial court awarded Mackereth (D) $2,100 in rent. Spiller (P) appealed.

■ **ISSUE**

Is a cotenant in possession of property liable to other cotenants for rent when there is no evidence the cotenant in possession has done anything to exclude the other cotenant from the property?

■ **DECISION AND RATIONALE**

(Jones, J.) No. The general rule is that in absence of an agreement to pay rent or ouster of a cotenant, a cotenant in possession is not liable to cotenants for the value of use and occupation of the property. The key here lies in the definition of the word "ouster." Ouster can refer to either the beginning of the running of the statute of limitations for adverse possession or the liability of an occupying cotenant for rent to other cotenant. The adverse possession aspect of the word is precluded here as Spiller (P) has acknowledged the existence of the cotenant relationship by filing a bill for partition. With regard to liability for rent, ouster is evidenced when an occupying cotenant refuses a demand of other cotenants to be allowed into use and enjoyment of the land. Here, Mackereth's (D) letter only demanded that Spiller (P) vacate or pay rent, and did not state any desire of Mackereth (D) to enter the premises. The letter was insufficient because Spiller (P), as an occupying cotenant holds title to the whole property and may rightfully occupy it until Mackereth (D), another cotenant, asserts possessory rights. Mackereth (D) claims Spiller's (P) use of new locks amounts to ouster. However, there is no evidence that the locks were used to do anything other than secure Spiller's (P) merchandise inside. There is also no

Also in SH6 P. 53

evidence that Mackereth (D) or any other cotenants asked for the keys to the locks or were prevented from entering the building because of the locks. Without evidence that he (P) intended to exclude the other cotenants, Spiller (P) is not liable for rent. Judgment reversed.

Analysis:

Some jurisdictions take the view that a cotenant in exclusive possession must pay rent to cotenants out of possession even when no ouster is established. This view may seem more fair to cotenants out of possession. When a cotenant occupies the property in question, it is essentially kept "off the market" and thus potential rent from a prospective renter is lost. However, the majority rule here would seem to encourage constructive use of property, as opposed to leaving it vacant and possibly unimproved until a new renter occupies the premises.

■ CASE VOCABULARY

OUSTER: The beginning of the running of the statute of limitations in cases of adverse possession; the liability of an occupying cotenant for rent to other cotenants.

PER MY ET PER TOUT: "By the half and by the whole;" term used to describe how each tenant in a tenancy in common or a joint tenancy holds a whole share of the property with regard to survivorship, but holds a share equal to other tenants with regard to the right to occupy.

Swartzbaugh v. Sampson

(Lessor's Wife) v. (Boxing Pavilion Lessee)

11 Cal.App.2d 451, 54 P.2d 73 (1936)

CALIFORNIA APPELLATE COURT HOLDS THAT EACH TENANT IN A JOINT TENANCY HAS THE RIGHT TO POSSESSION OF THE WHOLE PROPERTY, AND THUS CAN LEASE OUT OR TRANSFER HIS OR HER RIGHT TO OCCUPY OR USE AS HE OR SHE SEES FIT

■ **INSTANT FACTS** Mr. Swartzbaugh leased part of some land for a boxing pavilion, but Mrs. Swartzbaugh, the joint tenant, never signed the lease and wants to cancel it.

■ **BLACK LETTER RULE** A joint tenant, during the existence of a joint estate, has the right to convey or mortgage his or her interest in the property, even if the other joint tenant objects.

■ **PROCEDURAL BASIS**

Appeal from granting of motion for nonsuit in action to cancel leases.

■ **FACTS**

Mr. and Mrs. Swartzbaugh (D and P, respectively) owned sixty acres of land containing walnut trees. They owned this land as joint tenants with the right of survivorship. In December, 1933, Sampson (D) began negotiations with Mr. and Mrs. Swartzbaugh (D and P) to lease a fraction of the land in order to build a boxing arena. Mrs. Swartzbaugh (P) objected to making such a lease at all times. An option for a lease, dated January 5, 1934, was executed by Sampson and Mr. Swartzbaugh (D). Mrs. Swartzbaugh (P) was injured in February, 1934, and was confined to her bed for some time. The lease was executed by Mr. Swartzbaugh and Sampson (D) on February 2, 1934, and a second lease for property adjoining the boxing pavilion site was also signed after this date. Mrs. Swartzbaugh's (P) refused to sign these documents and her name does not appear on any of them. The walnut trees were removed from the leased premises against Mrs. Swartzbaugh's (P) wishes. Sampson (D) then went into possession and built the pavilion. Mrs. Swartzbaugh (P) filed suit on June 20, 1934. At trial she testified that she received no part of the $15 monthly rent, a rate which she considered too low when compared to the $10,000 needed to build the arena. She (P) also claimed that she did not want the arena on her land because "women and liquor followed." Sampson (D) filed for nonsuit and the motion was granted. Mrs. Swartzbaugh (P) appealed.

■ **ISSUE**

Can one joint tenant, who has not joined in the leases executed by a cotenant and a lessee in exclusive possession of the leased property, maintain an action to cancel the leases?

■ **DECISION AND RATIONALE**

(Marks, J.) No. In a joint tenancy, each joint tenant owns an equal interest in, and has an equal right to possession of, the whole property. This court has held that each joint tenant has the right convey or mortgage an equal share of the property, and can also pledge his or her interest in the property to another person. In addition, a joint tenant can make a lease to his or her share of the property, and such a lease would be valid as to his or her share. Even a lease to all of the joint property by one joint tenant would be a valid and supportable contract as far as

---

the lessor in the joint property is concerned. Thus, the leases from Mr. Swartzbaugh (D) to Sampson (D) are valid and existing contracts which give Sampson (D) the same right of possession of the leased property that Mr. Swartzbaugh (D) had. A joint tenant cannot recover exclusive possession of joint property from a cotenant. Because Sampson (D) has effectively the same rights to the leased property that Mrs. Swartzbaugh (P) had prior to the transaction, she (P) cannot cancel the leases. Mrs. Swartzbaugh (P) may fear that she may lose her interest in the premises by prescription. This fear is unfounded because a lessee cannot generally dispute a landlord's title or claim adverse possession while holding the property under the conditions of a lease. There is no evidence that Sampson (D) is holding adversely to her, nor that Mrs. Swartzbaugh (P) ever demanded entry into the premises. Judgment affirmed.

Analysis:

The rule of this case is pretty straightforward. Although Mrs. Swartzbaugh could attempt to prove ouster if Sampson resists her attempts to enter, she would only be entitled to one-half the reasonable rental value of the land. This may result in more money for Mrs. Swartzbaugh, but she would not be able to remove him or the boxing arena from the land. This would also lead to questions of who would be responsible for paying her the full value of rent; should it be Sampson, or Mr. Swartzbaugh, for agreeing to such a low monthly rent in the beginning? She may also consider trying a partition action as a remedy, but such measures would, in the end, give her a smaller parcel of land than the one she started with.

■ CASE VOCABULARY

MECHANIC'S LIEN: A claim created by state law which attaches to property and enables persons to have priority in receiving payment for work they performed in building, improving, or repairing a building or structure on that property.

MOIETY: Half of something; extent to which a joint tenant is said to hold an interest in property ("hold by moieties").

NONSUIT: Judgment against a plaintiff when he or she has failed to prove his or her case; a dismissal.

OPTION: Contract made for the purpose of keeping an offer of another contract open for a specified period of time.

PRESCRIPTION: A person's acquisition of the right to use property by virtue of his or her continuous use of that property.

Sawada v. Endo

(Judgment Winner) v. (Judgment Debtor)

57 Haw. 608, 561 P.2d 1291 (1977)

HAWAII SUPREME COURT HOLDS THAT THE CONVEYANCE OF MARITAL PROPERTY BY A HUSBAND AND WIFE TO THEIR SONS DID NOT DEFRAUD THE HUSBAND'S JUDGMENT CREDITORS BECAUSE A TENANCY BY THE ENTIRETY IS NOT SUBJECT TO THE CREDITORS OF ONE SPOUSE

■ **INSTANT FACTS** Kokichi and Ume Endo conveyed their property to their sons the same day that Kokichi got into an auto accident that injured the Sawadas.

■ **BLACK LETTER RULE** An estate by the entirety is not subject to the claims of creditors of only one of the spouses because neither spouse acting alone can transfer his or her interest.

■ FACTS

Kokichi (D) and Ume Endo, husband and wife, owned a parcel of real property as tenants by the entirety. On November 30, 1968, Masako and Helen Sawada (Ps) were injured when struck by car driven by Kokichi Endo (D). On June 17, 1969, Helen Sawada (P) filed her complaint against Kokichi Endo for damages. Mr. (D) and Mrs. Endo conveyed the property to their sons by a deed dated July 26, 1969. Masako Sawada (P) filed her suit against Kokichi Endo (D) on August 13, 1969. The complaint and summons in each suit was served on Kokichi Endo on October 29, 1969. The deed from Mr. (D) and Mrs. Endo to their sons was recorded on December 17, 1969. The sons paid no consideration for the conveyance. Both sons were aware at the time of conveyance that their father (D) had been in an auto accident and carried no liability insurance. Mr. (D) and Mrs. Endo continued to reside on the premises they conveyed to their sons. On January 19, 1971 judgment was entered in favor of Helen Sawada (P) against Kokichi Endo (D) for the sum of $8,846.46. Judgment was also entered in favor of Masako Sawada (P) for the sum of $16,199.28. Ume Endo died ten days later, and was survived by Kokichi Endo (D). The Sawadas (P) brought suit to set aside the conveyance of the marital property and satisfy their judgment. The trial court refused, and the Sawadas appealed.

■ ISSUE

Is the interest of one spouse in real property, held in tenancy by the entireties, subject to levy and execution by his or her creditors?

■ DECISION AND RATIONALE

(Menor, J.) No. Under the Married Women's Property Act, the interest of a husband or wife in an estate by the entireties is not subject to the claims of his or her individual creditors during the joint lives of the spouses. This is apparently the prevailing view of the lower courts of this jurisdiction. This jurisdiction has long recognized the tenancy by the entirety and its basis upon the legal unity of husband and wife and their single ownership of the estate. Tenants by the entirety are each considered to take the whole estate, so each spouse can have all the privileges that ownership confers. Despite this, however, neither spouse has a separate divisible interest in the property that can be conveyed or reached by execution of a judgment. While a joint tenancy may be severed by such a process, a tenancy by the entirety cannot. The estate is indivisible and this is an indispensable feature of the tenancy by the entirety. The estate can only be created with a married couple, and thus can only be destroyed by the actions of a married couple. There is nothing to prevent a creditor from insisting that a property held in such a tenancy be subject to levy before extending credit, of course. Also, tenancy by the entirety cannot be entered to defraud creditors. But if the tenancy already exists, the creditor presumably has notice of the characteristics of the estate which would limit the ability to reach the property. With regard to public policy, the property held by spouses in a tenancy by the entirety is often the single most important asset of the family unit. To allow third parties to become a joint tenant with a couple would severely hinder the use of this asset as security for loans on education and other family expenses. For these reasons, the conveyance of marital property by Mr. (D) and Mrs. Endo to their sons is not subject to the claims of the Sawadas (P), and moreover did not defraud the judgment creditors.

■ DISSENT

(Kidwell, J.) The majority's interpretation of the Married Women's Act equalizes the positions of the spouses by taking away the husband's right to transfer his interest. This position prevents the wife from exercising the same right that the husband once enjoyed for the sake of equality. It would have been better to say either spouse may levy and execute upon their rights of survivorship. Accordingly, the separate interest of Kokichi Endo (D) should be alienable by him and subject to attachment by his separate creditors. A voluntary conveyance by him (D) should be set aside when it is done to defraud his (D) creditors.

Analysis:

The majority of states do not allow a creditor of one spouse to reach a tenancy by the entirety, because one spouse acting alone cannot assign his or her interest. This aspect of the tenancy effectively protects the family home, as well as other property, from unwise transfer by one spouse and from creditors of one spouse. It is likely that this condition is one of the main reasons the tenancy by the entirety has endured.

■ CASE VOCABULARY

COVERTURE: Earlier status of married women under common law, when a wife possessed only the right of survivorship, and not the right to use and enjoyment and exercise of ownership, in the marital estate.

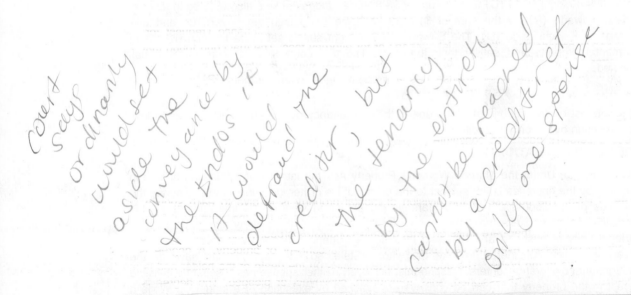

In re Marriage of Graham

(Stewardess Wife and Business Graduate Husband)

574 P.2d 75 (Colo. 1978)

COLORADO SUPREME COURT HOLDS THAT A MASTER'S DEGREE IN BUSINESS ADMINISTRATION AND THE INCREASED EARNING POWER IT PROVIDES DO NOT CONSTITUTE MARITAL PROPERTY AND THUS ARE NOT SUBJECT TO DIVISION UPON DIVORCE

■ **INSTANT FACTS** Flight attendant supports husband through business school, covering seventy percent of their expenses, and after he graduates they get a divorce.

■ **BLACK LETTER RULE** An educational degree is not property, and therefore is not subject to division upon divorce.

■ **PROCEDURAL BASIS**

Appeal from ruling in divorce action.

■ **FACTS**

Anne Graham (P) and Dennis Graham (D) were married on August 5, 1968. Throughout the six-year marriage, Anne Graham (P) was employed full-time as a flight attendant and continues in that profession. Dennis Graham (D) worked part-time for most of the marriage, and devoted his time to his education. He (D) attended school for about three and one-half years of the marriage, acquiring a bachelor's degree in engineering physics and a master's degree in business administration. After graduation, he obtained a corporate position at a starting salary of $14,000 per year. During the marriage, Anne Graham (P) contributed roughly seventy percent of the total income, which was used for family expenses and for Dennis Graham's (D) education. The couple accumulated no marital assets during the marriage. Anne Graham (P) also did the majority of the cooking and other housework. Both persons filed jointly for divorce on February 4, 1974. Anne Graham (P) made no claim for maintenance [request for her husband to provide her with financial support] or for attorney fees. The trial court found that, as a matter of law, an education obtained by one spouse during a marriage is jointly-owned property to which the other spouse has a property right. Anne Graham (P) was awarded $33,134 of Dennis Graham's (D) future earnings. The court of appeals reversed.

■ **ISSUE**

Does a person's education constitute property which can be divided between spouses in the event of a divorce?

■ **DECISION AND RATIONALE**

(Lee, J.) No. The purpose of the division of marital property is to give to each spouse the property that fairly belongs to him or her. There is no rigid formula that the court must follow in doing so. However, there are limits on what actually constitutes property. An educational degree is not encompassed even by very broad views of the concept of property. A degree is of personal value to the holder. The degree itself terminates on the death of the holder and is not inheritable. It cannot be assigned, sold, transferred, conveyed, or pledged. The degree is an intellectual achievement that may assist in the future acquisition of property, but it is not property in and of itself. A spouse who provides financial support while the other spouse acquires an education will have that contribution taken into consideration when marital property is to be divided. Here, though, no marital property has been accumulated by the Grahams. Judgment affirmed.

■ DISSENT

(Carrigan, J.) In a practical sense, the most valuable asset acquired during the Grahams' marriage was the husband's (D) increased earning capacity. This was undeniably the result of Dennis Graham's (D) obtaining the two degrees while married. In fact, Anne Graham's (P) earnings amounted to an investment in that she took on the brunt of financial responsibilities so Dennis Graham (D) would have the time and funds necessary to get a degree. In cases such as this, where the wife works to educate her husband but is rewarded with a divorce after the husband attains a degree, the court should go beyond narrow concepts of property in order to promote equity. The law of torts recognizes that the deprivation of future earnings is something that can be compensated for when impaired or destroyed. Thus, Anne Graham should be compensated for the loss of future earnings of her husband, which were made possible by her investment in his education.

Analysis:

A number of other states have agreed with the decision of the New Jersey court in *Mahoney v. Mahoney*, 91 N.J. 488, 453 A.2d 527 (1982), in which the court held that a professional degree is too speculative in value to be considered marital property. The court held that the working spouse should be awarded "reimbursement alimony." With this ruling, the working spouse would be repaid for covering the costs of the spouse's education, travel expenses to and from school, household expenses, and any other means of support he or she provided while the other spouse earned a degree. Some states have rejected this decision by the enactment of statutes specifically mandating a division of educational benefits. One problem, however, is whether or not to reimburse working spouses for the income the other spouses might have contributed if they had not devoted all their time to education.

■ CASE VOCABULARY

MAINTENANCE: Financial support or assistance paid by one spouse to another after divorce; alimony.

PLEDGE: The use of personal property as security for the payment of a debt.

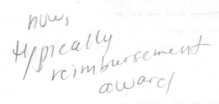

Elkus v. Elkus

(Opera Singer Wife) v. (Voice Coach Husband)

169 A.D.2d 134, 572 N.Y.S.2d 901 (1991)

NEW YORK SUPREME COURT, APPELLATE DIVISION, HOLDS THAT AN INCREASE IN THE VALUE OF ONE SPOUSE'S CAREER, WHEN BROUGHT ABOUT BY THE CONTRIBUTIONS OF THE OTHER SPOUSE, CONSTITUTES MARITAL PROPERTY

■ **INSTANT FACTS** Beginning opera singer marries a voice coach, and after her career skyrockets while he coaches her during marriage, he wants his share upon divorce.

■ **BLACK LETTER RULE** An increase in the value of one spouse's career, when it is the result of the efforts of the other spouse, constitutes marital property and is thus subject to equitable distribution.

■ **PROCEDURAL BASIS**

Appeal from order in divorce action.

■ **FACTS**

Frederica von Stade Elkus (P), a beginning opera singer, and her husband (D), a singer and teacher, were married on February 9, 1973. During the marriage, Mrs. Elkus (P) achieved tremendous success. Her (P) income went from $2,250 in 1973 to $621,878 in 1989. She (P) became an internationally known recording artist and performer, won numerous awards, and performed for the President of the United States. During the marriage, Mr. Elkus (D) traveled with her, attending and critiquing her (P) many performances and rehearsals throughout the world. He (D) photographed her for album covers and magazine articles. He (D) also served as her (P) voice coach and teacher for ten years of the marriage, and took care of their (P and D) two children. Mr. Elkus (D) claimed that he (D) sacrificed his own career as a singer and teacher to devote his time to her (P) career and to the children. Mrs. Elkus (P) claimed her career and celebrity status are not licensed, but rather are the products of her talent, and thus do not constitute property. However, because Mrs. Elkus' (P) celebrity status and career level increased in value in part because of his (D) efforts, Mr. Elkus (D) claimed he (D) was entitled to equitable distribution of this marital property (her career and/or celebrity status). The Supreme Court disagreed with Mr. Elkus (D), and Mr. Elkus (D) appealed.

■ **ISSUE**

Does an increase in the value of one spouse's career, when brought about by the efforts of the other spouse, constitute marital property which can be equitably divided?

■ **DECISION AND RATIONALE**

(Rosenberger, J.) Yes. Things of value that are acquired during marriage are marital property even if they do not fit the traditional definitions of property. Moreover, the property may be tangible or intangible. Such was the case in *O'Brien v. O'Brien*, 66 N.Y.2d 576, 498 N.Y.S.2d 743, 489 N.E.2d 712 [medical license constitutes marital property as it increases one's earning capacity]. There, the court also referred to New York Domestic Relations Law § 236 in its decision. That law states that when making an equitable distribution of marital property, the court shall consider any direct or indirect contribution a spouse makes "to the career or career potential of the other [spouse]." Thus, an interest in one's career counts as marital property, and this may be represented by contributions of the other spouse, including financial and non-financial contributions, such as caring for the home and family. The fact that Mrs. Elkus' (P's) career is not a licensed profession like medicine is irrelevant. It is not the license or degree, but rather the increased earning capacity, that constitutes marital property. Here, it is clear that Mr. Elkus (D) made direct and concrete contributions to Mrs. Elkus' (P's) career, and gave support through his time with the children. Though Mrs. Elkus (P) came into the marriage with her own genuine talent, and with a position in the Metropolitan Opera, her career had barely begun at that time. Mr. Elkus (D) was actively involved in her (P's) career through his critiquing, teaching, and coaching of her (P). Thus, to the extent the appreciation in Mrs. Elkus' (P's) career was due to Mr. Elkus' (D's) efforts, this appreciation constitutes marital property. Judgment reversed.

Analysis:

Some may find this decision to be unfair to Mrs. Elkus. Mr. Elkus claimed that, during the marriage, he served as Mrs. Elkus' voice coach and teacher, and sacrificed his own career to do so. The problem with this position is that Mr. Elkus already was a teacher at the time of the marriage. In essence, then, Mr. Elkus was able to keep his career, but then later enjoy a (presumably) comfortable lifestyle as he accompanied his only student all over the world for concerts and other performances. It would seem that Mr. Elkus has already enjoyed considerable acclaim and other benefits, not only as the husband, but as the teacher of an internationally known opera singer. The court's decision allowed him to continue reaping those benefits even though he no longer filled the role of husband or teacher. Other courts have found that an entertainer has "good will" that is a marital asset, regardless of the contributions of the other spouse.

Varnum v. Brien

(Same Sex Couples) v. *(County)*

763 N.W.2d 862 (Iowa 2009)

SAME SEX COUPLES MAY WED IN IOWA

■ **INSTANT FACTS** Six same sex couples sought marriage licenses from the county recorder, who refused to issue the licenses based on a state statute that provided that only a marriage between a male and a female is valid.

■ **BLACK LETTER RULE** A statute restricting civil marriage to a man and a woman violates the equal protection clause of the Iowa constitution.

■ **PROCEDURAL BASIS**

State supreme court review of summary judgment in favor of the plaintiffs.

■ **FACTS**

When six same sex couples in committed relationships applied for marriage licenses, the county recorder refused to issue the licenses because a state statute provided that only marriage between a male and a female was valid. The six couples met all the other requirements for a valid civil marriage. Thereafter, they commenced a civil rights action against the County (D), alleging that the same sex marriage ban violated certain liberty and equality rights under the Iowa Constitution. The matter came before the trial court on a summary judgment motion, with the County (D) presenting testimony in the form of affidavits and depositions of opinions of individuals that same sex marriage would harm the institution of marriage and children raised in such marriages. The couples produced evidence that sexual orientation and gender do not affect children raised by same sex couples, and that research repudiates the idea that children of dual sex parents become well-adjusted adults. The district court held that the challenged statute violated the due process and equal protection clauses of the state constitution and granted summary judgment for the couples.

■ **ISSUE**

Did statue statute limiting civil marriage to a man and a woman violate the Iowa Constitution as the trial court ruled?

■ **DECISION AND RATIONALE**

(Cady, J.) Yes. A statute restricting civil marriage to a man and a woman violates the equal protection clause of the Iowa constitution. The Iowa equal protection clause is essentially a mandate that all persons similarly situated be treated the same. We reject the County's (D) argument that same sex couples are not similarly situated to opposite sex couples because they cannot procreate naturally. The similarly situated requirement does not require similarity in every way. With respect to the purpose of Iowa's marriage laws, the couples here are similarly situated to heterosexual couples in that they are in committed, loving relationships, with many raising children.

For purposes of scrutinizing the challenged statute, we apply the "intermediate" or "heightened" scrutiny standard, which requires the County (D) to demonstrate that excluding same sex couples from civil marriage is substantially related to the achievement of an important

---

governmental objective. None of the following governmental objectives suggested by the County (D) could fairly be said to be advanced by the challenged statutory classification: (1) maintaining traditional marriage; (2) promoting the best environment to raise children; (3) promotion of procreation; (4) promotion of stability in heterosexual relationships; and (5) conservation of state resources, because if fewer people are allowed to marry the state's fiscal burden with respect to governmental benefits to married couples will be less. Because the exclusion of same sex couples from civil marriage does not substantially further any important governmental objective, the statue violates the equal protection clause of the Iowa Constitution.

Analysis:

The court also considered what it termed the unspoken reason for excluding same sex couples from civil marriage, religious opposition to such marriages. It noted that there were many varied religious views regarding marriage, but that the government can express no religious views in its legislation. Therefore, civil marriage may not be judged under religious doctrines or the religious views of individuals. Its decision would have no impact on how any religious institution defined marriage for its own purposes.

CHAPTER SIX

Tradition, Tension, and Change in Landlord-Tenant Law

Garner v. Gerrish

Instant Facts: Donovan leased house to Gerrish (D) for as long as Gerrish (D) wished.

Black Letter Rule: If a lessee has the option of terminating a lease when he pleases, a determinable life tenancy is created.

Hannan v. Dusch

Instant Facts: When Hannan's (P) lease was to begin, Dusch (D) failed to evict a hold-over tenant.

Black Letter Rule: A landlord only has a duty to deliver the right to possession of the premises to a tenant, not actual possession.

Ernst v. Conditt

Instant Facts: Rogers, the original lessee, transferred his interest to Conditt (D).

Black Letter Rule: In determining whether an assignment or a sub-leasing has occurred, the court looks to the intentions of the parties.

Kendall v. Ernest Pestana

Instant Facts: Ernest Pestana (D) demanded increased rent in exchange for consent to assign a lease.

Black Letter Rule: A lessor may not unreasonably and arbitrarily withhold his or her consent to an assignment.

Berg v. Wiley

Instant Facts: Wiley (D) changed the locks on property that he leased to Berg (P).

Black Letter Rule: A landlord may not use self-help to regain possession of his land.

Sommer v. Kridel

Instant Facts: Sommer (P) failed to make efforts to re-let an apartment when Kridel (D) abandoned it.

Black Letter Rule: A landlord is under a duty to mitigate damages by making reasonable efforts to re-let an apartment wrongfully vacated by the tenant.

Village Commons, LLC v. Marion County Prosecutor's Office

Instant Facts: After a series of water leaks in the leased premises, the local prosecutor's office moved out of the leased building and stopped paying rent; the landlord sued for breach of the lease based on the exclusive remedies provision included therein.

Black Letter Rule: A tenant is relieved of any obligation to pay rent if the landlord deprives the tenant of possession and beneficial use and enjoyment of any part of the demised premises by eviction.

Hilder v. St. Peter

Instant Facts: St. Peter (D) leased an apartment unfit for habitability to Hilder (P). Though Hilder (P) informed St. Peter (D) of these defects, he failed to remedy them.

Black Letter Rule: There is an implied warranty of habitability in every residential lease.

Chicago Board of Realtors v. City of Chicago

Instant Facts: Chicago enacted a rent control ordinance which made minor re-allocations of rights between landlords and tenants.

Black Letter Rule: A rent control ordinance which makes minor re-allocations of rights between landlords and tenants is reasonably related to a legitimate public goal.

Garner v. Gerrish

(Landlord) v. (Tenant)

63 N.Y.2d 575, 473 N.E.2d 223 (1984)

COURT REVERSES OLD COMMON LAW AND ALLOWS PARTIES TO CREATE A DETERMINABLE LIFE TENANCY

■ **INSTANT FACTS** Donovan leased house to Gerrish (D) for as long as Gerrish (D) wished.

■ **BLACK LETTER RULE** If a lessee has the option of terminating a lease when he pleases, a determinable life tenancy is created.

■ **PROCEDURAL BASIS**

Appeal from an order by the appellate court affirming a judgment in action to eject.

■ **FACTS**

In 1977 Donovan leased land to Gerrish (D) for $ 100 per month. The lease stated that Gerrish (D) had the option of terminating the lease at a date of his choice. Gerrish lived there without incident until 1981. In 1981, Donovan died, and Garner (P) became the executor of his estate. Garner (P) requested Gerrish (D) to quit the premises. When Gerrish (D) refused, Garner (P) commenced this action. Garner (P) contends that the lease created a tenancy at will since the length of the lease was indefinite. Gerrish (D) contends that the lease, by its language, created a determinable life tenancy.

■ **ISSUE**

If a lessee may terminate a lease when he pleases, is a determinable life tenancy created?

■ **DECISION AND RATIONALE**

(Wachtler, J.) Yes. At common law, the rule was that a lease for so long as the lessee shall please is a lease at will of both lessee and lessor. This rule had its origin in the ancient ritual of livery of seisin. Livery of seisin, the transfer of a clod of dirt, was required to create a life estate. Therefore, the common law did not allow the creation of a determinable life tenancy without livery of seisin. Hence the old rule: A lease for so long as the lessee shall please is a lease at the will of both lessee and lessor. In modern times, livery of seisin has been abandoned because it is out of step with the realities of modern life. In modern times, the courts look to the terms of the agreement to determine what type of lease has been created. In this case, the terms of the agreement clearly indicate that Donovan and Gerrish (D) agreed that Gerrish (D) would have a determinable life tenancy. Judgment reversed.

Analysis:

This case introduces the tension between property law and contract law that is present throughout all of landlord-tenant law. At early common law, a leasehold was viewed as an interest in property. Since it was a property interest, all of the rules of property law, not contract law, applied. For example, the premises were conveyed without warranty as to the condition of the premises, and breach of the agreement by the landlord did not excuse the tenant from paying rent. The view of a lease as a conveyance of an estate rather than as a contract has come under pressure because of the changing nature of society. As the next several cases demonstrate, courts have responded to this by incorporating many contract principles into the law of property. Thus, the law of leaseholds is a mixed bag of property law and contract law.

■ **CASE VOCABULARY**

LESSEE: One who leases land from another.

LESSOR: One who leases land to another.

QUIET ENJOYMENT: A covenant, implied if not expressly incorporated into a lease, which states that a lessor shall not interfere with the lessee's ability to enjoy the premises.

SUMMARY PROCEEDING: An expedited procedure for evicting a tenant.

TENANCY AT WILL: One who may possess land so long as both he and the landlord desire.

takeaway: today, tenancy at will is rare, it's attempted creation creates instead an implied periodic tenancy

Hannan v. Dusch

(Tenant) v. (Landlord)

154 Va. 356, 153 S.E. 824, 70 A.L.R. 141 (1930)

*[handwritten: * Landlord's duty to deliver possession of the premises at the start of the lease]*

COURT RULES THAT A LANDLORD NEED NOT PLACE A TENANT IN POSSESSION; THE LANDLORD NEED ONLY GIVE A RIGHT OF POSSESSION

■ **INSTANT FACTS** When Hannan's (P) lease was to begin, Dusch (D) failed to evict a hold-over tenant.

■ **BLACK LETTER RULE** A landlord only has a duty to deliver the right to possession of the premises to a tenant, not actual possession.

[handwritten: Manifestation of the so-called American rule — no duty to put new T in actual physical possession vs. English rule says there is a duty to deliver legal + actual possession]

■ **PROCEDURAL BASIS**

Appeal from the sustaining of a demurrer in action for damages for failure to deliver possession.

■ **FACTS**

Hannan (P) leased land from Dusch (D). When the lease was to begin, the tenant then in possession failed to vacate. Dusch (D) failed to put Hannan (P) in possession. Hannan (P) contends that Dusch (D) must deliver actual possession and that he should have evicted the holdover tenant. Dusch (D) contends that he need only deliver the legal right to possession. There is no covenant in the lease to the effect that Dusch (D) must put Hannan (P) in possession.

■ **ISSUE**

Must the landlord deliver actual possession to the tenant?

[handwritten: a term of years lease b/c we know the ending]

■ **DECISION AND RATIONALE**

(Prentis, J.) No. It is clear that a landlord must at least provide the legal right to possession. It is also clear that once the tenant takes possession, he is responsible for ejecting a trespasser. Were there a covenant in the lease stating either that the landlord did or did not have the duty to put the tenant in possession, that covenant would prevail. Where there is no covenant, there are two rules: (1) The English rule says that the landlord must place the tenant in possession and (2) The American rule says that the landlord must only give the tenant the right to possession. We must pick the one that we believe is better supported by reason. There are a couple of reasons why the English rule is good: (1) A tenant contracts for possession and not for a lawsuit to evict a hold-over; (2) The landlord is in a better position to assess whether a current tenant will in fact hold-over. However, we chose the American rule because it is unfair to hold the landlord liable for the wrong of another. Judgment affirmed.

Analysis:

As is apparent throughout landlord/tenant law, whether one views a lease as a contract or as a property interest greatly affects the rights and duties of the landlord and tenant. Treating a lease like an estate seems more proper if the tenant is a large corporation and the land will be used for commercial purposes. In that case, the corporation seeks not just possession, but also some form of title, albeit not a freehold title. Moreover, a corporation has more resources to vindicate

*[handwritten: * Today, the English rule is the majority U.S. rule]*

its rights. However, if the tenant is a family and the land will be used as a residence, the primary concern of the tenant is possession. In this case, the lease is more properly viewed as a contract where the landlord has the duty to deliver possession.

■ **CASE VOCABULARY**

OUST: To remove from possession.

Ernst v. Conditt

(Lessor) v. (Assignee)

54 Tenn.App. 328, 390 S.W.2d 703 (1964)

COURT APPLIES CONTRACT LAW IN LEASE AGREEMENT: IN DETERMINING WHETHER AN ASSIGNMENT OR A SUB-LEASE HAS OCCURRED, THE COURT WILL LOOK TO THE INTENTIONS OF THE PARTIES

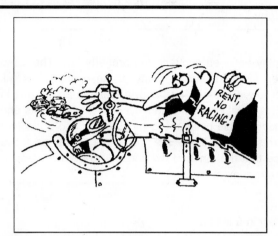

■ **INSTANT FACTS** Rogers, the original lessee, transferred his interest to Conditt (D).

■ **BLACK LETTER RULE** In determining whether an assignment or a sub-leasing has occurred, the court looks to the intentions of the parties.

■ **PROCEDURAL BASIS**

Appeal from judgment in action for damages for breach of lease agreement.

■ **FACTS**

Ernst (P) leased land to Rogers for a term of 1 year, 7 days. After Rogers operated a race track for a short time on the premises, he entered into negotiations with Conditt (D) for the sale of the business. The original lease was modified. The modified lease contained the following provisions: (1) The term of the lease was extended to 2 years; (2) Rogers was given the right to "sublet" the premises to Conditt (D) on the condition that Rogers remain personally liable for the performance of the terms of the lease. Subsequently, Rogers leased the premises to Conditt (D). In the contract between Rogers and Conditt (D), the term "sublet" was used. After Conditt (D) took possession, he operated the race track for a short time. Soon, however, Conditt (D) quit paying rent, but he remained in possession. Ernst (P) sues Conditt for rent owed. Ernst (P) contends that the agreement between Rogers and Conditt (D) is an assignment of the lease, which would render Conditt (D) liable to Ernst (P). Conditt (D) contends that the agreement between Rogers and him was a subletting.

■ **ISSUE**

In determining whether an assignment or a sub-leasing has occurred, must the court look to the intentions of the parties?

■ **DECISION AND RATIONALE**

(Chattin, J.) Yes. An assignment allows the land owner to recover from the assignee. A sublease does not allow the land owner to recover from sub-lessees. At common law, the following rule was used to determine whether a lessee assigned or sublet the premises: An assignment conveyed the entire interest in a lease; it left nothing to the original lessee. A sublease granted an interest that was less than that owned by the original lessee; the original lessee retained a reversionary interest. The modern method of determining whether there has been an assignment or sublease is to ascertain the intention of the parties. Under the common law rule, Conditt (D) is liable to Ernst (P) because he took Rogers' entire interest in the land. The fact that the modified contract between Rogers and Ernst (P) held Rogers to be personally liable to Ernst does not matter for the following reason: The liability of Rogers to Ernst (P) is not determined by an agreement between Rogers and Conditt (D). Also, the fact that the modified agreement between Rogers and Ernst (P) contained the word "sublet" does not matter. Ernst's consent to "sublet" has been held to be only a consent to one other than the original lessee to go into possession; it authorizes both a subletting and an assignment. In any case, Conditt (D) is liable to Ernst (P) under the modern rule. By the terms of the agreement between Rogers and Conditt (D), Rogers retained no reversionary interest; he conveyed all that he had. Thus, Rogers has assigned his lease. Judgment affirmed.

Analysis:

This case illustrates and introduces the interplay between contract and property law. The lease between the lessor and lessee creates duties for both parties. Many of these duties, as will become apparent, have derived from contract law. On the other hand, a lease is an interest in property, and as such it may be conveyed. However, when it is conveyed, often the rights and duties follow it, as when a lessee assigns a lease. This binds the original lessor into a landlord tenant relationship with the lessee. The terms of this lease are the same terms as those between the original lessor and lessee. Notice that the landlord did consent to the new tenant. Many landlords reserve the right to refuse an assignment.

■ CASE VOCABULARY

ASSIGN: To give to another one's entire interest in a lease.

PRIVITY OF CONTRACT: A relationship between parties that arises because they have entered into a contract with one another.

PRIVITY OF ESTATE: A relationship between parties that arises because they share an interest in property.

SUBLET: To transfer a portion of a lessee's interest in a lease to another.

pure at
p. 488 txtbk

— what the parties call the
arrangement doesn't matter —
not dispositive

Kendall v. Ernest Pestana

(Assignee) v. (Lessor)

40 Cal.3d 488, 709 P.2d 837, 220 Cal.Rptr. 818 (1985)

COURT DECLARES THAT LESSOR MUST ACT REASONABLY: A LESSOR MAY NOT ARBITRARILY WITHHOLD CONSENT TO AN ASSIGNMENT

■ **INSTANT FACTS** Ernest Pestana (D) demanded increased rent in exchange for consent to assign a lease.

■ **BLACK LETTER RULE** A lessor may not unreasonably and arbitrarily withhold his or her consent to an assignment.

■ **FACTS**

The city of San Jose leased a hangar to Perlitch. Perlitch sublet the premises to Bixler for a term of 25 years. The lease provided that written consent of the lessor was required before the lessee could assign his interest. Bixler was to run an airplane maintenance business. Subsequently, Perlitch assigned his interest to Ernest Pestana (D). Later, Bixler attempted to sell his interest to Kendall (P). Kendall (P) was more financially sound than Bixler. As per the terms of the original lease between Bixler and Perlitch, Bixler requested consent from Ernest Pestana (D) for the sublease. Ernest Pestana (D) demanded an increase in rent in exchange for consent. Ernest Pestana (D) contends that he may arbitrarily refuse consent. Kendall (P) contends that this provision is against public policy since it is an unreasonable restraint on alienation.

■ **ISSUE**

May a lessor unreasonably and arbitrarily withhold his or her consent to an assignment?

■ **DECISION AND RATIONALE**

(Broussard, J.) No. The law favors the free alienability of property, including a leasehold. However, alienability may be restricted by contract so as to protect the lessor. Such contracts are construed against the lessor, especially when the act of assigning terminates the lease. The majority rule allows the lessor to arbitrarily withhold consent. Even in the majority states, however, the lessor may waive his right or be estopped from asserting it. A growing trend asserts the following rule: A lessor may withhold consent only when he has a commercially reasonable objection to the assignment. We adopt this rule for the following reasons: (1) Public policy favors free alienability; (2) The relationship between lessor and lessee has become more and more impersonal. As a result, the lessor is just as likely to find a high quality tenant in the assignee as the lessee; (3) The lessor's interests are protected by the fact that the lessee remains contractually liable to the lessor; (4) A lease is increasingly viewed as a contract. As a result, since the lessor has discretion in withholding consent, the lessor can withhold consent only in good faith. The lessor may withhold consent in the following circumstances, for example: (1) The property is ill-suited for the proposed use; (2) The proposed use is illegal; (3) The proposed use requires altering the premises. The lessor cannot withhold consent solely on the basis of personal taste. Nor may he demand higher rent in exchange for consent. This is because the original lease already exhibits an agreement between lessor and lessee, and lessor

---

may not attempt to get more than he bargained for. There are four reasons advanced for allowing arbitrary withholding of consent: (1) Lessor has picked his tenant and he should not have to look elsewhere for the rent. This is unpersuasive because lessor may still refuse consent if it is reasonable. If an assignee is a poor financial risk, lessor may reasonably withhold consent. Moreover, the original lessee is still liable to the lessor; (2) The lessee could have bargained for a contract clause that provided that consent could be withheld only if reasonable; the court should not place this clause in the contract. This is rejected because the fact that the parties agreed to a consent requirement must mean that they contemplated that the lessee give some reason for withholding consent; (3) The court must follow the rule because of stare decisis. Rejected, because the court has never ruled on this issue; (4) The lessor has a right to realize the increased value of his property by demanding higher rent. Rejected because the lessee took the risk that property prices would fall. He is also entitled to any gain should prices rise. The lessor, as well as the lessee, must live with the risk incurred as a result of the contract made. Judgment reversed.

■ DISSENT

The terms of the contract should be honored. There was no requirement in the contract that withholding of consent had to be reasonable. Moreover, the legislature has already adopted the rule that consent may be withheld arbitrarily.

Analysis:

This case continues the development of contract doctrine in the law of property. In this case, the doctrine of good faith is applied. A lessor may withhold his or her consent to an assignment only with good reason. Notice that the contract doctrine of good faith helps achieve one of the goals of property law: It promotes the free alienability of property.

■ CASE VOCABULARY

APPROVAL CLAUSE: A clause requiring the lessors approval before a lease can be assigned or sub-let.

FORFEITURE RESTRAINT: A restraint on the alienation of property which, if breached, causes the breacher's entire interest to be forfeited.

MITIGATE DAMAGES: To prevent the accrual of damages.

SURETY: One who will respond in damages if another person causes the damages. An insurance company acts as a surety.

Berg v. Wiley

(Tenant) v. (Landlord)

264 N.W.2d 145 (Minn. 1978)

COURT GIVES ADDITIONAL RIGHTS TO TENANTS: LANDLORD MAY NOT USE SELF-HELP TO EVICT TENANT

■ **INSTANT FACTS** Wiley (D) changed the locks on property that he leased to Berg (P).

■ **BLACK LETTER RULE** A landlord may not use self-help to regain possession of his land.

■ **PROCEDURAL BASIS**

Appeal from directed verdict in action for damages for wrongful eviction.

■ **FACTS**

Wiley (D) leased land to Phillip Berg for a term of five years. The lease provided that no changes in the building structure should be made without Wiley's (D) consent. Wiley (D) reserved the right to retake possession should Phillip Berg fail to meet the terms and conditions of the lease. Subsequently, Phillip Berg assigned his lease to Berg (P). Without securing Wiley's (D) permission, Berg (P) began to remodel the premises to make them suitable for a restaurant. A dispute arose between Berg (P) and Wiley (D) as a result of Berg's (P) continued remodeling of the restaurant without permission and operation of the restaurant in violation of the health code. Wiley (D) demanded that the health code violations be remedied and that Berg (P) complete the remodeling within two weeks. At the close of two weeks, Berg (P) closed the restaurant, dismissed her employees, and placed a sign on the premises that read, "Closed for Remodeling." Also after two weeks, Wiley (D) attempted to change the locks on the doors, but ceased this attempt when Berg (P) arrived. Three days later, without Berg's (P) knowledge, Wiley (D) changed the locks. Berg (P) contends that she was wrongfully evicted. Wiley (D) raises the defense of abandonment. The trial court ruled Wiley's (D) entry was forcible.

■ **ISSUE**

May a landowner use self-help to retake possession of his property?

■ **DECISION AND RATIONALE**

(Rogosheske, J.) No. Though the testimony is in conflict, there is ample evidence to support the jury's finding that Berg (P) did not abandon the premises. At common law, a landlord could use self-help if: (1) The landlord is legally entitled to possession, such as when a tenant is a hold-over; and (2) the landlord's means of entry are peaceable. On the first requirement, Wiley (D) contends that he was entitled to possession since Berg (P) breached the lease. However, it is for the courts, not Wiley (D), to determine if a landlord is entitled to possession. Turning to whether entry was peaceable, Wiley (D) contends that only actual or threatened use of violence should give rise to liability. We are not convinced. There has been a public policy in this state, expressed by both the courts and the legislature, aimed at discouraging self-help. To discourage self-help, the legislature has created summary proceedings to help the landlord

---

regain possession quickly. To further discourage self-help, the legislature has provided treble damages for forced entry. In consideration of this policy, Wiley's (D) entry was not peaceable. Given the historical relations between Berg (P) and Wiley (D), the only reason violence did not erupt was because Berg (P) was not present when the locks were changed. Indeed, any use of self-help has the potential for violence. Therefore, unless the tenant has abandoned or surrendered the premises, a landlord may not use self-help. The landlord must resort to the judicial process to regain possession. Judgment affirmed.

Analysis:

Because Berg (P) had possession of the premises, the law gave her much protection. There are various reasons for protecting possessors on rented land: (1) As the court mentioned, it discourages the forcible taking of possession. The law always wants to deter violence. (2) It protects families from being left with no-where to go. Note, however, that protection of possessors comes at the expense of the landlord, who may be legally entitled to possession. As a compromise, some states forbid self-help to evict a residential tenant, but allow self-help for the eviction of a commercial tenant.

■ **CASE VOCABULARY**

ABANDON: To give up possession.

BREACH OF PEACE: The eruption of violence.

RE-ENTRY: To retake possession.

RESTRAINING ORDER: A judicial order preventing a person from performing some act.

SELF-HELP: Vindicating one's rights without going to a court.

SUMMARY PROCEDURE: An expedited method to evict one in possession.

SURRENDER: To give up possession.

UNLAWFUL DETAINER STATUTE: Statute detailing the procedures that must be followed to evict a tenant.

Sommer v. Kridel

(Landlord) v. (Tenant Who Has Abandoned)

74 N.J. 446, 378 A.2d 767 (1977)

COURT MAKES LEASE MORE LIKE A CONTRACT: LANDLORD NOW HAS DUTY TO MITIGATE DAMAGES

[handwritten: ← borrowed from contract law]

[handwritten: walked + then sued for a lump sum]

■ **INSTANT FACTS** Sommer (P) failed to make efforts to re-let an apartment when Kridel (D) abandoned it.

■ **BLACK LETTER RULE** A landlord is under a duty to mitigate damages by making reasonable efforts to re-let an apartment wrongfully vacated by the tenant.

■ **PROCEDURAL BASIS**

Appeal from an order by the appellate court reversing judgment in action for damages to recover back rent.

■ **FACTS**

Sommer (P) leased apartment 6–L to Kridel (D) for a term of 2 years. Kridel (D) paid the first month's rent plus a security deposit. Before Kridel (D) went into possession, however, he informed Sommer (P) by letter that he could no longer afford the lease. Sommer (P) did not respond to the letter. Subsequently, a third party inquired about apartment 6–L. Though the third party was ready, willing, and able to rent apartment 6–L, she was refused because it had already been rented to Kridel (D). Over a year later, the apartment was finally re-let for terms and conditions similar to those negotiated with Kridel (D). Sommer (P) sues for damages for rent due between the date Kridel (D) was to take possession and the date when the apartment was rented to the third party. Kridel (D) contends that there is no liability because Sommer (P) both failed to mitigate and accepted Kridel's (D) surrender of the premises. The companion case of *Riverview Realty Co. v. Perosio* has similar facts: Perosio (D) abandoned possession of a two-year lease after a one year occupancy.

[handwritten margin note: landlord is being mean here]

■ **ISSUE**

Is a landlord under a duty to mitigate damages by making reasonable efforts to re-let an apartment wrongfully vacated by the tenant?

■ **DECISION AND RATIONALE**

(Pashman, J.) Yes. The majority rule is that a landlord has no duty to mitigate. This is based on the property view of a lease. This view understands a lease to be a property interest which forecloses any control of the property by the landlord. For example, in *Muller v. Beck* [issue of whether landlord must mitigate when a tenant abandons] it was said that "the tenant has an estate with which the landlord cannot interfere." It was understood that when the tenant vacated, he could retake the premises when he wished. Since the landlord had no control, it would be silly to require him to mitigate. Modern social forces, however, have exerted pressure on the law of estates. The law of estates has responded by allowing specific clauses in contracts to deal with these forces. Since we now view a lease in large measure as a contract, we apply a contract principle: The landlord must mitigate damages. This rule derives from considerations of fairness. It would be unfair to allow a landlord to sit idly by and watch damages mount when he can prevent those damages. For example, in *Sommer v. Kridel*, Sommer (P) let over a year pass and allowed $4658.50 in damages to accrue before he made efforts to re-let. The landlord cannot argue that he will lose the opportunity to rent to another if he's required to first rent the apartment that has been abandoned. This is because each apartment has its unique characteristics, and there is no reason to believe that a tenant who wished to rent the apartment that has been abandoned also would have been willing to rent another vacant apartment. In fact, in *Sommer v. Kridel*, there was a specific request for the abandoned apartment. So the rule is: If the landlord has many vacant apartments, he must treat the abandoned apartment as one of his vacant stock and make reasonable efforts to re-let it. Since the landlord is in a better position to demonstrate that his efforts were reasonable, he shall have the burden of showing reasonable efforts to re-let. Judgment reversed.

Analysis:

Historically, a landlord did not have to mitigate the damages of an abandonment because he was not the possessor of the estate. To change this historical understanding of a leasehold, and to encourage the efficient use of property, the law of contracts was imported into the law of property. Contract law has placed many burdens and duties on both the landlord and tenant that were not present at common law. Whether these new duties, such as the implied warranty of habitability, are desirable is in dispute. The next several cases take up this issue.

■ **CASE VOCABULARY**

DEFAULTING TENANT: A tenant who abandons or does not do some other act required under a lease (including the failure to pay rent).

MITIGATE DAMAGES: To attempt to reduce the damages that occur as a result of a breach or abandonment.

REASONABLE DILIGENCE: That amount of diligence that an ordinary man would exercise under the circumstances.

RE-LET: To lease to another.

SECURITY DEPOSIT: A sum of money paid by a lessee to insure against damage to the premises.

tenant breaches, but remains in possession no problem
with vs.
tenant vacates without good cause

Village Commons, LLC v. Marion County Prosecutor's Office

(Landlord) v. (Tenant)

882 N.E.2d 210 (Ind. Ct. App. 2008)

BOTH ACTUAL AND CONSTRUCTIVE EVICTION MAY RELIEVE A TENANT OF THE OBLIGATION TO PAY RENT

commercial lease

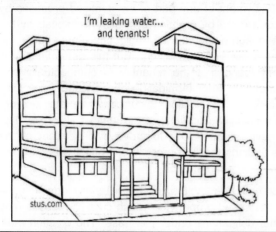

I'm leaking water... and tenants!

stus.com

Commercial lease

elements of constructive eviction

■ **INSTANT FACTS** After a series of water leaks in the leased premises, the local prosecutor's office moved out of the leased building and stopped paying rent; the landlord sued for breach of the lease based on the exclusive remedies provision included therein.

■ **BLACK LETTER RULE** A tenant is relieved of any obligation to pay rent if the landlord deprives the tenant of possession and beneficial use and enjoyment of any part of the demised premises by eviction.

■ **PROCEDURAL BASIS**

State appellate court review of a trial court judgment in the tenant's favor.

■ **FACTS**

The local prosecutor's office (D) entered into a lease with the plaintiff's predecessor, which continued when the plaintiff took ownership of the building. Pursuant to the lease, the landlord was required to maintain all building equipment and to maintain the premises in good condition. The tenant could sue for damages or injunctive relief in the event of the landlord's breach, but it could not terminate the lease and then abate any rent due thereunder. In 2001, the building experienced a series of water leaks that damaged the property of the prosecutor's office. The landlord took some initial steps, but delayed actually making repairs. In 2002, the main water line broke and caused a major leak in the prosecutor's evidence room. A mold remediation company detected mold in the evidence room and recommended remediation services. The landlord did not use the company's services, choosing instead to have its maintenance man perform some—but not all—of the recommended tasks. Leaks and water damage continued to occur over the next several months. The remediation company again recommended necessary steps and warned of possible allergic reactions to the mold. Even so, the landlord told the prosecutor's office employees that there were no health risks in the building, despite complaints from some employees of prolonged coughing and sneezing. One employee's doctor recommended his reassignment outside the building, and his symptoms subsided after he relocated. Another water leak ensued, causing the women's restroom to be closed for about three weeks, and a stream of water continued to pour into the evidence room. The landlord advised the tenant to avoid using those parts of the building that were most vulnerable to water damage.

Finally, in 2003, the prosecutor's office vacated the leased premises and stopped paying rent. The landlord sued for breach of the lease and sought damages for unpaid rent. The tenant counterclaimed for wrongful eviction, arguing that it had been constructively evicted. The trial court held that the prosecutor's defenses and counterclaim were not barred by the lease's exclusive remedies provisions; that the tenant was both actually evicted and constructively evicted; and that, even if the landlord could recover against the tenant, the landlord failed to mitigate its damages. The tenant was awarded damages and its costs.

■ ISSUE

Was the tenant constructively evicted and entitled to damages?

■ DECISION AND RATIONALE

(Riley, J.) Yes. A tenant is relieved of any obligation to pay rent if the landlord deprives the tenant of possession and beneficial use and enjoyment of any part of the demised premises by eviction. The landlord argues here that the court erred by granting a remedy prohibited by the exclusive remedies provision of the lease. We agree that the unambiguous language of the lease did not allow the tenant to terminate the lease or withhold rent. But this determination is not dispositive of the dispute. The trial court found that the tenant was both actually and constructively evicted because of the water damage. After termination of the lease, all liability under it for future rent is extinguished. Here, actual eviction occurred when the landlord informed the prosecutor's office to refrain from using the portions of the leased premises most vulnerable to water damage. The landlord advised the tenant to move evidence out of the evidence room. This supports the trial court's findings that the prosecutor's office was deprived of a material part of the leased premises by the water intrusions.

Constructive eviction occurs when an act or omission by the lessor materially deprives the lessee of the beneficial use or enjoyment of the leased property, in which case the lessee may elect to abandon the property and avoid further obligations under the lease. The election must occur within a reasonable time after the act or omission. It would be contrary to public policy to permit a landlord to completely eliminate a tenant's remedy for constructive eviction if the conditions are such that the leased property is unusable. But we do not need to rest on public policy here. The exclusive remedy provision did not prohibit the landlord from evicting the prosecutor, only the prosecutor's ability to terminate the lease and withhold rent. Upon the occurrence of eviction, either actual or constructive, it is the lessor's act or omission, not the lessee's, that ends the obligation to pay rent. Affirmed.

Analysis:

The court of appeals concluded in this case that the exclusive-remedy provision limited the prosecutor's office's ability to terminate the lease, not the landlord's, so an act of the landlord that actually or constructively evicted the prosecutor's office ended the obligation to pay rent. It was the landlord's own act or omission of not properly fixing the water leaks and preventing water damage that resulted in the prosecutor's office not having to pay future rent. The appellate court observed that the office was actually evicted in October 2002, when the landlord asked the office to stop using part of the space that was most vulnerable to the water leaks, and that the office was constructively evicted in January 2003, because of repeated water leaks that went unrepaired. The court of appeals allowed the prosecutor's office to bring its counterclaim and assert the defense that it had been evicted, despite a provision in the lease that the tenant's claims were barred after one year from the date of inaction or event complained of, because it was the landlord who initiated this case, so the prosecutor's office's defense and counterclaim were not barred by the lease.

■ CASE VOCABULARY

CONSTRUCTIVE: That which is not so in its essential nature, but which is regarded as such in the mind of the law; not actual, but legal. Constructive is used as an adjective with many terms to mean that which, through inference, presumption, or interpretation, the law holds as existing. "Constructive eviction" is a situation where a landlord causes a tenant to leave his premises without actually asking him to do so (*e.g.,* by turning off the heat in winter).

EVICTION: Dispossession; act of making a tenant surrender possession of property. Eviction may be by an assertion of paramount title, by disturbing a tenant's enjoyment of property thus causing him to leave, by reentry (for breach of a covenant in the lease), or by legal proceedings by the landlord.

constructive eviction

Hilder v. St. Peter

(Tenant) v. (Landlord)

144 Vt. 150, 478 A.2d 202 (1984)

COURT MAKES LIFE EASIER FOR RENTERS: THERE IS AN IMPLIED COVENANT OF HABITABILITY IN EVERY LEASE

[handwritten: Implied warranty of habitability]

■ **INSTANT FACTS** St. Peter (D) leased an apartment unfit for habitability to Hilder (P). Though Hilder (P) informed St. Peter (D) of these defects, he failed to remedy them.

■ **BLACK LETTER RULE** There is an implied warranty of habitability in every residential lease.

[handwritten: suitable for basic human dwelling]

■ **PROCEDURAL BASIS**

Appeal from judgment in action for damages for breach of implied covenant of habitability.

■ **FACTS**

In 1974 Hilder (P) and her three children rented an apartment from St. Peter (D) for $140 per month. Hilder (P) has paid all rent due. Upon taking possession of the apartment, Hilder (P) discovered a broken kitchen window. St. Peter (D) promised to repair it but failed to do so. Eventually, Hilder (P) repaired the window at her own expense because she was concerned that one of her children might get cut. There was also no key to the door. St. Peter (D) promised to provide a key, but never did. The toilet was clogged and was filled with feces; it would only flush if water was poured down it. The bathroom light and wall outlet were inoperable. In order to have light in the bathroom, Hilder (P) attached an extension cord to an outlet in an adjoining room and ran it to the bathroom. Water leaked into the apartment from an apartment above. As a result, a large section of plaster fell onto Hilder's (P) bed and her grandson's crib. Also, there was a strong and offensive odor in the apartment. All of these things St. Peter (D) promised to remedy, but never did. The trial court ruled these faults breached the warranty of habitability and awarded Hilder (P) the total rent paid. St. Peter contends that it was error to award the full rent because Hilder (P) never vacated. Hilder (P) contends that abandoning the premises is not required.

■ **ISSUE**

Is there an implied warranty of habitability in every residential lease?

■ **DECISION AND RATIONALE**

(Billings, J.) Yes. Historically the rule was that the lessee took possession in whatever state the premises were in. The landlord had no duty to make the premises habitable unless there was an express covenant in the lease. This is because a leasehold was viewed as an estate in land: The land was the essence of the conveyance, not the dwelling. The tenant was excused from paying rent only if the landlord ousted the tenant. In modern times, a tenant leases land for a safe, sanitary dwelling, not for arable land. Moreover, the characteristics of today's tenant has changed. The tenant of the middle ages was a farmer who was capable of making necessary repairs himself. In contrast, today's tenant is a city dweller who is unable to repair complex living units. On the other hand, landlords are in a much better position to repair residential units.

Given these changes, we now hold that there exists in every residential lease an implied covenant of habitability. Moreover, this warranty cannot be waived by a tenant. In determining whether this warranty has been breached, the courts may look to the local municipal housing code or to the minimum state housing code standards, for example. These codes and standards need not be dispositive, however. These standards should be used to determine if the premises are safe. Once the warranty has been breached, the tenant must notify the landlord and allow him time to remedy the defect. If the defect is not remedied, the tenant may pursue rescission, reformation, and damages. Damages awarded shall be the difference between the value of the residence as warranted and the value of the residence as defective. The tenant may recover for discomfort and annoyance, and he may repair the defect and deduct the expense from the rent. The tenant may also withhold rent until damages are calculated. The burden of bringing suit will then be on the landlord, who can better afford to bring the action. Finally, the plaintiff may pursue punitive damages. Judgment affirmed in part and remanded for a calculation of damages.

Analysis:

The implied warranty is often hailed as a victory for renters, but this is in dispute. First, as with the doctrine of constructive eviction, landlords may increase the rent, since they must now warrant the premises. This increase in rent will make housing less affordable, which is surely not a victory for tenants. Second, since the warranty is not waivable, it decreases renters' bargaining power. Should an informed renter, willing to live in an unfit house for a reduction in rent, be denied the opportunity to live there? The answer often given is that the courts should not permit conduct that debases human dignity.

■ CASE VOCABULARY

CAVEAT LESSEE: Literally, let the lessee beware; a doctrine which asserts that the lessee takes the premises as he finds it, whether fit for human habitation or not.

DE MINIMIS: A small amount not recognized by the law as significant.

IMPLIED WARRANTY OF HABITABILITY: A warranty implied in every contract for the lease of a residential dwelling to the effect that the landlord will maintain the premises fit for human habitability.

INTERDEPENDENT CONSIDERATIONS: Doctrine asserting that if landlord breaches a term of the lease, including the implied warranty of habitability, the tenant's duty to pay rent ceases.

PUNITIVE DAMAGES: Money awarded to plaintiff for the sole purpose of punishing defendant.

REFORMATION: The re-working of a contract.

RESCISSION: To voiding of a contract.

implied warranty of habitability (use that term b/c borrows from contract law

Chicago Board of Realtors v. City of Chicago

(Land Owners) v. (City)

819 F.2d 732 (7th Cir. 1987)

COURT UPHOLDS RENT ORDINANCE, BUT IS NOT HAPPY ABOUT IT

■ **INSTANT FACTS** Chicago enacted a rent control ordinance which made minor re-allocations of rights between landlords and tenants.

■ **BLACK LETTER RULE** A rent control ordinance which makes minor re-allocations of rights between landlords and tenants is reasonably related to a legitimate public goal.

■ **PROCEDURAL BASIS**

Appeal from denial of preliminary injunction in action to declare rent control ordinance unconstitutional.

■ **FACTS**

In 1986, Chicago enacted a Residential Landlord and Tenant Ordinance which essentially codified the implied warranty of habitability. It also contained new landlord responsibilities and tenant rights, such as: (1) a tenant may withhold rent if the landlord violates a term of the lease; (2) the landlord must pay interest on security deposits; (3) the security deposit must be held in an Illinois bank; and (4) a landlord is forbidden from charging more than $10 for late rent. Chicago Board of Realtors contends that the ordinance violates the contracts clause of the Constitution, procedural and substantive due process, equal protection clause, and it is void for vagueness.

■ **ISSUE**

Is a rent control ordinance which makes minor re-allocations of rights between landlords and tenants reasonably related to a legitimate public goal?

■ **DECISION AND RATIONALE**

(Cudahy, J.) Yes. [Judge Cudahy's constitutional analysis is omitted. Instead, the policy analysis of Judge Posner is included].

■ **CONCURRENCE**

(Posner, J.) We agree that the ordinance is reasonable. But a strong case can be made for its unreasonableness because it re-allocates rights between landlords and tenants. Though the stated purpose of the ordinance is to promote social welfare, this is probably not the true motivation. Moreover, it is not likely to be the actual result because, if landlords cannot charge more than $10 for late rent and if tenants can withhold rent, landlords will not improve housing as much, since it will no longer pay. In addition, landlords will try to raise rents. This will hurt tenants and force those who cannot pay the higher rent to go homeless. If the landlords can't raise rent, they will devote more resources to condominiums, reducing the stock of housing. The provision that requires that security deposits be placed in Illinois banks serves only to transfer wealth from landlords and out-of-state banks to tenants and local banks. This is class legislation and protectionism. This will really benefit the middle class, not the poor. This is

---

because the middle class will get preferential treatment by the landlords because they are a better risk against late rent. Further, the middle class will benefit from over-supplied and lower priced condominiums. This ordinance transfers wealth from out-of-state banks and tenants to the middle class. This becomes clear when one realizes that out of state individuals can't vote in Chicago elections and that the poor rarely vote.

Analysis:

Judge Posner articulates the argument against rent control and doctrines such as the implied warranty of habitability. Though such attempts are noble, he says, they have the opposite effect of that intended. Courts are reasonably free to develop doctrines to help the plight of the poor, and the implied warranty of habitability is an example of such an attempt. However, the courts are almost powerless in striking down attempts by the legislature to help the poor, even when these attempts have the opposite effect of that intended. As the Supreme Court has said many times, it is not for the courts to judge the propriety of the legislature's actions.

■ CASE VOCABULARY

CLASS LEGISLATION: Legislation designed for the sole purpose of aiding a particular class of individuals.

CONTRACTS CLAUSE: Constitution clause forbidding the government from interfering with contractual obligations.

PROCEDURAL DUE PROCESS: Clause of the constitution mandating that no life, liberty or property shall be taken without a fair chance for an individual to be heard.

REBUTTABLE PRESUMPTION: A presumption against a party which he may overcome by the introduction of evidence.

SUBSTANTIVE DUE PROCESS: Clause of the constitution (same clause as procedural due process) requiring that fundamental rights shall not be infringed upon unless the government has a compelling reason to do so.

TAKINGS CLAUSE: Clause of the constitution that requires that the government pay for land that it appropriates from private citizens.

VOID-FOR-VAGUENESS DOCTRINE: Doctrine which asserts that any law that is so vague that a reasonable person would not know how to avoid criminal behavior is void.

CHAPTER SEVEN

The Land Transaction

Licari v. Blackwelder

Instant Facts: Two real estate brokers associated with the listing agent on the Licaris' (P) property purchased the property and sold it for a profit six days later.

Black Letter Rule: As fiduciaries, real estate brokers must place their clients' interests above their own, act in good faith, and disclose all information that is or may be material to their clients' rights and interests.

Hickey v. Green

Instant Facts: The Hickeys (P) sold their house in reliance on an oral agreement with the owner of Lot S, Mrs. Green (D). Mrs. Green rescinded the agreement.

Black Letter Rule: When there is a clear oral promise, partial payment, plus an act made in reliance, a land transfer is sufficient to overcome the Statute of Frauds requirement that contracts for the sale of land must be in writing.

Lohmeyer v. Bower

Instant Facts: Prior to transfer of property, a title search showed that the property in question had two encumbrances upon it, both of which were being violated.

Black Letter Rule: Marketable title to real estate is title that does not expose the buyer to litigation.

Stambovsky v. Ackley

Instant Facts: Ackley (D) sells house that she has widely publicized as a haunted house to Stambovsky (P), who is from a different city and does not know that it is haunted.

Black Letter Rule: Where a seller has created a condition that materially alters the value of the contract for sale of real property, and the condition is uniquely within the knowledge of the seller and unlikely to be discovered by a careful buyer, failure to disclose that condition creates a basis for rescission as a matter of equity.

Johnson v. Davis

Instant Facts: Davis (P), with representation from Johnson (D) that a roof did not leak, buys home with a leaky roof.

Black Letter Rule: Sellers of real property have a duty to disclose to prospective buyers material facts affecting the value of the property, when those facts are not known or readily observable to the buyer.

Lempke v. Dagenais

Instant Facts: Lempke (P) purchases a house that has a garage that has been recently built, and later discovers the garage roof is defective.

Black Letter Rule: Privity of contract is not necessary to maintain a cause of action for the implied warranty of workmanship and good quality against a builder for latent defects.

Jones v. Lee

Instant Facts: After Lee (D) reneged on a purchase agreement, Jones (P) sued him for the difference between the asking price and eventual sale price.

Black Letter Rule: Under the "loss of the bargain rule," a seller's damages are measured by the difference between the purchase price and the market value of the property at the time the contact was breached.

Kutzin v. Pirnie

Instant Facts: Kutzin (P) and Pirnie (D) each claimed to be entitled to a $36,000 deposit paid pursuant to a contract for the purchase of Kutzin's (P) house.

Black Letter Rule: If a party justifiably refuses to perform on the ground that his remaining duties of performance have been discharged by the other party's breach, the party in breach is entitled to restitution for any benefit that he has conferred by way of part performance or reliance in excess of the loss that he caused by his own breach.

Brown v. Lober

Instant Facts: The Bosts sold land to the Browns, but conveyed only a one-third interest in the mineral rights to the Bosts.

Black Letter Rule: A covenant of quiet enjoyment can be breached by constructive eviction, but unless the covenantee's right of possession is interfered with, there is no constructive eviction, and, therefore, no breach of the covenant.

Frimberger v. Anzellotti

Instant Facts: After purchasing property, Frimberger (P) discovered that the home on the property violated state environmental protection statutes.

Black Letter Rule: A latent violation of a restrictive land use statute does not constitute a violation of the warranty against encumbrances.

Rockafellor v. Gray

Instant Facts: Rockafellor (P) purchases land and agrees to assume mortgage to Gray (D). Gray (D) forecloses on the mortgage.

Black Letter Rule: The covenant of seisin does run with the land, and is broken the moment the conveyance is delivered, becoming a chose in action held by the covenantee.

Sweeney, Administratrix v. Sweeney

Instant Facts: Maurice Sweeney deeded his property to his brother John (D), and had the deed recorded. Simultaneously, John (D) deeded the property back to Maurice and did not record the deed.

Black Letter Rule: Where a deed is handed to grantee, but evidence shows it is to take effect only upon the death of the grantor, the deed is considered properly delivered.

Rosengrant v. Rosengrant

Instant Facts: An elderly couple attempted to deliver a deed to their nephew, but they stated that the deed would be effective only upon their deaths. After their deaths, an interested relative challenged the "delivery" because it was not a valid present transfer.

Black Letter Rule: Where a grantor delivers a deed but retains a right of retrieval and states that the deed is operative only after the grantor's death, the delivery is not legally sufficient.

Murphy v. Financial Development Corp.

Instant Facts: Financial Development Corporation foreclosed on Murphy's mortgage, but concluded the foreclosure sale after only one $27,000 bid was made on the $54,000 house.

Black Letter Rule: A mortgagee executing a power of sale has a duty to protect the interests of the mortgagor and exercise good faith and due diligence in obtaining a fair price for a mortgagor's property.

Commonwealth v. Fremont Investment & Loan

Instant Facts: The state attorney general brought a consumer protection enforcement action against a bank that originated and serviced subprime loans in the state.

Black Letter Rule: A lender commits an unfair trade practice when it makes adjustable rate home mortgage loans reasonably knows that the terms of the loan are such that the borrower will default if the loan is not refinanced after the introductory interest rate period expires.

U.S. Bank Natl. Assn. v. Ibanez

Instant Facts: U.S. Bank (P) and Wells Fargo Bank (P) foreclosed on two properties, purchased them back at the foreclosure sale, and then brought a quiet title action seeking a judicial declaration that they were the fee simple owners of the property; the court held that the lenders had failed to make the requisite showing that they were entitled to clear title.

Black Letter Rule: One who sells under a power of sale must strictly adhere to its terms.

Bean v. Walker

Instant Facts: Walker defaulted on an installment land sale contract after paying Bean nearly half of the purchase price, and Bean sued to retake possession.

Black Letter Rule: The buyer under an installment land sale contract acquires equitable title which must be extinguished before the seller can retake possession, and so the buyer's payments cannot be forfeited where there would be an inequitable disposition of property and exorbitant money loss by the buyer.

Licari v. Blackwelder

(Property Owners) v. (Real Estate Broker)

539 A.2d 609 (Conn. App. Ct. 1988)

REAL ESTATE BROKERS MUST DISCLOSE PROSPECTIVE PURCHASERS AND NOT ENGAGE IN SELF-DEALING

This, of course, is the dark day on which courts started holding us to fiduciary standards.

stus.com

■ **INSTANT FACTS** Two real estate brokers associated with the listing agent on the Licaris' (P) property purchased the property and sold it for a profit six days later.

■ **BLACK LETTER RULE** As fiduciaries, real estate brokers must place their clients' interests above their own, act in good faith, and disclose all information that is or may be material to their clients' rights and interests.

■ **PROCEDURAL BASIS**

On appeal from a trial court judgment for the plaintiffs.

■ **FACTS**

The Licaris (P), six brothers and sisters who had inherited property in Westport, Connecticut, from their parents, contacted Schwartz, a Norwalk, Connecticut, real estate broker, to sell the property. Unfamiliar with the real estate market in Westport, Schwartz consulted with Blackwelder (D) and Opert (D), who were Westport brokers experienced in that market. As a result, Schwartz, Blackwelder (D), and Opert (D) entered into an agreement whereby Schwartz's Westport listings would be shared by all three, with commissions split evenly. Blackwelder (D) and Opert (D) then requested that Schwarz secure the listing on the Licaris' (P) property so that they could show it to a prospective purchaser at $125,000. However, Blackwelder (D) and Opert (D) made their own offer for $115,000, without negotiating with other prospective purchasers or advising the Licaris (P) of the value of the property to others. As a result, the Licaris (P) accepted the offer, believing it to be at fair market value. Six days after title was transferred, the defendants sold the property for $160,000 to a buyer previously known to them to be interested in purchasing the property. The plaintiffs sued Blackwelder (D) and Opert (D) for breach of duty for withholding information related to the negotiations with the eventual purchaser, and misleading them into selling the property at a lower price. At trial, the court found that the defendants' relationship with Schwartz created an obligation to the plaintiffs to act in their best interests and refrain from self-dealing. Judgment was awarded to the plaintiffs for $45,000.

■ **ISSUE**

Did the defendant real estate agents breach fiduciary duties owed to the sellers by purchasing the property themselves, knowing that there was another interested buyer who would pay more for it?

■ **DECISION AND RATIONALE**

(Bieluch, J.) Yes. Real estate brokers are fiduciaries who must place their clients' interests above their own, act in good faith, and disclose all information that is or may be material to their clients' rights and interests. As subagents under Schwartz, Blackwelder (D) and Opert (D) owed these duties to the plaintiffs. These duties are codified in the real estate licensing law. By withholding the identity of the eventual purchaser from the plaintiffs, the defendants breached this duty and are liable for the damages. Affirmed.

Analysis:

Imagine the process of selling a house if the real estate broker were not under a fiduciary duty to the seller. Often, real estate brokers are instrumental in assisting the seller in determining the appropriate market value, and thus the asking price, of his or her property. If the broker himself were able to place a value on the house, purchase it, and resell it at a profit, sellers would gain no benefit from utilizing the services of a real estate broker.

■ CASE VOCABULARY

BROKER: An agent who acts as an intermediary or negotiator, especially between prospective buyers and sellers; a person employed to make bargains and contracts between other persons in matters of trade, commerce, and navigation.

FIDUCIARY: One who owes to another the duties of good faith, trust, confidence, and candor.

SELF-DEALING: Participation in a transaction that benefits oneself instead of another who is owed a fiduciary duty.

Hickey v. Green
(Potential Buyer) v. (Seller)

14 Mass.App.Ct. 671, 442 N.E.2d 37 (1982)

SHG p. 106

oral sale agreement partial performance

MASSACHUSETTS COURT HOLDS THAT PARTIAL PERFORMANCE OF AN ORAL LAND SALE AGREEMENT IS SUFFICIENT TO REMOVE THE TRANSACTION FROM THE STATUTE OF FRAUDS

■ **INSTANT FACTS** The Hickeys (P) sold their house in reliance on an oral agreement with the owner of Lot S, Mrs. Green (D). Mrs. Green rescinded the agreement.

■ **BLACK LETTER RULE** When there is a clear oral promise, partial payment, plus an act made in reliance, a land transfer is sufficient to overcome the Statute of Frauds requirement that contracts for the sale of land must be in writing.

■ **PROCEDURAL BASIS**

Appeal from an order granting specific performance to plaintiff.

■ **FACTS**

The Hickeys (P) negotiated with Mrs. Green (D) to purchase Lot S from her. There were no lawyers involved in the negotiations. They orally agreed on a price of $15,000, and the Hickeys (P) put down a $500 deposit, which Mrs. Green (D) accepted. But, she did not cash the check. The Hickeys advised Mrs. Green that they intended to sell their home and build on Lot S. The Hickeys (P) sold their home very quickly. Two weeks after putting down the deposit with Mrs. Green (D), she (D) informed them that she no longer wished to sell, as she had another buyer willing to pay $16,000. Hickey (P) told Mrs. Green (D) that they had already sold their house and offered to pay $16,000, but Mrs. Green (D) refused to sell to him. The Hickeys (P) sued, seeking specific performance of the oral agreement.

■ **ISSUE**

In a land transfer where the Statute of Frauds is at issue, can a party be granted specific performance if they have substantially relied on the oral agreement?

■ **DECISION AND RATIONALE**

(Cutter, J.) Yes. Restatement (Second) of Contracts, § 129 sets forth the rule regarding specific performance. It requires that the party seeking specific enforcement must show reasonable reliance and that he or she has so changed his or her position that injustice can be avoided only by specific enforcement. The provisions of § 129 have traditionally been enforced very strictly in Massachusetts. The comments to § 129 illustrate that payment of the purchase price alone is not sufficient to constitute part performance. However, the requirement of part performance has been satisfied where the buyer makes payment and takes possession of the property. Here, there is evidence that both parties intended the sale of Lot S to be very quick. For that reason, the Hickeys (P) reasonably attempted to quickly sell their house, without seeking the assurance of a written document. The absence of a lawyer suggests that the parties did not intend to formalize their agreement. Additionally, the Hickeys' (P) acceptance and endorsement of a deposit for their house probably left them open to a suit if they had attempted to avoid transfer of their home. Mrs. Green (D) does not deny that there was an oral

(X) supplements doctrine of part performance w/ detrimental reliance (add to notes)

A little bit different then what stated in SHG p. 106

[handwritten top margin: I may need to go in book + look at this case]

[handwritten left margin: Justice Cardozo's doctrine of detrimental reliance]

agreement. This is significant because it shows injustice, and it shows that the reliance by the Hickeys (P) was reasonable and appropriate. Judgment affirmed.

Analysis:

Comment b to Restatement (Second) of Contracts § 129 articulates the two policy reasons for awarding specific performance based on reliance. First, such an award is justified based on the extent to which the parties' actions satisfy the evidentiary goals of the Statute of Frauds. In other words, the purpose of the Statute of Frauds is to provide concrete evidence that an agreement was made. If the parties' actions, through part performance, demonstrate good evidence of an agreement, courts are more likely to overlook the writing requirement. Second, the buyer's reliance may display the buyer's expectations as to what he thought the parties agreed upon. This provides to courts of equity more of a basis for enforcing the agreement than mere testimonial evidence.

■ CASE VOCABULARY

ESTOPPEL: A party is prevented by his own acts from asserting a right that will result in detriment to the other party.

RESCISSION OF A CONTRACT: To nullify or void a contract. The right of rescission is the right to cancel a contract upon default of some kind by the other party. Rescission may be effected by the mutual agreement of the parties.

SPECIFIC PERFORMANCE: Where money damages would be inadequate compensation, a court will compel a breaching party to perform specifically what he has agreed to do. These are considered appropriate remedies for buyers in land transfer cases, where each plot of land is considered "unique."

[handwritten: Specific performance is the preferred remedy for a land contract]

[handwritten: Money wouldn't made the aggrieved party whole]

[handwritten: Whether the Hickeys are liable on the oral contract to sell their home as well. If so, then, doctrine of part performance next, so injunction]

Lohmeyer v. Bower

(Buyer) v. (Seller)

170 Kan. 442, 227 P.2d 102 (1951)

[handwritten: Marketable title]

STATE SUPREME COURT DEFINES THE FACTORS THAT MAKE A TITLE UNMARKETABLE

■ **INSTANT FACTS** Prior to transfer of property, a title search showed that the property in question had two encumbrances upon it, both of which were being violated.

■ **BLACK LETTER RULE** Marketable title to real estate is title that does not expose the buyer to litigation.

[handwritten: SHG p. 107-108]

[handwritten: seller's]

■ **PROCEDURAL BASIS**

Appeal from judgment awarding specific performance to defendant on cross-complaint.

■ **FACTS**

Lohmeyer (P) entered into a contract whereby he was to purchase Lot 37, on which there was a house in a subdivision from Bower (D). The contract provided that the conveyance of the title was subject to Bower (D) producing a merchantable title, showing it was free and clear of all encumbrances. Restrictions and easements of record applying to the property, however, would not prevent the conveyance. Additionally, Bower (D) was to have reasonable time to correct any defects in the title. The abstract of title showed that there was a restrictive covenant on the property, requiring that all houses be two stories. Additionally, a municipal ordinance applying to the property provided that no house was to be less than three feet from a side or rear lot line. The house on Lot 37 violated both restrictions. Lohmeyer (P) sought to rescind the contract, not based on the existence of the restrictions, but on the fact that those restrictions were violated.

[handwritten: — SHG P. 108]

■ **ISSUE**

Does the violation of valid restrictions render a title unmerchantable?

[handwritten: merchantable/ Marketable title]

[handwritten: p. 108 encumbrances zoning violations]

■ **DECISION AND RATIONALE**

[handwritten: public vs. private]

(Parker, J.) Yes. The weight of the case law is clear that a buyer may not rescind a contract to purchase land where the encumbrance on the title is the result of a municipal ordinance. A buyer may ordinarily rescind a contract based on the existence of private covenants, but Lohmeyer (P) agreed to accept private covenants. Lohmeyer's (P) case is premised on the fact that the house on Lot 37 violates these restrictions, thus leaving him open to litigation. The case of *Peatling v. Baird* clarifies what constitutes merchantable title. *Peatling v. Baird* holds that "A marketable title to real estate is one which is free from unreasonable doubt, and a title is doubtful if it exposes the party holding it to the hazard of litigation." Property that is violating both a private covenant and a municipal requirement will expose Lohmeyer (P) to litigation. According to the contract, Bower (D) is entitled to have time to remedy the restrictions. While he may purchase more land to remedy the lot line problem, building a second floor onto the house would be too much to require.

Analysis:

The court points out that there is a different standard for marketable title in the case of ordinances than there is for private covenants. In other words, if a zoning ordinance required houses in a certain area to be of a certain type, a buyer, absent an agreement otherwise, cannot rescind the contract. On the other hand, if there is a private covenant running with the land that houses must be of that type, a buyer may rescind. The legal basis for this distinction is unclear. One reason might be that individuals may have greater notice of the existence of municipal ordinances before entering into the agreement. On the other hand, most citizens are not aware of the municipal ordinances in their city, especially as pertain to specified areas. A buyer might be more likely to notice that every house in a subdivision is two stories tall than that they are all equally distant from the lot line of the property.

■ **CASE VOCABULARY**

EASEMENT: A right of use of a property by someone other than the owner, *e.g.*, the right to use a waterway or path that extends over another's property; generally for the benefit of neighbors.

SPECIFIC PERFORMANCE: Where money damages would be inadequate compensation, a court will compel a breaching party to perform specifically what he has agreed to do. These are considered appropriate remedies for buyers in land transfer cases, where each plot of land is considered "unique."

Stambovsky v. Ackley

(Buyer) v. (Seller)

169 A.D.2d 254, 572 N.Y.S.2d 672 (1991)

IN SPITE OF THE DOCTRINE OF CAVEAT EMPTOR, NEW YORK COURT FINDS THAT SELLER HAD A DUTY TO INFORM BUYER THAT HOUSE WAS HAUNTED

■ **INSTANT FACTS** Ackley (D) sells a house that she has widely publicized as a haunted house to Stambovsky (P), who is from a different city and does not know that it is haunted.

■ **BLACK LETTER RULE** Where a seller has created a condition that materially alters the value of the contract for sale of real property, and the condition is uniquely within the knowledge of the seller and unlikely to be discovered by a careful buyer, failure to disclose that condition creates a basis for rescission as a matter of equity.

■ PROCEDURAL BASIS

Appeal from dismissal of a complaint.

■ FACTS

Ackley (D) sold her house in the Village of Nyack to Stambovsky (P), a resident of New York City. Stambovsky (P) then discovered that the house was known in the area to be haunted. Ackley (D) had perpetuated that rumor by reporting the presence of ghosts in her local newspaper and to Reader's Digest, and by including the home in a walking tour of Nyack. She had not told Stambovsky (P) that the house was haunted. Stambovsky (P) sought to rescind the contract, but the trial court dismissed the cause of action because of the doctrine of caveat emptor.

■ ISSUE

Where the seller creates a condition that materially affects the value of land, and where the buyer has acted with reasonable prudence, can nondisclosure be the basis for rescission of the contract of sale?

■ DECISION AND RATIONALE

(Rubin, J.) Yes. Preliminarily, the impact of the house's ghostly reputation goes to the very essence of the bargain. As Ackley (D) was responsible for circulating the folklore that the house was haunted, it is not for the court to decide whether there are, in fact, poltergeists in the house. Rather, Ackley (D) is estopped to deny the existence of ghosts, and the house is, as a matter of law, haunted. While the real estate broker, as agent for the seller, was under no duty to disclose the existence of poltergeists, equitable considerations suggest that the contract should be rescinded. It is difficult, and unusual, for a prospective buyer to order an inspection for ghosts. Additionally, we do not want to create a precedent that suggests that buyers should inspect for ghosts. Caveat emptor is appropriate where the buyer has equal opportunity to discover information about the house. A traditional means of refuting the doctrine was to show that the seller actively concealed a material fact. Here, while Ackley (D) did not actively conceal the existence of ghosts, she took unfair advantage of the Stambovsky's (P) ignorance of the folklore of the Village of Nyack. Enforcing this contract is offensive to the sense of equity. Judgment modified.

■ **DISSENT**

(Smith, J.) This court should not overturn the doctrine of caveat emptor because of the purported existence of poltergeists.

Analysis:

The court's decision rests upon the idea that the policy reasons for the doctrine of caveat emptor are not met in the case of a haunted house. The court finds that the existence of poltergeists is a material issue in the sale. And the court implies that it would be undesirable to require all buyers to bring mediums or psychics to every house they purchase. For this reason, to best provide protection for the buyer and to avoid ridiculous consequences, the court is willing to make a substantial inroad into the destruction of the doctrine of caveat emptor.

■ **CASE VOCABULARY**

DOCTRINE OF CAVEAT EMPTOR: "Let the buyer beware." A maxim that a purchaser must judge, test and examine the quality of an item for himself.

Johnson v. Davis

(Seller) v. (Buyer)

480 So.2d 625 (Fla. 1985)

[handwritten: duty to disclose, caveat emptor]

STATE SUPREME COURT FURTHER DESTROYS THE DOCTRINE OF CAVEAT EMPTOR IN LAND TRANSACTIONS

[handwritten: SHG p. 107-109, esp. p.109]

■ **INSTANT FACTS** Davis (P), with representation from Johnson (D) that a roof did not leak, buys home with a leaky roof.

■ **BLACK LETTER RULE** Sellers of real property have a duty to disclose to prospective buyers material facts affecting the value of the property, when those facts are not known or readily observable to the buyer.

[handwritten: again p. 108 seller's duty to disclose, responsible for material lies as well as material omissions]

■ **PROCEDURAL BASIS**

Appeal from a judgment for plaintiff for rescission of contract.

■ **FACTS**

Johnson (D) contracted to sell his home to Davis (P). Although Johnson (D) knew that the roof leaked, he affirmatively represented to Davis (P) that it did not. Several days later, Davis (P) discovered water gushing in to the home, resulting from heavy rain. Davis (P) sued to rescind the contract.

■ **ISSUE**

Where a seller is aware of a material fact that is not known or readily observable to the buyer, does the seller have a duty to disclose that fact?

■ **DECISION AND RATIONALE**

(Adkins, J.) Yes. The affirmative representation that the roof was sound was a material misrepresentation. Consequently, Davis (P) was entitled to rescission. Even if Johnson (D) had not affirmatively lied, Davis (P) should be entitled to recovery. Where the failure to disclose a material fact is calculated to induce a false belief, the distinction between concealment and affirmative representations is tenuous. The doctrine of caveat emptor, however, relieves a seller from liability for concealing material facts. This notion is out of date and undesirable. A seller should not take advantage of a buyer's ignorance. Therefore, where a seller of a home knows of facts that are material to the value of the property, and where these facts are not readily observable to the buyer, the seller has a duty to disclose these material facts. Judgment affirmed.

[handwritten margin: court says we rescind the contract b/c we don't condone fraud]

Analysis:

This case is one of many that carve away at the doctrine of caveat emptor. Many courts and legal scholars take the position that, in today's society, the doctrine is inappropriate. In today's society, most people have specialized skills and do not have a lot of experience or knowledge about construction. Moreover, it is often impossible to discover defects until a period of time has elapsed and the buyer has experience with the property. For these reasons, a majority of states impose a duty on the seller to disclose latent defects.

[handwritten: important]

[handwritten margin: to avoid post-sale litigation]

■ CASE VOCABULARY

MATERIAL FACT: A fact which is significant enough to influence the bargain; if one of the parties had known this fact, there position in the land transfer would have changed.

MISFEASANCE: The improper performance of an act.

NONFEASANCE: Failure to perform an act that a person ought to do.

Lempke v. Dagenais

(Buyer) v. (Builder)

130 N.H. 782, 547 A.2d 290 (1988)

COURT FINDS THAT PRIVITY OF CONTRACT IS NOT NECESSARY FOR IMPLIED WARRANTIES IN SALE OF LAND

■ **INSTANT FACTS** Lempke (P) purchases a house that has a garage that has been recently built, and later discovers the garage roof is defective.

■ **BLACK LETTER RULE** Privity of contract is not necessary to maintain a cause of action for the implied warranty of workmanship and good quality against a builder for latent defects.

■ **PROCEDURAL BASIS**

Appeal from dismissal of plaintiff's complaint.

■ **FACTS**

Lempke's (P) predecessors in title contracted with Dagenais (D) to build a garage on their property. Lempke (P) bought the property six months later. After they purchased the home, the Lempkes (P) noticed structural defects in the garage's construction. They sued Dagenais (D) based on three grounds: 1) breach of the implied warranty of workmanlike quality, 2) negligence, and 3) breach of assigned contract rights.

■ **ISSUE**

Does a successor in title have a cause of action for the implied warranty of workmanship and quality against a prior builder?

■ **DECISION AND RATIONALE**

(Thayer, J.) Yes. The lower court's decision relied on the opinion in *Ellis v. Morris,* which held that, absent privity of contract, a successor in interest could not recover for economic loss for the implied warranty of workmanship and good quality. Because privity was the major factor, we first consider that issue. The case *Norton v. Burleaud* established a cause of action for the implied warranty of quality. Courts and legal scholars have debated over which theory of liability the implied warranty of quality is based. Regardless of whether it is a tort, contract or hybrid, however, the implied warranty is a public policy doctrine that exists independently of any legal theory or of any agreement between the parties. The purposes of implied warranties are to protect purchasers from latent defects in their houses. To so protect purchasers, we hold that the privity requirement of the implied warranty of quality should be abandoned, where a subsequent purchaser suffers economic loss from a latent defect. To hold otherwise would leave innocent homeowners without a remedy. It would not be fair to relieve a contractor from liability for unsound workmanship simply because a house has changed hands. Finally, the builder is in a better position to prevent the damage from occurring. There are several overriding policy reasons behind implied warranties that support extension of the doctrine to successors in title. First, latent defects in a house often do not manifest themselves for a long period of time. Second, society is changing. People are less likely to stay in one place for long periods. Therefore, the ordinary buyer is not in a position to discover latent defects. Third, subsequent

---

purchasers have little opportunity to inspect, and they have little knowledge about construction. In today's society, people rely on the craftsmanship of builders. Fourth, there is no unfairness to the builder, because he or she has a duty of workmanship to the first owner. Fifth and lastly, insulating only the first buyer might encourage "sham" first sales to protect contractors from liability. Finally, we address the issue of whether the extension of the implied warranty of workmanship and quality to successors in title should extend to purely economic loss. Most courts that have allowed recovery for economic loss have done so because of the difficulty in drawing the line between property damage and economic loss. We agree with these courts, finding the distinction between economic loss and personal injury or property damage is arbitrary. Note that there are limitations on our holding. We do not expect builders to act as insurers. The extension of the doctrine is limited to *latent* defects, where the buyer did not and, with an adequate inspection, should not have reasonably known of the defect. Additionally, the extension is limited to a reasonable period, and the plaintiff bears the burden of showing the defect was a result of the builder's poor workmanship. The duty to builders is to perform competently, according to acceptable standards.

■ DISSENT

(Souter, J.) I am not satisfied that there is adequate justification to overturn the rationale in *Ellis v. Robert C. Morris.*

Analysis:

Note that the policy justifications for extending implied warranties overlap with the policy justifications for abrogating the doctrine of caveat emptor. In both instances, courts look to fairness and changing society as a basis for imposing liability. The court points out that these doctrines are being abrogated in the area of sales as well. Consider the court's reassurance that the warranty of quality will extend only for "a reasonable time." Does this create more uncertainty on the part of the builders? Even if courts are unwilling to impose liability for defects that are discovered several years after the home or structure has been built, allowing a cause of action for successors in interest may increase the number of actions brought against builders.

■ CASE VOCABULARY

ECONOMIC HARM: Includes recovery for costs of repair and/or replacement of defective property, as opposed to simply decrease in value or personal injuries.

Jones v. Lee

(Seller) v. (Buyer)

971 P.2d 858 (N.M. Ct. App. 1998)

SELLERS MAY RECOVER FOR THE LOSS OF THEIR BARGAIN WHEN BUYERS REFUSE TO PERFORM

So, how are you doing with calculating damages in my real estate breach of contract case?

stus.com

■ **INSTANT FACTS** After Lee (D) reneged on a purchase agreement, Jones (P) sued him for the difference between the asking price and eventual sale price.

■ **BLACK LETTER RULE** Under the "loss of the bargain rule," a seller's damages are measured by the difference between the purchase price and the market value of the property at the time the contact was breached.

■ PROCEDURAL BASIS

On appeal to review a trial court judgment for the plaintiff.

■ FACTS

Jones (P) entered into a contract to sell his home to Lee (D) for $610,000, whereby Lee (D) paid $6000 in earnest money. Several weeks later, Lee (D) informed Jones (P) that, for financial reasons, he was unable to purchase the home, and he proposed a termination agreement under which he forfeited his earnest money to void the contract. Jones rejected the termination agreement and relisted the property when it appeared that Lee (D) would not perform, and he eventually sold the home for $540,000. After the sale, Jones (P) sued Lee (D) to recover the $70,000 difference between the original and ultimate sale prices, plus special and punitive damages. After trial, the court awarded Jones (P) $70,000 in compensatory damages and $87,118.94 in special and punitive damages. Lee (D) appealed, arguing that the trial court erred in awarding special and punitive damages and used an incorrect method for calculating compensatory damages.

■ ISSUE

Did the court properly calculate the plaintiff's damages by basing its award of compensatory damages on the difference between the sale prices, plus special and punitive damages?

■ DECISION AND RATIONALE

(Donnelly, J.) No. When a purchaser defaults on a real estate contract, the seller generally has three options: (1) seek rescission of the contract, (2) seek specific performance of the contract, and (3) retain the property and seek damages for breach of contract. Here, Jones (P) elected to seek damages. New Mexico law follows the "loss of the bargain rule," under which the seller's damages are measured by the difference between the purchase price and the market value of the property at the time the contact was breached. The evidence here clearly demonstrated that the purchase price of the property was $540,000. The plaintiff failed, however, to present evidence that the market value of the property was $610,000 at the time of the breach. While the parties stipulated by contract that the market value was $610,000 at the time of the contract, no evidence was offered that the value of the home remained $610,000 when the breach occurred. Accordingly, the court used an improper method to calculate compensatory damages, if any, owed to the plaintiff.

Lee (D) also claims that the court erred in awarding special damages and punitive damages to Jones (P), but here the court was correct. Special damages may be recovered for those losses that are the natural and probable consequence of the breach and were known or reasonably foreseeable by the parties at the time of the contract. Included in the special damages awarded by the court are charges for an inspection of the solar system, a consultation on the solar system, and a heating warranty incident to the sale of the home. Because these charges were contemplated by the terms of the contract, the court correctly found them a reasonably foreseeable consequence of the breach. Likewise, the additional mortgage interest Jones (P) paid due to the delay in selling the home is a reasonably foreseeable damage.

Finally, at trial, the court awarded Jones (P) punitive damages based on Lee's (D) fraudulent conduct in attempting to persuade Jones (P) to cancel the purchase agreement. The court found that the Lees (D) reasonably frightened Mrs. Jones by their conduct and misrepresented facts regarding their financial ability to purchase the home. Under such circumstances, punitive damages were warranted.

Affirmed in part, remanded in part.

Analysis:

To grant the seller the true loss of his bargain, wouldn't a more appropriate measure of damages be the contractual price, rather than the market value at the time of the breach? Perhaps Jones (P) negotiated a great deal when he contracted with Lee (D) to sell the house for $610,000. If the house were in fact worth only $540,000 at that time, as well as at the time of the breach, Jones's (P) actual damages using the court's methodology are zero. Yet, he has arguably lost $70,000, taking his negotiated bargain into consideration.

■ **CASE VOCABULARY**

COMPENSATORY DAMAGES: Damages sufficient in amount to indemnify the injured person for the loss suffered.

EARNEST MONEY: A deposit paid (usually in escrow) by a prospective buyer (especially of real estate) to show a good-faith intention to complete the transaction, and ordinarily forfeited if the buyer defaults.

LOSS-OF-BARGAIN RULE: The doctrine that damages for a breach of a contract should put the injured party in the position it would have been in if both parties had performed their contractual duties.

PUNITIVE DAMAGES: Damages awarded in addition to actual damages when the defendant acted with recklessness, malice, or deceit.

RESCISSION: A party's unilateral unmaking of a contract for a legally sufficient reason, such as the other party's material breach.

SPECIFIC PERFORMANCE: A court-ordered remedy that requires precise fulfillment of a legal or contractual obligation when monetary damages are inappropriate or inadequate, as when the sale of real estate or a rare article is involved.

Kutzin v. Pirnie

(Seller) v. (Buyer)

591 A.2d 932 (N.J. 1991)

BUYERS ARE ENTITLED TO RESTITUTION OF ANY CONTRACTUAL DEPOSIT THAT EXCEEDS THE SELLER'S ACTUAL DAMAGES

■ **INSTANT FACTS** Kutzin (P) and Pirnie (D) each claimed to be entitled to a $36,000 deposit paid pursuant to a contract for the purchase of Kutzin's (P) house.

■ **BLACK LETTER RULE** If a party justifiably refuses to perform on the ground that his remaining duties of performance have been discharged by the other party's breach, the party in breach is entitled to restitution for any benefit that he has conferred by way of part performance or reliance in excess of the loss that he caused by his own breach.

■ **PROCEDURAL BASIS**

On appeal from a New Jersey Appellate Division decision for the plaintiff.

■ **FACTS**

Pirnie (D) contracted to purchase Kutzin's (P) house for $365,000. Under the contract, Pirnie (D) was required to pay a deposit of $36,000 toward the purchase price, but the contract included no liquidated damages or forfeiture provision in the event that Pirnie (D) breached the contract. Instead, the contract merely stated that in the event of a breach, the deposit would be disbursed as directed by both parties. Pirnie (D) breached the contract, and Kutzin (P) sued for damages after selling the house for $352,500. The trial court ruled that the parties entered into a binding contract and awarded Kutzin (P) $17,325 in damages—$12,500 for the difference in the sale prices and $3,825 in utility, real estate tax, and insurance expenses incurred as a result of the delayed sale, plus $1000 for carpet Kutzin (P) installed to make the house more marketable. The court denied Kutzin's (P) claim for interest on the $12,500 award and damages for an increase in capital-gains tax due to the breach. The remainder of the $36,000 deposit was ordered returned to Pirnie (D). Both parties appealed. Kutzin (P) claimed he should recover the lost interest and increased capital gains taxes, or, alternatively, be allowed to retain the entire deposit. Pirnie (D) argued he should retain the entire deposit because the contract had been rescinded. The appellate division held that an enforceable contract existed, but that Kutzin (P) was not entitled to the damages sought on appeal. However, the court concluded that Kutzin (P) was entitled to the entire deposit, but no additional damages.

■ **ISSUE**

Is a seller entitled to retain a deposit when a buyer breaches a contract that does not include a liquidated-damages or forfeiture clause?

■ **DECISION AND RATIONALE**

(Clifford, J.) No. At common law, when a buyer made a partial payment toward the purchase of real property and breached the contract without lawful excuse, he was not entitled to recover the deposit, regardless of the actual damages suffered by the seller. More recently, however, a judicial recognition of the unfairness of the common law rule has emerged. Under this modern

---

movement, a buyer is entitled to restitution of any deposit unless: (1) the seller has not rescinded the contract and maintains a right of specific performance against the buyer; (2) the buyer has not shown that the deposit exceeds the seller's actual damages; or (3) the contract expressly provides that the seller may retain the deposit in the event of a breach, and the facts demonstrate that the retention serves as liquidated damages and not a penalty or forfeiture. Section 374 of the Restatement (Second) of Contracts illustrates this principle. "If a party justifiably refuses to perform on the ground that his remaining duties of performance have been discharged by the other party's breach, the party in breach is entitled to restitution for any benefit that he has conferred by way of part performance or reliance in excess of the loss that he had caused by his own breach." To the extent that New Jersey law follows the common-law rule, it is overruled and the modern trend of the Restatement is adopted. Applying this rule, Pirnie (D) is entitled to restitution of any portion of the deposit exceeding Kutzin's (P) actual damages, given the absence of a liquidated damages or forfeiture clause in the contract. The decision of the appellate division is modified to reinstate the trial court's award. Affirmed as modified.

Analysis:

Note that the court carefully clarified its decision to illustrate the importance of a liquidated damages clause to its reasoning. Where the parties agree by the terms of the contract that the seller will be allowed to retain any deposit regardless of his actual damages, the buyer would not be entitled to any restitution. In some states, however, liquidated damage or forfeiture clauses are entirely unenforceable. In others, they are enforceable if their terms are reasonable.

■ CASE VOCABULARY

FORFEITURE CLAUSE: A contractual provision stating that, under certain circumstances, one party must forfeit something to another.

LIQUIDATED DAMAGES: An amount contractually stipulated as a reasonable estimation of actual damages to be recovered by one party if the other party breaches. If the parties to a contract have agreed on liquidated damages, the sum fixed is the measure of damages for a breach, whether it exceeds or falls short of actual damages.

PENALTY CLAUSE: A contractual provision that assesses an excessive monetary charge against a defaulting party. Penalty clauses are mostly unenforceable.

RESTITUTION: Return or restoration of some specific thing to its rightful owner or status.

SPECIFIC PERFORMANCE: A court-ordered remedy that requires precise fulfillment of a legal or contractual obligation when monetary damages are inappropriate or inadequate, as when the sale of real estate or a rare article is involved.

Brown v. Lober

(Land Buyer) v. (Bosts' Executor)

75 Ill.2d 547, 389 N.E.2d 1188 (1979)

THE COVENANT OF QUIET ENJOYMENT CAN ONLY BE BREACHED BY DISTURBING THE COVENANTEE'S RIGHT OF POSSESSION

■ **INSTANT FACTS** The Bosts sold land to the Browns, but conveyed only a one-third interest in the mineral rights to the Bosts.

■ **BLACK LETTER RULE** A covenant of quiet enjoyment can be breached by constructive eviction, but unless the covenantee's right of possession is interfered with, there is no constructive eviction, and, therefore, no breach of the covenant.

■ **PROCEDURAL BASIS**

Appeal from judgment for damages in action for breach of the covenant of quiet enjoyment.

■ **FACTS**

William and Faith Bost had eighty acres of land conveyed to them in 1947. The previous owner of this land had reserved a two-thirds interest in the mineral rights, thus conveying only a one-third mineral interest to the Bosts. In 1957, the Bosts conveyed this same land to James R. Brown and his wife (P) by a general warranty deed with no exceptions. In 1974, the Browns (P) contracted to sell their (P) mineral rights to Consolidated Coal Co. for $6,000. Consolidated Coal, however, renegotiated the contract to provide for payment of only $2,000 to the Browns (P) after learning the Browns (P) possessed only one-third of the mineral rights. The initial owner made no attempt whatsoever to exercise his mineral rights to the land. The Browns (P) sued Lober (D), the executor of the then-deceased Bosts, for $4,000 in damages for the breach of the covenant of quiet enjoyment. The trial court ruled for Lober (D), and the appellate court reversed.

■ **ISSUE**

Is the covenant of quiet enjoyment breached when a covenantee has not been prevented from enjoying possession of his or her interest in the given property?

■ **DECISION AND RATIONALE**

(Underwood, J.) No. A covenant of quiet enjoyment can be breached by constructive eviction, but unless the covenantee's right of possession is interfered with, there is no constructive eviction, and, therefore, no breach of the covenant. This court's earlier decision in Scott v. Kirkendall [breach of covenant of quiet enjoyment of surface rights rejected because Scott could have taken possession at any time] is controlling in this case. There, Kirkendall granted title to Scott, even though others had paramount title. This was not a breach of the covenant of quiet enjoyment because the other parties never tried to assert the adverse title. The land in question had always been vacant, and Scott could have taken peaceable possession of it at any time. While that case dealt with surface rights, and not mineral rights, its reasoning is still applicable here. Here, no one tried to remove the minerals from the ground or do anything else to inform the community that the mineral interest was being exclusively used or enjoyed. The mineral estate of the land in this case was vacant, just as the surface land was in Scott. Likewise, the

---

Browns (P) could have taken peaceable possession of it at any time, without any hindrance from anyone else. Until the Browns (P) meet such resistance in exercising this right of possession, there is no breach of the covenant of quiet enjoyment. Granted, there is a breach of the covenant of seisin involved here that results from the Bosts' deed to the Browns (P), but the Browns (P) did not raise a suit as to this issue within the ten years' statute of limitations. Moreover, the fact that Consolidated Coal modified the contract with the Browns (P) does not constitute a breach of the covenant of quiet enjoyment. Judgment of appellate court reversed.

Analysis:

One way a person can be constructively evicted is by being forced to buy superior title to keep from actually being physically evicted from the property. Another form of constructive eviction occurs when an owner is enjoined from using the property in a way that violates an earlier restrictive covenant on the property. If any of these situations were to arise, then the owner's right of possession would be considered "disturbed," and thus a "future" covenant would be breached. Because some form of eviction is needed for breach, even if not an actual "loss" of possession, the statute of limitations against bringing an action to challenge the breach would not run until the date of the eviction. Note that, in this case, there was no eviction, so the statute of limitations was never really an issue.

Frimberger v. Anzellotti

(Buyer) v. (Seller)

25 Conn.App. 401, 594 A.2d 1029 (1991)

THE WARRANTY AGAINST ENCUMBRANCES MAY NOT BE USED TO CURE VIOLATIONS OF A RESTRICTIVE LAND USE STATUTE

■ **INSTANT FACTS** After purchasing property, Frimberger (P) discovered that the home on the property violated state environmental protection statutes.

■ **BLACK LETTER RULE** A latent violation of a restrictive land use statute does not constitute a violation of the warranty against encumbrances.

■ **PROCEDURAL BASIS**

Appeal from trial court judgment awarding damages to plaintiff.

■ **FACTS**

Anzellotti's (D) brother began to develop a property that, because it was adjacent to tidal wetlands, was subject to restrictive land use statutes. He then transferred the property to Anzellotti (D). Anzellotti (D) sold the property to Frimberger (P), free and clear of all encumbrances but subject to all building line and zoning restrictions. Frimberger (P) hired engineers to make improvements on the property. The engineers discovered that the improvements to the property made by the original owner violated the restrictive land use statutes. The Department of Environmental Protection ("DEP") informed Frimberger (P) that he could submit an application to the DEP, explaining the necessity of maintaining the improvements. The DEP did not fine Frimberger (P) or subject him to any sanctions for the violations. Nevertheless, Frimberger (P), without submitting the application to the DEP, sued Anzellotti (D) for breach of the warranty against encumbrances.

■ **ISSUE**

Can a latent violation of a land use statute, existing at the time a seller conveys a title, be considered an encumbrance violating the warranty against encumbrances?

■ **DECISION AND RATIONALE**

(Lavery, J.) No. This is a case of first impression in Connecticut. However, a survey of other jurisdictions reveals that most jurisdictions find that statutes, ordinances or regulations do not affect marketability and should not be considered an encumbrance. The New Jersey case of *Fahmie v. Wulster* has a very similar fact pattern to this one. In *Fahmie,* a previous owner of a property had enclosed a stream in a manner that violated a New Jersey statute. The buyer of the property sued the seller for breach of the warranty against encumbrances. The New Jersey court held that to extend the warranty against encumbrances to land use violations would cause too much uncertainty in the law of conveyancing and title insurance. This uncertainty would result because neither a title search nor a physical examination of the premises would disclose the violation. The court decided that explicit contract provisions between private parties were the better method of protecting buyers. This case raises the same issues and concerns. Anzellotti (D) did not know of the defects in the property; they were discoverable only by consulting the

---

DEP. Additionally, prior cases in Connecticut have held that for a title to be rendered unmarketable, the defect must subject the plaintiff to a real and substantial probability of litigation and loss. Here, the DEP, the entity charged with enforcement of the regulations, has taken no official action, and has even granted Frimberger (P) with a means to remedy his problem. Although the trial court awarded damages based on projected costs, there is no true means of awarding damages here, because Frimberger (P) has not yet been subjected to any real injury. Finally, Frimberger (P), an attorney and land developer, could have taken steps to protect himself before buying the property. He could have required a survey to ensure compliance, or he could have inserted protective provisions in the deed to protect him from liability for violations. The trial court further erred in finding Anzellotti (D) liable for innocent misrepresentation. The court's based its finding on its determination that Anzellotti (D) breached the warranty against encumbrances. Because we have found he did not breach the warranty against encumbrances, there was no innocent misrepresentation.

Analysis:

Recall the case of *Lohmeyer v. Bower,* where the court found that a prospective buyer could rescind his agreement upon a finding that the property violated a local zoning ordinance. These cases appear to be inapposite. In that case, the court allowed the buyer to rescind the contract because he was subject to a real and substantial probability of litigation or loss at the time of the conveyance. This case can be distinguished for two reasons. One, the state and municipal violations at issue here are latent; in other words, they do not show up on land records and are not known by the seller. Secondly, the agency charged with enforcement has taken no official action. Based on the facts of *Lohmeyer* and the language of the court's opinion here, it appears that both of these conditions must be met to be protected from rescission.

■ CASE VOCABULARY

ENCUMBRANCE: Every right or interest in the land which may exist in third persons, to the diminution of the value of the equity in the land, but consistent with the passing of the fee by the conveyance.

RESCISSION OF A CONTRACT: To nullify or void a contract; the right of rescission is the right to cancel a contract for cause. Rescission may be effected by the mutual agreement of the parties.

Rockafellor v. Gray

(Owner of Land) v. (Creditor)

194 Iowa 1280, 191 N.W. 107 (1922)

STATE SUPREME COURT HOLDS THAT THE COVENANT OF SEISIN MAY BE ASSIGNED TO REMOTE BUYERS

■ **INSTANT FACTS** Rockafellor (P) purchases land and agrees to assume mortgage to Gray (D). Gray (D) forecloses on the mortgage.

■ **BLACK LETTER RULE** The covenant of seisin does run with the land, and is broken the moment the conveyance is delivered, becoming a chose in action held by the covenantee.

■ **PROCEDURAL BASIS**

Appeal by cross-defendant from a judgment in favor of cross-complainant.

■ **FACTS**

Rockafellor (P) bought a parcel of property from Doffing and took over (assumed) a $500.00 mortgage to Gray (D). Subsequently, Gray (D) initiated foreclosure proceedings against Doffing, which culminated in a sheriff's deed, which was executed and delivered to Connelly. Connelly conveyed the property to Dixon. The deed contained the typical covenants of warranty, and Dixon paid $4000 consideration for the deed. Dixon conveyed the premises to Hansen & Gregerson for a consideration of $7000.00. Rockafellor (P) brought suit to vacate and set aside the foreclosure sale, on the grounds that the court did not obtain jurisdiction over Rockafellor (P). Hansen & Gregerson then cross-complained against Connelly on the ground that the covenant of seisin in his deed to Dixon also applied to Hansen & Gregerson.

■ **ISSUE**

Does the covenant of seisin run with the land, so that an action may be maintained by a remote grantee?

■ **DECISION AND RATIONALE**

(Faville, J.) Yes. Although most American courts hold that the covenant of seisin does not run with the land, we adopt the English Rule. The English Rule states that the covenant of seisin does run with the land, and is broken the instant the conveyance is delivered, and then becomes a chose in action held by the covenantee in the deed. A deed by the covenantee operates as an assignment of such chose in action to a remote grantee. The remote grantee, on the basis of that assignment can then maintain an action against the grantor in the original deed. Connelly, however, contends that because he was never in possession of the land, the covenant cannot run with the land. Connelly's argument is that because seisin requires possession, he never had seisin of the land. Seisin is what gives rise to the idea that the covenant of seisin runs with the land. This argument is flawed, however, because we hold that the covenant of seisin exists as a chose in action. Connelly does not argue that Dixon was not protected by the covenant of seisin. Because Dixon himself was protected by the covenant of seisin, he could assign the covenant as a chose in action. Hansen & Gregerson are entitled to

---

recovery of the consideration recited in the original grant from Connelly to Dixon. Judgment affirmed.

Analysis:

What is the significance of the court holding that the covenant of seisin is broken, but allowing it to be maintained as a chose in action? One reason is illustrated by this case—to avoid issues of possession. For a covenant to "run with the land," the grantor must convey either title or possession, something to which a covenant can "attach." A chose in action is a personal right to sue that is not attached to property. Because a chose in action is not an interest in real property, calling the covenant a chose in action also may avoid issues raised by the Statute of Frauds.

■ CASE VOCABULARY

CHOSE IN ACTION: A right of bringing an action or right to recover a debt or money.

COVENANT OF SEISIN: An assurance to the purchaser that the grantor has the very estate in quantity and quality which he purports to convey.

SEISIN: Possession of real property under claim of freehold estate.

Sweeney, Administratrix v. Sweeney

(Estranged Widow) v. (Brother)

126 Conn. 391, 11 A.2d 806 (1940)

A TRANSFER INTENDED ONLY TO TAKE EFFECT UPON THE TRANSFEROR'S DEATH IS VALID IF THE DEED IS DELIVERED DIRECTLY TO THE TRANSFEREE

■ **INSTANT FACTS** Maurice Sweeney deeded his property to his brother John (D), and had the deed recorded. Simultaneously, John (D) deeded the property back to Maurice and did not record the deed.

■ **BLACK LETTER RULE** Where a deed is handed to grantee, but evidence shows it is to take effect only upon the death of the grantor, the deed is considered properly delivered.

■ **PROCEDURAL BASIS**

Appeal from a judgment for defendant.

■ **FACTS**

Maurice deeded his property, which included a tavern, to his brother John (D) so that he would have it in case Maurice died. Maurice wanted to also protect himself in case John died, so he had John execute a deed transferring the property back to Maurice. The first deed was recorded; the second was not. The second deed [from John (D) back to Maurice] was ultimately burned in a fire. Maurice continued to run the tavern with only a little help from John (D). Upon Maurice's death, his estranged wife (P), claimed the property, by virtue of the second deed.

■ **ISSUE**

Where a deed is handed to a grantee, but the intention of the grantor is that it is to take effect only upon the grantor's death, will the court consider a valid delivery to have been made?

■ **DECISION AND RATIONALE**

(Jennings, J.) Yes. Although Maurice intended the tavern to belong to John (D), the second deed, made by John (D) back to Maurice is valid. All of the elements of a good delivery were present: a deed had been executed and Maurice continued to possess the premises, pay fixed charges, receive rents and exercise full dominion over it until his death. Possession of the premises is not conclusive proof that the deed was delivered. John (D) may introduce evidence that the terms of the deed were not met. However, the evidence shows that John (D) intended to grant the property to Maurice. Additionally, The fact that the deed benefitted Maurice is prima facie evidence that he assented to it. These presumptions can be defeated only by evidence that John (D) did not intend to deliver the deed to Maurice. Maurice said that he requested the deed to protect himself, and this purpose would have been defeated had the deed not been delivered. This is conclusive proof that John (D) intended to deliver the deed. John's (D) final contention is that if there was a delivery, it was conditional on John's (D) death predating Maurice's. However, deliveries can only be conditional if the grantor delivers the deed into the hands of a third party. Here, the grantor delivered the deed into the hands of the grantee himself. Although the evidence suggests the intention of the parties was to make the deed

---

conditional, we cannot bend the rules of property to fit this situation. To do so would open the doors of the court to fraud and fabrication of evidence. Judgment reversed and case remanded.

Analysis:

A number of courts have decided exactly the opposite of the court in *Sweeney*. The jurisdictions are split into three groups, some following the rule in *Sweeney,* some finding that these types of grants are testamentary and therefore invalid, and some ruling as to the intention of the parties. This latter group, illustrated by the Maryland case *Chillemi v. Chillemi,* reason that a deed can be held in escrow by the grantee as a conditional grant just as easily as by a third party. The court in *Chillemi* noted that decisions regarding traditional conditional grants are made by adhering to the intentions of the individual parties.

■ **CASE VOCABULARY**

TESTAMENTARY: Made in lieu of a will; not to take effect until after death.

Rosengrant v. Rosengrant

(Deed Challenger) v. (Purported Grantee)

629 P.2d 800 (Okla. Ct. App. 1981)

SHG p. 109-110 delivery of a deed

DELIVERY REQUIRES A PRESENT INTENT TO PASS TITLE, EVEN THOUGH POSSESSION MAY BE POSTPONED

[handwritten: → solely a test of present intent, need not be actually or literally transferred]

■ **INSTANT FACTS** An elderly couple attempted to deliver a deed to their nephew, but they stated that the deed would be effective only upon their deaths. After their deaths, an interested relative challenged the "delivery" because it was not a valid present transfer.

■ **BLACK LETTER RULE** Where a grantor delivers a deed but retains a right of retrieval and states that the deed is operative only after the grantor's death, the delivery is not legally sufficient.

[handwritten: not proper delivery of the deed]

[handwritten: important, add to outline]

■ PROCEDURAL BASIS

Appeal of verdict setting aside the transfer of a warranty deed to real property.

■ FACTS

Mildred and Harold Rosengrant were an elderly couple who desired to transfer their farm to their nephew, Jay Rosengrant (D), upon their deaths. Jay (D) accompanied Harold and Mildred to the bank, where the couple signed the deed and handed it to Jay "to make this legal." They then instructed Jay (D) to return the deed to the banker, who put it in an envelope labeled "J.W. Rosengrant or Harold H. Rosengrant" in a safe deposit box. Harold and Mildred told Jay (D) that he could record the deed when they died. After Mildred died, Jay (D) consulted an attorney concerning the legality of the transaction. The attorney said the delivery should be sufficient but told Harold he could draw up a will. After Harold died (presumably without a will), Jay (D) obtained the deed from the bank and recorded it. Another Rosengrant (P) relative challenged the transfer, filing a petition to cancel and set aside the deed. Rosengrant (P) argued that the deed was void because it was never legally delivered and that the deed was really a testamentary instrument which was void for failure to comply with the Statute of Wills. The trial court agreed and found the deed null and void. Jay (D) appealed.

[handwritten: on the envelope, bank wrote to Harold or to Jay; this created the impression that the deed was revocable by Harold]

■ ISSUE

Where a grantor delivers a deed but retains a right of retrieval and states that the deed is operative only after the grantor's death, is the delivery legally sufficient?

■ DECISION AND RATIONALE

(Boydston, J.) No. Where a grantor delivers a deed but retains a right of retrieval and states that the deed is operative only after the grantor's death, the delivery is not legally sufficient. Harold and Mildred intended to comply with the legal aspects of delivery by handing the deed to Jay (D). However, after the "transfer" Harold continued to live on, farm, and pay taxes on the land. The words written on the envelope create an inescapable conclusion that the deed was retrievable by Harold any time before his death. There was an agreement that the deed was to take effect only upon the death of Harold and Mildred. Thus, the "transfer" to Jay (D) was only a pro forma attempt to comply with the legal aspects of delivery. The grantor clearly intended to exercise control over the land and had the power to revoke the transfer at any time. We agree with the trial court that the deed was not properly delivered. Affirmed.

[handwritten: so not proper delivery → revocable by Harold]

[handwritten bottom: a revocable transfer is NOT delivery]

■ CONCURRENCE

(Brightmire, J.) A valid conveyance requires actual or constructive delivery of the deed, plus an intention by the grantor to divest himself of the conveyed interest. Here there was no valid delivery. If the grantors intended to convey the property prior to their deaths, they should have given Jay (D) the deed and told him to record it. The continued occupation and possession by the grantors indicates that they did not intend to create a present transfer. Moreover, Jay's testimony regarding the "delivery" is self-serving and suspicious. I agree that the deed failed as a valid conveyance. Affirmed.

Analysis:

This case underscores the importance of complying with the strict requirements of delivery. Harold and Mildred clearly intended for Jay (D) to take the property upon their deaths. Even though they attempted to legally deliver the deed, they failed to comply with the requirements. Harold and Mildred could have handled the situation in at least two other ways in order to accomplish their goals. First, they could have simply created a will that transferred the property upon their deaths to Jay (D). The will would have had to comply with the Statute of Wills (*i.e.*, be in writing, signed, and witnessed appropriately). Second, if they wished to avoid probate associated with a will, they could have established a revocable trust on their farm. They would hold their farm in trust, retaining the right to possession and all rents and profits for their joint lives and the life of the survivor. A life estate would have been created in Harold and Mildred for the life of the survivor, with the remainder to Jay (D) upon their deaths. They would have then maintained the power to revoke the transfer at any time during their lives. This trust would have avoided probate and would be valid in all states.

■ CASE VOCABULARY

DE FACTO: As a matter of fact (as opposed to a matter of law).

IN PRAESENTI: At the present time.

PRO FORMA: As a matter of form or based upon assumed facts.

Murphy v. Financial Development Corp.

(Unemployed Borrower) v. *(Lending Institution)*

126 N.H. 536, 495 A.2d 1245 (1985)

A MORTGAGEE CONDUCTING A FORECLOSURE SALE MUST EXERCISE GOOD FAITH AND DUE DILIGENCE IN OBTAINING A FAIR PRICE FOR A MORTGAGOR'S PROPERTY

■ **INSTANT FACTS** Financial Development Corporation foreclosed on Murphy's mortgage, but concluded the foreclosure sale after only one $27,000 bid was made on the $54,000 house.

■ **BLACK LETTER RULE** A mortgagee executing a power of sale has a duty to protect the interests of the mortgagor and exercise good faith and due diligence in obtaining a fair price for a mortgagor's property.

■ **PROCEDURAL BASIS**

Appeal from judgment in action to set aside foreclosure sale or to obtain money damages.

■ **FACTS**

In 1966, Richard Murphy and his wife (P) bought a house and financed it with a mortgage loan. In March 1980, the Murphys (P) refinanced the loan, executing a new promissory note and a power of sale mortgage, with Financial Development Corporation (FDC) (D) as the mortgagee. In February 1981, Richard Murphy (P) became unemployed, and the Murphys (P) went on to fall seven months behind on their (P) mortgage payments. FDC (D) discussed proposals to assist the Murphys (Ps) in making their payments, but none were implemented. On October 6, 1981, FDC (D) gave notice of its (D) intent to foreclose. The Murphys (P) soon paid the late mortgage payments, but not the costs and legal fees of the foreclosure proceedings. FDC (D) scheduled the foreclosure sale for November 10, 1981 at the property itself. FDC (D) fulfilled all the statutory requirements for notice. At the Murphys' (P) request, FDC (D) postponed the sale until December 15, 1981. Notice of this sale was posted at the property on November 10, and later at the local city hall and post office and for three weeks in the local newspaper. Further attempts to postpone the sale were unsuccessful. At the scheduled time of the sale at 10:00 a.m. on December 15, the roads were clear and the weather was warm. The only people present at the sale were the Murphys (P), an FDC (D) representative, and Morgan Hollis, an attorney filling in for the FDC (D) attorney who had been "apprehensive" about the snowy weather the night before. The FDC (D) representative made the only bid at the sale, which was for $27,00 owed on the mortgage and costs and fees. The sale ended with the acceptance of this bid. Later that day, one of Hollis' clients, a corporation represented by William Dube, offered to buy the property from FDC (D) for $27,000. FDC (D) countered with an offer of $40,000, and two days later, sold the property for $38,000. The Murphys (P) sued FDC (D) on February 5, 1982, and FDC (D) moved to dismiss. The master found that FDC (D) failed to exercise good faith and due diligence in obtaining a fair price for the property. Finding the fair market value to be $54,000, the master assessed damages at $27,000, and also legal fees on account of bad faith. FDC (D) appealed.

■ **ISSUE**

Is a mortgagee required to exercise good faith and due diligence to obtain a fair price when conducting a foreclosure sale of mortgaged property?

■ DECISION AND RATIONALE

(Douglas, J.) Yes. The mortgagor's duty should be considered to be that of a fiduciary, as the trend has been to liberally define the term "fiduciary" in order to prevent unjust enrichment. Thus, a mortgagee executing a power of sale has a duty to protect the interests of the mortgagor and exercise good faith and due diligence in obtaining a fair price for a mortgagor's property. The question of what is a fair price, or whether a mortgagor must set a minimum price or make other similar efforts to assure a fair price, depends on the circumstances of each case. It is important to note that the duties of good faith and due diligence are distinct. There must be "an intentional disregard of duty or a purpose to injure" for there to be bad faith. Here, FDC (D) complied with the statutory requirements of notice and conducted the sale in compliance with similar provisions. FDC (D) also postponed the sale once, did nothing to discourage other buyers, and made its (D) bid without knowledge of any other immediate buyer. These facts demonstrate the lack of bad faith by FDC (D). FDC (D) clearly failed, however to exercise due diligence in obtaining a fair price. The test is whether a reasonable person in the lenders' place would have adjourned the sale. The house had been appraised at $46,000 in 1980. Even though FDC (D) did not have the house appraised again for the sale, a reasonable person would have known the Murphys' (P) equity in the home was at least $19,000. This considerable equity, FDC's (D) knowledge of the value of the property, and the Murphys' (P) efforts to pay the late installments all show that FDC (D) had a duty to protect the Murphys' (P) equity by obtaining a fair price. The $27,000 bid did not provide for this, and instead was meant only to make FDC (D) "whole" with regard to the amount owed on the mortgage. In addition, FDC (D) did not give the same notice to the December 15 postponement that it gave to the November 10 sale. With only the postings at the house and the public buildings, and the resulting absence of bidders at the sale, FDC (D) was able to buy the house at a low price and make a quick profit. Granted, FDC (D) did not have an actual, specific buyer for the property at the time of the sale. Despite this, the fact that FDC (D) sold the house for so much more than it (D) had paid supports the view that FDC (D) had reason to know it (D) could make such a profit. This kind of knowledge is the most conclusive evidence that, in following the letter of the law, that FDC (D) violated its spirit. Further, damages should be assessed in the amount of the difference between a fair price for the property and the price obtained at the sale. Judgment reversed in part, affirmed in part, and remanded.

Analysis:

Some state legislatures have passed different laws to protect mortgagors. One type of statute enacts fair market value limitations in order to protect mortgagors from low foreclosure sale prices when the real estate market happens to be depressed. This statute enables a mortgagee to get a deficiency judgment only for the difference between the debt of the mortgagor and the fair market value of the property at the time of foreclosure, as determined by the court. Some other states have legislation that bars deficiency judgments by mortgagees on ordinary purchase money mortgages. These laws were the product of the Great Depression, after widespread promotion schemes caused people to engage in very shaky property investments throughout the 1920s. Further, many states provide for a statutory right of redemption, which may allow a mortgagor to stay in possession of the property until a set period of time has expired. In that extra time after foreclosure, the mortgagor can gather money, redeem from the purchaser at the foreclosure sale, and get the property back.

Commonwealth v. Fremont Investment & Loan

(State) v. (Mortgage Lender)

897 N.E.2d 548 (Mass. 2008)

THE ORIGINATION OF SUBPRIME MORTGAGE LOANS CONSTITUTED AN UNFAIR TRADE PRACTICE

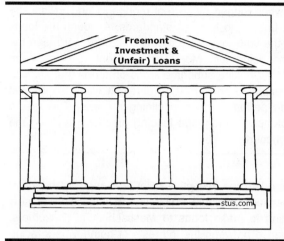

■ **INSTANT FACTS** The state attorney general brought a consumer protection enforcement action against a bank that originated and serviced subprime loans in the state.

■ **BLACK LETTER RULE** A lender commits an unfair trade practice when it makes adjustable rate home mortgage loans reasonably knows that the terms of the loan are such that the borrower will default if the loan is not refinanced after the introductory interest rate period expires.

■ **PROCEDURAL BASIS**

Direct appellate review by the state supreme court of a preliminary injunction issued by the trial court.

■ **FACTS**

Fremont Investment Loan (D) originated thousands of subprime residential mortgage loans in Massachusetts between 2004 and 2007. Those loans had four characteristics that made it almost certain that the borrower would default, leading to foreclosure: (1) they were adjustable rate mortgage (ARM) loans with an introductory rate period of three years or less; (2) the introductory rate was at least three percentage points below the fully indexed rate; (3) the loans were made to borrowers for whom the debt-to income ratio would exceed fifty percent if the borrower's debt had been measured by the monthly payments due at the fully indexed rate, instead of by the monthly payments due under the introductory rate; and (4) the loan-to-value ratio was one hundred percent, or the loan featured a substantial prepayment penalty. The trial court held that under all the attendant circumstances, Fremont (D) acted unfairly, in violation of the consumer protection statute, in making such loans, and the Attorney General (AG) (P) was entitled to a preliminary injunction requiring Fremont (D) (1) to give advance notice of its intent to foreclose on any home loan mortgage; (2) as to loans with the four described characteristics, to work with the AG (P) to resolve their differences regarding foreclosure, through a restructuring or workout; and (3) if resolution did not occur, to obtain court approval for foreclosure. Fremont (D) appealed from the order granting preliminary injunctive relief.

■ **ISSUE**

Did the trial court err in restricting foreclosure of certain subprime loans determined to be presumptively unfair?

■ **DECISION AND RATIONALE**

(Botsford, J.) No. A lender commits an unfair trade practice when it makes adjustable rate home mortgage loans and reasonably knows that the terms of the loan are such that the borrower will default if the loan is not refinanced after the introductory interest rate period expires. We agree with the lower court that Fremont (D) reasonably recognized that based on the first three characteristics of the loans, they were doomed to foreclosure unless the borrower could refinance at the end of the introductory-rate period and obtain a new and low introductory

---

rate. However, the fourth characteristic made refinancing of such subprime loans almost impossible unless housing prices increased. Without an increase in the home's value, a borrower was not likely to have the equity or financial capacity to obtain a new loan. Issuing a home loan when the success of the loan depends on the unsupported hope that fair market values will increase during the introductory period is presumptively unfair. We reject Fremont's (D) argument that the loans were not unfair when judged by current mortgage lending industry standards, and that the trial judge applied ex post facto fairness standards. Although the loans were not considered unfair by the industry at the time they were made, that does not mean the converse, that the loans were recognized as being fair. Moreover, Fremont (D) had been warned prior to 2004 by regulatory agencies that making subprime loans on terms that showed that borrowers would be unable to pay was unsound and probably unfair. It was also warned before 2004 that it needed to consider loan performance in declining markets. The record established the unfairness of Fremont's (D) subprime mortgage lending practices, entitling the AG (P) to the injunctive relief given by the trial court.

Analysis:

The court disposed of Fremont's (D) contention that the injunctive relief fashioned by the lower court did not promote the public interest because it would result in the imposition of new standards, which would make lenders unwilling to make loans to Massachusetts consumers. According to the court, the order struck a balance between the interests of homeowners facing possible foreclosure under the terms of a presumptively unfair mortgage and a lender's interest in recovering the value of its loan. The order did not bar foreclosure as a lender remedy, and it did not relieve borrowers of their obligation to pay the loan. If the court ultimately does not approve a foreclosure, that simply leaves the preliminary injunction in place until the AG (P) has an opportunity to prove that that specific loan violates the unfair trade practices statute.

U.S. Bank Natl. Assn. v. Ibanez

(Trustee of Mortgages) v. (Mortgagor)

941 N.E.2d 40 (Mass. 2010)

A LENDER CANNOT FORECLOSE IF IT DOES NOT HAVE AN EFFECTIVE ASSIGNMENT OF THE MORTGAGE

■ INSTANT FACTS U.S. Bank (P) and Wells Fargo Bank (P) foreclosed on two properties, purchased them back at the foreclosure sale, and then brought a quiet title action seeking a judicial declaration that they were the fee simple owners of the property; the court held that the lenders had failed to make the requisite showing that they were entitled to clear title.

■ BLACK LETTER RULE One who sells under a power of sale must strictly adhere to its terms.

■ PROCEDURAL BASIS

State appellate court review of a trial court decision against the banks.

■ FACTS

Ibanez (D) took out a mortgage from Rose Mortgage, Inc. to purchase a home. The mortgage was assigned to Option One, then to Lehman Brothers, and then to the Structured Asset Securities Corporation, which transferred the Ibanez (D) mortgage, along with many others, to U.S. Bank as trustee. The mortgages were pooled into a trust and converted into securities. In 2007, U.S. Bank (P) filed a complaint to foreclose on the Ibanez (D) mortgage, representing that it was the owner and present holder of the mortgage. U.S. Bank (P) itself purchased the property at the foreclosure sale, for an amount far less than the mortgage debt and fair market value of the property. More than a year after the sale, American Home Mortgage Servicing, the successor in interest to Option One (which was until then the actual record holder of the Ibanez (D) mortgage) executed a written assignment of the mortgage to U.S. Bank as trustee. A similar process ensued with regard to Wells Fargo (P) in respect to the LaRace (D) mortgage. The lenders brought a quiet title action seeking a declaration that the mortgagors' titles had been extinguished.

■ ISSUE

Were U.S. Bank (P) and Wells Fargo (P) entitled to clear title to the foreclosed properties?

■ DECISION AND RATIONALE

(Gants, J.) No. One who sells under a power of sale must strictly adhere to its terms. One of the restrictions that must be adhered to relates to who is entitled to foreclose. Any effort to foreclose by a party lacking authority to carry out a foreclosure is invalid. Another strict requirement relates to notice. Because only a present holder of the mortgage is authorized to foreclose on the mortgaged property, and because the mortgagor is entitled to know who is foreclosing on and selling the property, the failure to identify the holder in the notice of sale may render the notice defective and the foreclosure sale void.

The plaintiffs in this case had the burden of demonstrating their entitlement to clear title. Like the sale of land itself, the assignment of a mortgage is a conveyance that requires a writing signed by the grantor. U.S. Bank (P) offered the trust agreement as the required writing, but

---

that agreement only referenced the intent to assign mortgages to U.S. Bank in the future. U.S. Bank (P) failed to furnish any evidence that Structured Asset Securities Corp, which assigned the mortgage to U.S. Bank (P), ever held the mortgage to be assigned. The last assignment on record was from Rose Mortgage to Option One. This is not enough. The same can be said with regard to Wells Fargo (P) and the LaRace (D) loan. When a plaintiff files a complaint asking for a declaration of clear title after a mortgage foreclosure, the judge is entitled to ask for proof that the foreclosing entity was the mortgage holder at the time of the notice of sale and foreclosure, or was one of the parties authorized to foreclose. The judge did not err in concluding that the securitization documents submitted by the plaintiffs failed to demonstrate that they were the holders of the foreclosed mortgages at the time of publication of the notices and the sales in this case. Because the plaintiffs failed to make the requisite showing, they failed to demonstrate that they acquired fee simple title to the properties by purchasing them at the foreclosure sale. Judgment against the plaintiffs was not in error. Affirmed.

■ CONCURRENCE

(Cordy, J.) There is no dispute that the mortgagors had defaulted and that the properties were subject to foreclosure. Before commencing such an action, however, the holder of an assigned mortgage needs to make sure that its paperwork is in order. The plaintiff banks who brought these cases to clear title have failed to prove that the underlying assignments of the mortgages, which would have entitled them to foreclose, ever existed in any legally cognizable form before they exercised the power of sale.

Analysis:

When a mortgage grants a mortgage holder the power of sale, after the mortgagor defaults in the performance of the underlying note the mortgage holder may sell the property at a public auction and convey the property to the purchaser in fee simple. Such a sale forever bars the mortgagor and all persons claiming under him from any right to and interest in the mortgaged premises. The problem in this case was that the mortgage holder did not have any written evidence establishing that status at the time of sale, and therefore it could not prove its entitlement to clear title.

■ CASE VOCABULARY

ASSIGNMENT: The transferring to another of one's rights or property interest.

FORECLOSURE: Cutting off or termination of a right to property. "Foreclosure" describes both the process and the result and is usually done by the person who holds the mortgage. In addition to taking the property away from the mortgagor and ending his rights in it, the property is usually sold publicly to the highest bidder to pay off the mortgage debt.

MORTGAGE: 1. Security for a loan. 2. An interest in real property given by the debtor (the mortgagor) to the creditor, loan company, or bank (the mortgagee) to secure payment of the loan. At common law, the mortgagee had the legal right to possession. Today, in most states a mortgage is a lien, therefore, the mortgagee may only have the legal right to possession after a foreclosure hearing with proof of default in payments by the debtor.

MORTGAGEE: The party who holds the mortgage; one who lends the money to a mortgagor and then takes a security interest in the mortgagor's real property.

MORTGAGOR: The party who borrows money from a mortgagee. The mortgagor secures the debt with real property owned by the mortgagor.

Bean v. Walker

(Home Seller) v. (Home Buyer)

95 A.D.2d 70, 464 N.Y.S.2d 895 (1983)

WHEN A BUYER DEFAULTS ON AN INSTALLMENT LAND SALE CONTRACT, HIS OR HER PAYMENTS ARE NOT FORFEITED AS LONG AS HE OR SHE HAS ALREADY PAID A SUBSTANTIAL AMOUNT ON THE CONTRACT

■ **INSTANT FACTS** Walker defaulted on an installment land sale contract after paying Bean nearly half of the purchase price, and Bean sued to retake possession.

■ **BLACK LETTER RULE** The buyer under an installment land sale contract acquires equitable title which must be extinguished before the seller can retake possession, and so the buyer's payments cannot be forfeited where there would be an inequitable disposition of property and exorbitant money loss by the buyer.

■ **PROCEDURAL BASIS**

Appeal from summary judgment in action for ejectment.

■ **FACTS**

In January 1973, the Beans (P) agreed to sell a house to the Walkers (D) for $15,000. The sale contract provided that the $15,000 was to be paid over a 15-year period at 5% interest, in monthly installments of $118.62 each. The Beans (P) retained legal title and would convey it to the Walkers (D) upon full payment of the purchase price according to the terms of the contract. The Walkers (D) were entitled to possession of the property. Under the contract, if the Walkers (D) defaulted in making payment and failed to cure that default within 30 days, the Beans (P) could demand the rest of the balance or terminate the contract and repossess the premises. If this latter choice were made, then the Beans (P) could retain all the money paid by the Walkers (D) to that point as "liquidated damages" under a forfeiture clause. These payments would then be considered as going towards rent, and not as any kind of penalty. The Walkers (D) went into possession of the house in January 1973. They (D) went on to make substantial improvements to the property. They (D) made all their (D) required payments under the contract until August 1981. Then, the Walkers (D) defaulted after Carl Walker (D) became injured. By that time, the Walkers (D) had paid the Beans (P) $12,099.24, with $7,114.75 of it being applied to the $15,000 principal. Thus, nearly half of the principal had been paid by the Walkers (D). The Beans (P) waited 30 days and then filed this action, seeking a judgment granting them (P) possession of the property. The court granted summary judgment to the Beans (P).

■ **ISSUE**

Does the buyer in an installment land sale contract automatically forfeit his or her payments to the seller, and lose possession of the property to the seller, if he or she defaults in making payment?

■ **DECISION AND RATIONALE**

(Doerr, J.) No. The buyer under an installment land sale contract acquires equitable title which must be extinguished before the seller can retake possession, and so the buyer's payments cannot be forfeited where there would be an inequitable disposition of property and exorbitant money loss by the buyer. In the similar case of Skendzel v. Marshall [vendee in land sale contract acquires equitable title when contract is consummated], the Indiana Supreme Court found that the status of the parties in an installment land sale contract is like that of a mortgagor and mortgagee. This status strongly suggests that the concept that equity deems that which ought to be done as done should be applied here. Numerous cases of this state [New York] have already demonstrated that parties to such an installment contract occupy the position of mortgagor and mortgagee at common law. The common law mortgagor also acquires equitable title. This form of title gives its owner the right to any increase in the value of the property, and allows the owner's interest to be treated as real property. The seller's interest, by contrast, is personal property, namely the right to receive money. Because the buyer possesses equitable title, the seller must first extinguish the equitable owner's equity of redemption to resume possession. There is no reason why the Beans (P) and Walkers (D) should be treated differently than the mortgagee and mortgagor at common law. The question that must be decided is whether the buyer in a land sale contract has obtained the kind of property interest that must be extinguished before the seller may resume possession. The Walkers (D) do have such an interest as they (D) acquired equitable title and the Beans (P) held the legal title in trust for them (D). Thus, the Beans (P) had to foreclose the equitable title or bring an action at law for the purchase price in order to resume possession. The Beans (P) sought neither of these remedies. The lower court judgment would allow the Beans (P) to retake the property, after improvements by the Walkers (D), along with over $11,000 in principal and interest payments. This result would clearly be inequitable; equity should be used when a forfeiture would lead to such an unfair disposition of property and an exorbitant loss of money would occur. Judgment reversed, motion denied, and matter remitted.

Analysis:

Most states currently require a seller to give notice of a possible forfeiture. This notice must conform to either legislative or judicial standards for notice, depending on the particular state. In some states, a seller may waive future rights to forfeiture by accepting late payments, because this may lead a buyer to think that promptness is not necessary under the contract. Defaulting buyers may also have the right to specific performance in the event that all, or possibly a specified amount over fifty percent, of the purchase price is paid. In addition, a seller's declaration of forfeiture may bar any suit for the remainder of the purchase price. Indeed, a buyer, even one who willingly defaults on the contract, could get restitution of payments to cover his or her loss, even if such distribution is unfair to the seller.

■ **CASE VOCABULARY**

EJECTMENT: A cause of action raised by a person entitled to possession of property in order to retake such possession.

EQUITY OF REDEMPTION: A mortgagor's right to reclaim property after it has been forfeited.

CHAPTER EIGHT

Title Assurance

Luthi v. Evans

Instant Facts: Owens and others assigned all their oil and gas interests in the county to Tours, and Burris found no record of this when inspecting title.

Black Letter Rule: A Mother Hubbard clause is upheld as between the parties to the instrument that contains it, but is insufficient to give constructive notice to subsequent purchasers without actual notice of it.

Orr v. Byers

Instant Facts: Byers was unaware of Orr's lien on Elliott's property because Elliott's name was misspelled on the abstract of judgment, causing misspellings in the title index.

Black Letter Rule: Requiring a title searcher to examine title records for other spellings of the grantor's name would be an undue burden on the transfer of property.

Messersmith v. Smith

Instant Facts: After a first deed was found to be incorrect, Messersmith took a second deed to a notary public, who got Messersmith's acknowledgment over the telephone.

Black Letter Rule: An instrument that is not properly acknowledged is not entitled to be recorded.

Board of Education of Minneapolis v. Hughes

Instant Facts: Hughes obtained title first, but recorded second; Duryea and Wilson obtained title second, but recorded third; the Board obtained title third, but recorded first.

Black Letter Rule: A deed from a grantor outside the chain of title, even if recorded, is treated as though it were unrecorded and gives no constructive notice.

Guillette v. Daly Dry Wall, Inc.

Instant Facts: Daly Dry Wall, Inc. tried to build an apartment building on a lot in a subdivision which was restricted to single-family houses.

Black Letter Rule: A subsequent purchaser from a common grantor in a subdivision has constructive notice of the restrictions on the rest of the subdivision, and thus acquires title subject to those restrictions.

Daniels v. Anderson

Instant Facts: A person who possessed the right of first refusal on a piece of property sues a subsequent buyer who purchased the property and took possession without allowing the prior buyer to exercise his preemptive option.

Black Letter Rule: Bona fide purchaser status attaches only when the full purchase price has been paid.

Lewis v. Superior Court

Instant Facts: A couple purchased property by giving a note to the seller one day before the lis pendens of a party claiming a hostile interest was properly indexed.

Black Letter Rule: A seller need not be paid in full before the buyer can be considered a bona fide purchaser.

Harper v. Paradise

Instant Facts: The Paradises, who claim title to property dating back to a 1928 deed, are challenged by Clyde Harper (P), who asserts that the Paradises had notice of a prior deed in which Clyde (P) was the remainderman.

Black Letter Rule: Subsequent grantees are held to inquiry notice of the contents of prior recorded deeds in the chain of title for purposes of a race-notice recording act.

Waldorff Ins. and Bonding, Inc. v. Eglin National Bank

Instant Facts: A bank attempts to foreclose on mortgages secured by condominiums, executed when one of the condo units subject to the mortgage was openly possessed and owned by another party.

Black Letter Rule: Actual possession gives constructive notice to the world of any right which the person in possession is able to establish.

Walker Rogge, Inc. v. Chelsea Title and Guaranty Co.

Instant Facts: Chelsea did not inform Walker Rogge when a prior deed indicated that the tract being insured was about seven acres smaller than what Walker Rogge believed.

Black Letter Rule: If a title company fails to conduct a reasonable title examination, or having conducted such an examination, fails to disclose the results to the insured, then it runs the risk of liability under the terms of the insurance policy and not under tort for negligence.

Lick Mill Creek Apartments v. Chicago Title Insurance Co.

Instant Facts: The apartment owners tried to have the title company indemnify them for the costs of cleaning up and removing the hazardous substances under their property.

Black Letter Rule: Title insurance policies are intended to protect the condition of an owner's title to land, and not provide coverage for the physical condition of the land itself.

Luthi v. Evans

(Subsequent Assignee) v. ("Mother Hubbard" Assignee)

223 Kan. 622, 576 P.2d 1064 (1978)

INSTRUMENTS RECORDED WITH "MOTHER HUBBARD" CLAUSES ARE VALID WITH REGARD TO THE PARTIES TO IT, BUT DO NOT PROVIDE CONSTRUCTIVE NOTICE FOR SUBSEQUENT PURCHASERS

[handwritten: notice]

■ **INSTANT FACTS** Owens and others assigned all their oil and gas interests in the county to Tours, and Burris found no record of this when inspecting title.

■ **BLACK LETTER RULE** A Mother Hubbard clause is upheld as between the parties to the instrument that contains it, but is insufficient to give constructive notice to subsequent purchasers without actual notice of it.

[handwritten: Burns wasn't given appropriate notice SDG P.115-116]

■ **PROCEDURAL BASIS**

Appeal from judgment to quiet title.

■ **FACTS**

Grace V. Owens owned interests in several oil and gas leases in Coffey County, Kansas. On February 1, 1971, she assigned all of these oil and gas interests to International Tours, Inc. (Tours) through a written instrument. This document stated that the Owens and the other assignors intended to convey "all interest whatsoever of working nature in all working interests and overriding royalty interest in all Oil and Gas Leases in Coffey County, Kansas." This sort of clause, conveying all of a grantor's property in a certain county, is commonly referred to as a "Mother Hubbard" clause. This assignment was recorded in the county office of the register of deeds on February 16, 1971. In addition to the seven leases specifically outlined in the agreement, Owens owned a working interest in an oil and gas lease known as the Kufahl lease. This lease was also located on land in Coffey County. Although it was not specifically described in the assignment, the Kufahl lease nonetheless fit the description in the Tours assignment. On January 30, 1975, Owens executed and delivered a second assignment of her interest in the Kufahl lease to J.R. Burris (P). Before this assignment took place, Burris (P) personally checked the records in the office of the register of deeds. After the assignment, he (P) obtained an abstract of title to the same property. Neither his inspection nor the abstract revealed the prior assignment to Tours. Tours contends that the 1971 assignment effectively conveyed Owens' interest in the Kufahl lease to Tours, and that its recordation with the county gave constructive notice to all subsequent purchasers, including Burris. Burris, however, asserts that the language of the assignment provided an inadequate description of the interests conveyed. Burris prevailed in district court. On appeal, the general description in the 1971 assignment was held to be sufficient, when recorded, to provide constructive notice.

[handwritten: p.114 Appears that in a notice jurisdiction, Burns is a bona fide purchaser + doesn't matter who (Burns or Tours) records first]

■ **ISSUE**

[handwritten: prevailed]

Is an instrument using a Mother Hubbard clause to describe assigned interests sufficient to provide constructive notice to subsequent purchasers?

■ DECISION AND RATIONALE

(Prager, J.) No. A Mother Hubbard clause is upheld as between the parties to the instrument that contains it, but is insufficient to give constructive notice to subsequent purchasers without actual notice of it. This court agrees with both parties that the 1971 assignment constituted a valid transfer of Owens' interest in the Kufahl lease to Tours, but only as between the two parties to that assignment. Likewise, a single instrument can convey separate tracts by specific description, and by general description which can be made specific. This can be done when the language of the assignment expresses that clear intent. The state statutes, however, require the register of deeds to keep a general index of title that records a description of each tract conveyed when appropriate. Further, county commissioners are required to record a numerical index of all deeds, complete with brief descriptions of the properties involved. It is clear that these statutes are intended to notify a subsequent purchaser regarding instruments which affect the title to a specific tract of land. Thus, the legislature likely intended that recorded instruments describe the conveyed land well enough so that it could be identified later on. An instrument using a Mother Hubbard clause is ineffective as to subsequent purchasers unless they have actual knowledge of the transfer. A Mother Hubbard clause can be used in the event of emergency, so long as the grantee takes steps to protect his or her title against subsequent purchasers. These steps could include taking possession of the property or filing an affidavit with the county containing a more appropriate description of the property. Here, because Burris had no actual notice of the 1971 assignment to Tours, the assignment to Burris prevails. Judgment of district court affirmed.

Analysis:

There are two systems for governmental description of "official" parcels of land. The first official method is the Government Survey System, which was devised by Thomas Jefferson and adopted by the Continental Congress in 1785. It is generally available throughout the country except along the East Coast and Kentucky, Tennessee, and West Virginia. The System is based on thirty-six sets of north-south Principal Meridians and east-west Base Lines. East-west lines running every six miles split the sections into Townships, while similar north-south lines divide the land into Ranges. With this System, lands can be described by citing an intersection number for the Meridian and Line, and then numbers for the Township and the Range. The other system, recognized in every state, is the plat. A plat is a map drawn to specific standards of form and accuracy. Though approved by and filed with an appropriate government body, it is drawn up by an engineer or surveyor hired by the landowner. The plat must contain references to recognized landmarks outside the property, so the land itself can be located. The plat can then serve as the basis for description of subdivisions of the land.

■ CASE VOCABULARY

MOTHER HUBBARD CLAUSE: Language used in a conveyance which describes the property to be conveyed as all of the grantor's property in a certain county; reference is to a nursery rhyme describing Mother Hubbard going to her cupboard, "and when she got there, the cupboard was bare," the idea being a grantor's interests in a county are similarly cleared out by this clause.

Orr v. Byers

(Judgment Winner) v. (Property Buyer)

198 Cal.App.3d 666, 244 Cal.Rptr. 13 (1988)

A TITLE SEARCHER IS NOT REQUIRED TO SEARCH FOR MISRECORDED INSTRUMENTS

■ **INSTANT FACTS** Byers was unaware of Orr's lien on Elliott's property because Elliott's name was misspelled on the abstract of judgment, causing misspellings in the title index.

■ **BLACK LETTER RULE** Requiring a title searcher to examine title records for other spellings of the grantor's name would be an undue burden on the transfer of property.

■ **PROCEDURAL BASIS**

Appeal from judgment denying declaratory relief.

■ **FACTS**

In October 1978, James Orr (P) obtained a judgment against William Elliott (D) in excess of $50,000. Orr's (P) attorney prepared a written judgment against Elliott (D), but misspelled his name with only one "t." That November, an abstract of the judgment was recorded in the Orange County Recorder's Office, with "Elliott" being misspelled as "Elliot" and "Eliot." This abstract was listed in the County's Grantor-Grantee Index under those names only. Elliott (D) later obtained title to a parcel of property. This property became subject to Orr's (P) lien. Elliott (D) sold that property to Rick Byers (D) in July 1979, but a title search failed to reveal the abstract of judgment. Thus, the preliminary title report did not disclose Orr's (P) judgment lien against Elliott (D), and the sale of Elliott's land to Byers (D) was not used to satisfy Orr's (P) judgment lien. In February 1981, Orr (P) filed suit against Byers, Elliott, and two local financial institutions (D), seeking a declaration of the rights and duties of all parties. In effect, Orr (P) sought judicial foreclosure of his (P) judgment lien. Orr (P) argued that the others (D) had constructive notice of the abstract of judgment through the doctrine of idem sonans. The trial judge ruled that the doctrine was inapplicable and denied Orr's (P) request for declaratory relief. A formal judgment was filed in February, 1986, and Orr (P) appealed.

■ **ISSUE**

Is a title searcher required to examine the records for alternative spellings of a grantor's name under the doctrine of idem sonans?

■ **DECISION AND RATIONALE**

(Sonenshine, J.) No. Requiring a title searcher to examine title records for other spellings of the grantor's name would be an undue burden on the transfer of property. Under the doctrine of idem sonans, the identity of a person whose name has been inaccurately written will be presumed from the similarity of sounds between the pronunciations of the correctly and incorrectly spelled names. This doctrine, however, is inapplicable when it is the written, not the spoken, name that is material. Here, the written name is clearly material. Requiring Byers (D) or any title searcher to "comb the records" for alternative spellings of a given name would place an undue burden on the transfer of property. Indeed, adding that burden to the already potentially daunting task of searching title for all those who have identical names would be unjustifiable. Already, not every name uncovered by a search pertains to the person subject to a particular lien. Checking for liens against those with similarly spelled names, and checking to see if those liens affected the desired property, would make the problem worse. While new software and computer systems are now used in title searches, these measures could generate even more extraneous names, particularly if the name in question is a common one in a large county. The burden should rest with the judgment creditor, Orr (P), to take appropriate action to ensure the judgment will be satisfied. That action includes spelling the names of the debtor properly on official documents. Judgment affirmed.

Analysis:

The cases are divided on the issue of misrecorded instruments, and often depend on the specific language of the governing statutes, as was demonstrated by the court here. The majority of states regard the mere act of copying the deed or other instrument into the official record as a sufficient recording to uphold it. The modern trend, however, has been to decide along the line of *Orr* and treat misindexed instruments as unrecorded. Practically speaking, this is the more logical view, as there is no reasonable way to locate such an instrument until it has been properly filed and indexed.

■ **CASE VOCABULARY**

ABSTRACT: An abridged summary; less detailed than a transcript.

IDEM SONANS: "Having the same sound"; Latin term given to doctrine that states though a person's name has been inaccurately written, the person's identity will be presumed from the similarity of pronunciation between the correct and incorrect spellings of the person's name.

Messersmith v. Smith

(Title Grantor) v. (Title Grantee)

60 N.W.2d 276 (N.D. 1953)

AN IMPROPERLY ACKNOWLEDGED INSTRUMENT SHOULD BE CONSIDERED AS UNRECORDED

■ **INSTANT FACTS** After a first deed was found to be incorrect, Messersmith took a second deed to a notary public, who got Messersmith's acknowledgment over the telephone.

■ **BLACK LETTER RULE** An instrument that is not properly acknowledged is not entitled to be recorded.

■ **PROCEDURAL BASIS**

Appeal from finding in statutory action to quiet title.

■ **FACTS**

Caroline Messersmith and her nephew, Frederick Messersmith (P), each owned an undivided one-half interest in three sections of land in Golden Valley County, North Dakota. On May 7, 1946, Caroline executed and delivered a quitclaim deed to the property to Frederick (P) which was not recorded until July 9, 1951. From January to April 1951, oil fever hit the County, as brokers, oil men, and speculators flocked to North Dakota. On April 23, 1951, she met with Herbert J. Smith, Jr. (D) to discuss a gas and oil lease to the properties. Caroline claimed that only royalties were negotiated, while Smith (D) claimed the matter of the mineral deed was discussed. On May 7, 1951, Caroline executed a mineral deed for an undivided one-half interest in the oil, gas and minerals under the three sections of land. Caroline claims that she thought she was signing a transfer of royalties only. Smith (D) paid a consideration of $1,400 for the deed. After leaving, Smith (D) discovered that the deed incorrectly stated the term "his heirs" instead of "her heirs." Smith (D) returned to Caroline's home the same day and explained the mistake to her. He (D) then tore up the deed and prepared another one in the same form and with the error corrected. Smith (D) then, according to his (D) testimony, took the deed to the same notary public to whom Caroline acknowledged the first deed. The notary called Caroline for her acknowledgment over the telephone, and then placed his seal and signature on the deed. Two days later, Smith (D) executed a mineral deed conveying the interest conveyed by Caroline to E.B. Seale. Both deeds were recorded May 26, 1951. Seale apparently relied on the second deed between Caroline and Smith (D) when making his purchase of the one-half interest. Frederick Messersmith (P) filed action to quiet title to the land. Seale (D) answered by claiming he (D) was a purchaser without actual or constructive notice of Frederick's (P) claim. Frederick (P) further answered by claiming Seale's (D) mineral deed was never acknowledged, not entitled to be recorded and was obtained by fraud, deceit and misrepresentation. Smith (D) defaulted.

■ **ISSUE**

Is a deed which is improperly acknowledged entitled to be recorded?

■ **DECISION AND RATIONALE**

(Morris, J.) No. An instrument that is not properly acknowledged is not entitled to be recorded. The trial court found that the deeds were not executed through fraud or false representation, and there is no reason to disturb that finding. Caroline's mineral deed to Smith (D) however, was invalid, for she had already conveyed her interest to her nephew (P). Smith's (D) conveyance to Seale (D) was also invalid. The only way Seale (D) can assert title to any interest in the property is by citing the fact that Frederick's (P) deed was not recorded until July 1951. This reasoning is insufficient, however, to support Seale's (D) claim because Seale's (D) deed was nonetheless improperly executed. Under the governing state statutes, a deed to real property cannot be recorded without proper acknowledgment by the parties. Caroline did not appear before the notary and acknowledge she executed the deed that was recorded; she allegedly did so over the telephone. Because the deed was not entitled to be recorded, the record then did not constitute notice of its execution. Because the record did not constitute notice, the purchaser, Seale (D), did not become a subsequent purchaser in good faith within the meaning of the statutes. The right Seale (D) tries to claim is dependent on compliance with the recording statutes. It is likewise dependent on the deed that was actually recorded, not the one that was destroyed. Judgment reversed.

Analysis:

Most courts hold that an individual has notice of documents in his or her own chain of title even if they are not recorded. The idea behind this is simply that a purchaser can reasonably be expected to know, and usually does know, about the history of his or her title. While this position does give a strong incentive for ensuring that the public records are complete, it is somewhat illogical and impractical. A potential purchaser would have no notice of prior adverse claims or conveyances to the title if such were unrecorded, and there would be no place to begin following up on those claims. The *Messersmith* case is an extreme example of this position, though it is by no means unanimously followed by the states.

■ **CASE VOCABULARY**

NOTARY PUBLIC: A public officer with the duty of authenticating and acknowledging certain documents, including deeds and other instruments of conveyance.

QUITCLAIM DEED: A conveyance of title without any warranties or guarantees for the title or that the grantor's title is even valid.

Board of Education of Minneapolis v. Hughes

(Third Deed Grantee) v. (First Deed Grantee)

118 Minn. 404, 136 N.W. 1095 (1912)

A DEED FROM A GRANTOR WHO IS NOT PART OF THE CHAIN OF TITLE DOES NOT COUNT AS A RECORDED DEED AND ITS RECORDING DOES NOT GIVE CONSTRUCTIVE NOTICE

■ **INSTANT FACTS** Hughes obtained title first, but recorded second; Duryea and Wilson obtained title second, but recorded third; the Board obtained title third, but recorded first. (Got it?)

■ **BLACK LETTER RULE** A deed from a grantor outside the chain of title, even if recorded, is treated as though it were unrecorded and gives no constructive notice.

■ **PROCEDURAL BASIS**

Appeal from order denying new trial in action to determine adverse claim.

■ **FACTS**

The facts are not in controversy and are as follows: On May 16, 1906, Carrie B. Hoerger, a resident of Faribault, owned the lot in question, which was vacant and subject to unpaid delinquent taxes. Defendant L.A. Hughes offered to pay $25 for this lot. His offer was accepted, and he sent his check for the purchase price of this and two other lots bought at the same time to Ed Hoerger, husband of the owner, together with a deed to be executed and returned. The name of the grantee in the deed was not inserted; the space for the same being left blank. It was executed and acknowledged by Carrie B. Hoerger and her husband on May 17, 1906, and delivered to defendant Hughes by mail. The check was retained and cashed. Hughes filled in the name of the grantee, but not until shortly prior to the date when the deed was recorded, which was December 16, 1910. On April 27, 1909, Duryea & Wilson, real estate dealers, paid Mrs. Hoerger $25 for a quitclaim deed to the lot, which was executed and delivered to them, but which was not recorded until December 21, 1910. On November 19, 1909, Duryea & Wilson executed and delivered to plaintiff a warranty deed to the lot, which deed was filed for record January 27, 1910. It thus appears that the deed to Hughes was recorded before the deed to Duryea & Wilson, though the deed from them to plaintiff was recorded before the deed to defendant.

■ **ISSUE**

Does a deed granted by an individual outside the chain of title count as a properly recorded deed and give constructive notice to subsequent purchasers?

■ **DECISION AND RATIONALE**

(Bunn, J.) No. A deed from a grantor outside the chain of title, even if recorded, is treated as though it were unrecorded and gives no constructive notice. First, a preliminary issue must be discussed. The initial deed to Hughes (D) did become operative when he (D) put his name on it before recording it. Before that name was filled in, the deed itself was a nullity. Hughes (D) had implied authority to fill in the blank. It is to be presumed that the grantee has the authority to do this when the grantor retains the consideration for the deed, and delivers the deed to the grantee, just as the Hoergers did here. Turning to the issue of the deed to the Board (P), the facts support Hughes' (D) claim to title. When Duryea and Wilson deeded the property to the Board (P) in November 1909, there was no record showing they had any title to convey. The Duryea and Wilson deed was not recorded until December 21, 1910. By contrast, Hughes (D) was a subsequent purchaser, and is protected by the fact that his (D) deed was recorded five days before the deed from the Hoergers to Duryea and Wilson. At the time Hughes (D) recorded his deed, Duryea and Wilson were still not a record owner anywhere in the chain of title. Hughes (D) was thus the rightful owner of the lot. Order reversed, and new trial granted.

Analysis:

The problem presented here is often referred to as the "wild deed." Generally, it is a deed to property that is recorded, but not within the chain of title because neither the grantor nor the grantee is known to the searcher of title in official records. Here, the term "wild deed" refers to the deed from Duryea and Wilson to the Board. There are three other similar, generic problems of title recordation. One occurs when title is recorded too late, as when a grantee in one deed fails to record it until after the grantor's deed to a second grantee is recorded. Another problem results when a grantee records a deed before the grantor actually obtains title to the property in question. Still another problem arises when the owner of two or more parcels includes, in a deed to one parcel, language that encumbers title to any other commonly owned parcel. In all four of these chain of title problems, the courts have favored title searchers by treating the given conveyances as if they were unrecorded and as providing no constructive notice. Almost invariably, the grantee is spared the burden of discovering all claims to the title in question, as the four recording problems mentioned above render the task of finding all adverse claims to title incredibly difficult.

■ CASE VOCABULARY

WARRANTY DEED: A conveyance which explicitly lists covenants concerning the quality of title being conveyed; by this deed, the grantor conveys good, clear title.

Guillette v. Daly Dry Wall, Inc.

(Neighboring Lot Owner) v. (Would-Be Apartment Builder)

367 Mass. 355, 325 N.E.2d 572 (1975)

A PURCHASER OF A LOT IN A SUBDIVISION HAS CONSTRUCTIVE NOTICE OF RESTRICTIONS ON NEIGHBORING LOTS

■ **INSTANT FACTS** Daly Dry Wall, Inc. tried to build an apartment building on a lot in a subdivision which was restricted to single-family houses.

■ **BLACK LETTER RULE** A subsequent purchaser from a common grantor in a subdivision has constructive notice of the restrictions on the rest of the subdivision, and thus acquires title subject to those restrictions.

■ **PROCEDURAL BASIS**

Appeal from final decree in action for injunctive relief.

■ **FACTS**

Wallace L. Gilmore sold lots in a subdivision to Mr. and Mrs. Guillette (P) in May 1968, by a deed referring to a plan dated in March 1968. Earlier, the Walcotts (P) purchased a lot in August 1967, by a deed referring to a plan dated in July 1967. Both these plans are essentially the same and mention no restrictions. In June 1968, the Paraskivas (P) purchased a lot in the subdivision by a deed referring to the 1968 plan. These three deeds, along with five other deeds to lots in the subdivision, set out or refer to restrictions on the respective lots. Gilmore and at least the three sets of neighbors (P) intended to keep the subdivision limited to single-family residential use. In April 1972, Daly Dry Wall, Inc. (Daly) (D) purchased a lot from Gilmore. This deed contained no reference to any restrictions, but it did refer to the 1968 plan. Daly (D) made no inquiry regarding restrictions on the property and did not know of any development pattern in the subdivision. Daly (D) learned of the restrictions in August 1972 after a title examination was made. Daly (D) later obtained a building permit for thirty-six apartment-type units. Guillette (P), the Walcotts (P), and the Paraskivas (P) brought suit to enjoin Daly (D) from constructing the apartment building on its (D) lot. A final decree was entered enjoining Daly (D) from building any structures which did not conform to the restrictions contained in the deed from Gilmore to the Guillettes (P). Daly (D) appealed.

■ **ISSUE**

Is a subsequent purchaser of a lot in a subdivision bound by restrictions contained in deeds to neighboring landowners when the purchaser took title without knowledge of the restrictions?

■ **DECISION AND RATIONALE**

(Braucher, J.) Yes. A subsequent purchaser from a common grantor in a subdivision has constructive notice of the restrictions on the rest of the subdivision, and thus acquires title subject to those restrictions. The deed from Gilmore to the Guillettes (P) conveyed more than just the described lot. It also conveyed an interest in the land then owned by Gilmore. That remaining land owned by Gilmore was subject to the same restrictions as the rest of the land. Thus, when Daly (D) purchased part of the land, it (D) took title subject to those restrictions. Daly (D) argues that charging it (D) with notice would impose a nearly impossible burden of searching each and every deed given in the subdivision. The Daly (D) deed, however, referred to the same plan mentioned in the Guillette (P) deed. A search for such deeds would not be impossible. Decree affirmed.

Analysis:

This case is an example of the fourth generic chain of title problem discussed in the previous brief. It is important to note the difficulty that a subsequent purchaser in a subdivision faces in learning of the restrictions on neighboring lots and how they affect his or her lot. In many states that rely on name indexes to record title, the index books include a column where a brief description can be included for each affected parcel. This method is not mandatory, however, and is often maintained only as a favor to title searchers. Even if this column is present in the record, there is no guarantee that those in the recording office will accurately summarize which properties are affected by a given set of restrictions. This is particularly true if the restriction's effect on other parcels is very complex or not very obvious. A title searcher may only be legally entitled to rely on the comments in this brief description column if it is legally required to be included in the index. If it is not, then a searcher would have to go through every conveyance by the grantor. Granted, that task seemed fairly easy here, but if the grantor is a large-scale developer or real estate dealer, the number of conveyances could go well into the hundreds, making the task an enormous one. The courts are pretty evenly split on this issue, with some holding that this burden of title searching is too excessive, and some imposing this burden on the searcher anyway.

Daniels v. Anderson

(Option Holder) v. (Not Stated)

162 Ill.2d 47, 642 N.E.2d 128 (1994)

COURT ADOPTS STRICT TEST FOR BONA FIDE PURCHASER STATUS

■ **INSTANT FACTS** A person who possessed the right of first refusal on a piece of property sues a subsequent buyer who purchased the property and took possession without allowing the prior buyer to exercise his preemptive option.

■ **BLACK LETTER RULE** Bona fide purchaser status attaches only when the full purchase price has been paid.

■ **PROCEDURAL BASIS**

Appeal from order affirming verdict of specific performance of preemptive option in land sale.

■ **FACTS**

In 1977 William Daniels (P) bought two lots from Stephen Jacula (D). The contract of sale gave Daniels (P) the right of first refusal if Jacula (D) ever decided to sell an adjacent parcel (the "Contiguous Parcel") for the same price as any prospective buyer offered. Daniels (P) received and recorded the deed, which did not mention the right of first refusal. The contract of sale was not recorded. In 1985, Zografos (D) contracted with Jacula (D) to buy the Contiguous Parcel for $60,000. Daniels (P) was not notified of the offer. Zografos (D) paid Jacula (D) $10,000 and gave Jacula (D) a note for the balance. Zografos (D) paid $30,000 more in early 1986. In June 1986 Daniels' (P) wife gave Zografos (D) notice of the right of first refusal. In August 1986 Zografos (D) paid the remaining $20,000 to Jacula (D). Zografos (D) received and recorded the deed to the Contiguous Parcel. Daniels (P) sued Jacula (D) and Zografos (D) for specific performance of the preemptive option. Zografos (D) contended that he was a bona fide purchaser without notice of the option. The trial court held that Zografos (D) was not a subsequent bona fide purchaser because he had actual notice of the option at the time he took title. The court ordered Zografos (D) to convey the Contiguous Parcel to Daniels (P), and ordered Daniels (P) to pay Zografos (D) the full purchase price of $60,000 plus $11,000 in property taxes Zografos (D) had paid on the Contiguous Parcel. Zografos (D) appealed on grounds that he became a bona fide purchaser because he took equitable title prior to receiving actual notice of Daniels' (P) interest, even though he did not take legal title until after he had notice. The appellate court affirmed, holding that Zografos (D) waived this theory because he did not assert it at any time prior to the appeal. Zografos (D) appeals to the Supreme Court of Illinois.

■ **ISSUE**

Where a buyer receives notice of an outstanding interest subsequent to paying some, but not all, of the full purchase price, is the buyer considered a bona fide purchaser?

■ **DECISION AND RATIONALE**

(Freeman, J.) No. Where a buyer receives notice of an outstanding interest subsequent to paying some, but not all, of the full purchase price, the buyer is not considered a bona fide purchaser. A bona fide purchaser, by definition, takes title to real property without notice of the

---

interests of others. Some appellate courts have held that partial payment of the consideration is insufficient to render the buyer a bona fide purchaser. A majority of jurisdictions have relaxed this harsh rule and have applied a pro tanto rule, which protects the buyer to the extent of the payments made prior to notice, but no further. Courts can exercise considerable latitude in reaching an equitable resolution. We hold that the trial court's disposition of the issue between Zografos (D) and Daniels (P) was fair and not an abuse of discretion. Affirmed.

Analysis:

This case tackles the difficult question of when a buyer becomes a bona fide purchaser. The question is very important. If a subsequent buyer is considered a bona fide purchaser, he can take title despite a previous hostile interest in the same property. Clearly, where a party pays full consideration and takes legal title without actual or constructive notice of prior interests, that party is a bona fide purchaser and is protected. Conversely, where the new buyer has notice of the prior interest, he commits fraud upon the holder of the prior interest by consummating the purchase. But should a bona fide status attach prior to taking actual legal title? Without stating any policy justification, the opinion concludes that it should not. Some courts award the land to the prior holder and refund any payments the subsequent buyer made. Another option is to divide the land between the two purchasers. Perhaps this approach would have been more fair in this case, assuming the property could be subdivided.

■ CASE VOCABULARY

EQUITABLE CONVERSION: The doctrine that vests equitable title to property in the purchaser once a binding land sale contract is executed.

PRO TANTO: Partial payment made on a claim or purchase.

SPECIFIC PERFORMANCE: The remedy of requiring performance of a contract under the exact terms of the agreement.

Lewis v. Superior Court

(Purchaser) v. (Court)

30 Cal.App.4th 1850, 37 Cal.Rptr.2d 63 (1994)

COURT OVERRULES ANTIQUATED "PAYMENT OF VALUE" RULE TO DETERMINE A BONA FIDE PURCHASER

■ **INSTANT FACTS** A couple purchased property by giving a note to the seller one day before the lis pendens of a party claiming a hostile interest was properly indexed.

■ **BLACK LETTER RULE** A seller need not be paid in full before the buyer can be considered a bona fide purchaser.

■ **PROCEDURAL BASIS**

Appeal from denial of motion for summary judgment in action to quiet title and expunge lis pendens.

■ **FACTS**

In February 1991, Robert and Josephine Lewis contracted to buy a residence for $2.3 million. On February 24, Fontana Films (D) recorded a lis pendens on the property. On February 25, the Lewises (P) paid $350,000. Escrow closed on February 28, 1991, when the Lewises (P) gave the seller a note for $1.95 million. The Lewises (P) had neither actual nor constructive notice of the lis pendens at this time. On February 29, 1991, the lis pendens was indexed. Within the next year, the Lewises (P) paid the note in full and spent over $1 million in renovating the property. In September 1993, the Lewises (P) were served with Fontana's (D) lawsuit and learned about the lis pendens. The Lewises (P) brought suit to remove the lis pendens and clear their title. Fontana (D) contends that even if the Lewises (D) took title before the indexing of the lis pendens, they nevertheless were not bona fide purchasers because they did not fully pay for the property until after indexing. The trial court denied the Lewises' (P) motion for summary judgment, and they appeal.

■ **ISSUE**

Must a seller be paid in full before the buyer can be considered a bona fide purchaser?

■ **DECISION AND RATIONALE**

(Woods, J.) No. A seller need not be paid in full before the buyer can be considered a bona fide purchaser. Fontana (D) relies on our antiquated holding in *Davis v. Ward* [a buyer becomes a bona fide purchaser only upon payment in full]. The *Davis* payment of value rule cannot be reconciled with modern real property law and practice. The *Davis* rule was premised in part on the assertion that a purchaser who loses his property is "not hurt" if he has not fully paid for the land. This claim is inconsistent with modern market considerations. Any purchaser without notice who makes a down payment and unequivocally obligates himself to pay the balance has every reason to believe that, if he makes the payments when due, his right to the property will be secure. Such a purchaser may drastically alter his position by, for example, selling his prior residence and making significant improvements to the property. The landowner cannot be adequately redressed by simply returning the money he paid so far. Real property is

---

unique and its loss cannot be compensated in money. Furthermore, the *Davis* holding cannot rationally be applied to cases involving only constructive notice. A completely innocent purchaser who has only partially paid should not be punished for simply living up to his payment obligations. Moreover, he should not be required to undertake a title search before each and every payment (360 title searches for a typical 30-year note). Finally, applying *Davis* would unfairly penalize the Lewises for paying cash for the property, rather than financing the purchase price. In *Davis,* the court recognized that if the buyer had taken out a mortgage and given a note to the bank, he could be a bona fide purchaser because the seller would have been fully paid. On the other hand, a buyer who gives a note to the seller would only be considered a bona fide purchaser when he made his final payment to the seller. This distinction makes no sense. It unfairly penalizes a buyer who arranges a cash transaction with the seller rather than taking out a mortgage. We therefore issue a peremptory writ of mandate directing the superior court to vacate its order denying the Lewises (P) motion for summary judgment, and thereafter issue a new order granting the motion and expunging the lis pendens.

Analysis:

This well-reasoned holding effectively overrules the "payment of value" rule. In modern real property transactions, few buyers can make a full cash payment at the time of the sale. Rather, buyers typically finance the purchase price, either through the seller or by taking out a mortgage with a bank. In either case, the buyer is entitled to take possession of the property even though he has not yet fully paid the price. While the buyer does not have legal title until he pays off the mortgage or the note, he is in every other way the true owner of the property. When considering whether a buyer is a bona fide purchaser, it should make no difference when the seller is fully paid. The opinion raises some strong policy justifications for the court's holding. Buyers who take possession under a note or mortgage often drastically alter their position based on the understanding that they own the property. Buyers sell their prior residences, move their families, and improve the new property even though they do not yet have legal title. The unique nature of real property makes it impossible to compensate the buyer merely by refunding what he has already paid. The opinion can be questioned only for failing to take into account the equitable considerations involving Fontana Films' (D) interest. Apparently, Fontana (D) could not record its lis pendens until it knew that someone was trying to buy the property over which Fontana (D) purportedly held an interest. Fontana (D) recorded its lis pendens immediately, and it probably was not Fontana's (D) fault that the lis pendens was not indexed until after the Lewises (P) gave the seller their note.

■ CASE VOCABULARY

EXPOSTULATING: Reasoning in an effort to dissuade or correct.

LIS PENDENS: A notice of lawsuit affecting title to property.

Harper v. Paradise

(Remaindermen) v. (Subsequent Grantees)

233 Ga. 194, 210 S.E.2d 710 (1974)

SUBSEQUENT GRANTEES ARE HELD TO INQUIRY NOTICE OF THE CONTENTS OF
PRIOR RECORDED DEEDS IN THE CHAIN OF TITLE

■ **INSTANT FACTS** The Paradises, who claim title to property dating back to a 1928 deed, are challenged by Clyde Harper (P), who asserts that the Paradises had notice of a prior deed in which Clyde (P) was the remainderman.

■ **BLACK LETTER RULE** Subsequent grantees are held to inquiry notice of the contents of prior recorded deeds in the chain of title for purposes of a race-notice recording act.

■ **PROCEDURAL BASIS**

Appeal from directed verdict determining title to land.

■ **FACTS**

In 1922, Susan Harper conveyed a deed for a farm to Maude Harper, for life with remainder in fee simple to Maude's named children, including Clyde (P). The deed was misplaced and not recorded until 1957, when Clyde (P) found the deed in a trunk and recorded it. Susan died in or about 1925 and was survived by her heirs. In 1928, all of the heirs except one (John Harper) executed a deed to Maude. The language of this deed, which was recorded in 1928, expressly noted that the prior deed from Susan to Maude had been lost. In 1933, Maude executed a deed which purported to convey the property to Ella Thornton as security for a loan. When Maude defaulted on the loan, Ella foreclosed. Ella received a sheriff's deed in 1936, which she recorded in 1936. An unbroken chain of title existed between Ella and the Paradises (D), who were grantees to a 1955 deed which was recorded in 1955. The Paradises (D) also assert title by adverse possession which began in 1940. The Paradises (D) claim their direct title from the 1928 deed from Susan's heirs to Maude. Clyde (P) alleges that the Paradises (D) do not hold valid title because the 1928 deed provided notice of the prior 1922 deed to Maude. Maude died in 1972. From a directed verdict in favor of the Paradises (D), Clyde (P) appeals.

■ **ISSUE**

Are subsequent grantees held to have inquiry notice of the contents of prior recorded deeds?

■ **DECISION AND RATIONALE**

(Ingram, J.) Yes. Subsequent grantees are held to have inquiry notice of the contents of prior recorded deeds. The 1928 deed, on which the Paradises (D) rely to establish their chain of title, expressly referenced the 1922 deed to Maude. Thus, Maude is bound to have taken the 1928 deed with knowledge of the 1922 deed. The recitals in the 1928 deed put any subsequent purchaser on notice of the earlier misplaced or lost deed. Thus, the 1928 deed is not entitled to priority, even though it was recorded years before the 1922 deed. Furthermore, the Paradises (D) cannot rely on the 1922 deed, because any interest they may have obtained under this deed would only be Maude's life estate, which terminated upon her death in 1972. We conclude that it was incumbent upon the Paradises (D) to ascertain through diligent inquiry the contents of the 1922 deed. The 1928 deed provides constructive notice of the 1922 deed. However, the

---

Paradises (D) did not make any effort to inquire as to the interests conveyed in the 1922 deed when they purchased the property in 1955. Furthermore, the Paradises (D) cannot claim title by adverse possession from 1940 to 1955, because the adverse possession period would not have begun to run until Maude's death in 1972. Reversed and remanded with judgment to be entered in favor of Clyde (P).

Analysis:

The 1928 deed to Maude stated, on its face, that a prior deed existed. Even though the 1928 deed was recorded first, it cannot take priority over the 1922 deed because there was not a lack of notice. Thus, at its foundation, this case deals with the issue of notice. A subsequent purchaser for value is protected by a race-notice statute only if he acquires title without notice of the prior deed and if he records first. The notice need not be actual notice. Subsequent grantees must make some effort to determine if prior deeds existed. A simple analysis of the language of the 1928 deed would have revealed the prior 1922 deed, and thus the Paradises (D) do not meet the "notice" requirement of the recording statute.

■ CASE VOCABULARY

PLAT: A map of a parcel of property, showing boundaries and location.

REMAINDERMAN: The person who gains title to property once the prior tenancy ends, *e.g.*, by death of a life tenant.

Waldorff Ins. and Bonding, Inc. v. Eglin National Bank

(Condominium Owner) v. (Mortgagee)

453 So.2d 1383 (Fl. Dist. Ct. App. 1984)

ACTUAL POSSESSION GIVES CONSTRUCTIVE NOTICE TO ALL WHO MAY CLAIM AN
ADVERSE INTEREST

■ **INSTANT FACTS** A bank attempts to foreclose on mortgages secured by condominiums, executed when one of the condo units subject to the mortgage was openly possessed and owned by another party.

■ **BLACK LETTER RULE** Actual possession gives constructive notice to the world of any right which the person in possession is able to establish.

■ **FACTS**

Choctaw Partnership developed certain properties in Okaloosa County, Florida by constructing condominiums. In June 1972, Choctaw executed a promissory note and mortgage on the properties. The $1.1 million note and mortgage was eventually assigned to Eglin National Bank (Bank) (P) in January 1975, when less than $42,000 remained due on the note and mortgage. In April 1973, Waldorff Insurance and Bonding, Inc. (D) entered into a purchase agreement with Choctaw to buy Condo Unit 111. Waldorff (D) began occupancy of the unit immediately, continually occupying and maintaining the unit until the date of the hearing. In October 1973, Choctaw executed another note and mortgage for $600,000 in favor of the Bank (P). Unit 111 was included in this mortgage. In June 1974, Choctaw executed yet another note and mortgage in favor of the Bank for $95,000, securing a number of units including Unit 111. In March 1975, Choctaw, an insurance client of Waldorff (D), agreed to consider the purchase price of Unit 111 paid in full in exchange for a past due debt for insurance premiums owed by Choctaw to Waldorff (D). Waldorff (D) wrote off the debt on their taxes, and Choctaw executed a quitclaim deed in favor of Waldorff (D). In 1976, the Bank brought a foreclosure action against Choctaw. A final judgment of foreclosure was entered in September 1976, but this judgment explicitly retained jurisdiction to determine the ownership of Unit 111. Finally, in February 1983, a hearing on this issue was held. The trial court determined that the Bank's (P) ownership interest was superior to Waldorff's (D). The court held that Waldorff (D) did not have superior title, finding that Waldorff's (D) occupancy of Unit 111 was equivocal because Choctaw allowed several other condo units to be used for free, and finding that Waldorff (D) did not pay adequate consideration for Unit 111 so its quitclaim deed was void. Waldorff (D) appealed.

■ **ISSUE**

Does actual possession give constructive notice to all who claim an adverse ownership interest in a piece of property?

■ **DECISION AND RATIONALE**

(Shivers, J.) Yes. Actual possession gives constructive notice to all who claim an adverse ownership interest in a piece of property. In the situation at hand, Waldorff (D) openly and exclusively occupied and possessed Unit 111 at the time Choctaw executed the October 1973 and June 1974 mortgages to the Bank (P). Thus, the Bank (P) is held to have had constructive notice of Waldorff's (D) adverse title, so the Bank (P) cannot claim the benefit of the recording

---

act. It is irrelevant that several other condo units were occupied by persons who possessed no legal or equitable title to the units. The units were intended to be conveyed as separate parcels, and thus the status of the other units is inconsequential. The Bank (P) contends that it would have been difficult to ascertain whether Waldorff (D) actually had a claim of ownership interest over Unit 111. Although it would be inconvenient for the Bank (P) to inquire as to the ownership of Unit 111, we follow the holding in *Phelan v. Brady* [actual possession of real estate is sufficient to a person proposing to take a mortgage on the property, and to all the world, of the existence of an right which the person in possession is able to establish]. In addition, we hold that the trial court erred in finding that the conveyance from Choctaw to Waldorff (D) was void due to lack of consideration. Although Waldorff (D) may have erred in taking a "bad debt" tax deduction for the cancellation of its debt, the fact that Choctaw was relieved from payment of the debt constituted valuable consideration. All in all, only the Bank's (P) 1972 mortgage lien is superior to Waldorff's (D) interest, and the satisfaction of this lien can come from the 1976 foreclosure sale of the other condo units. Waldorff's (D) title is superior to the other mortgages. Reversed and remanded.

Analysis:

Here is yet another factually complicated case that can be reduced to a relatively simple holding. In brief, this case involves three mortgages that the condo developer executed in favor of the Bank (P) (presumably in exchange for loans from the Bank (P) to the developer). As a security for the loans, the developer pledged the condo units. However, the developer did not own exclusive title to at least one of the units, Unit 111, when the second and third mortgages were executed. Waldorff (D), who held equitable title to Unit 111, should not have his interest taken away merely because the developer defaulted on his loans. Further, the holding is fair because the Bank (P) could have done a little research and determined that Waldorff (D) was openly possessing Unit 111 and held an equitable interest in the unit. The Bank (P) should have assumed that anyone occupying a condo had a legal interest therein until it could conclusively determine otherwise.

■ CASE VOCABULARY

EQUIVOCAL: Ambiguous, doubtful, open to question.

Walker Rogge, Inc. v. Chelsea Title and Guaranty Co.

(Property Owner) v. (Title Insurer)

116 N.J. 517, 562 A.2d 208 (1989)

A TITLE COMPANY CAN BE HELD LIABLE UNDER A TITLE POLICY IF IT FAILS TO CONDUCT OR DISCLOSE THE RESULTS OF A REASONABLE TITLE EXAMINATION

■ **INSTANT FACTS** Chelsea did not inform Walker Rogge when a prior deed indicated that the tract being insured was about seven acres smaller than what Walker Rogge believed.

■ **BLACK LETTER RULE** If a title company fails to conduct a reasonable title examination, or having conducted such an examination, fails to disclose the results to the insured, then it runs the risk of liability under the terms of the insurance policy and not under tort for negligence.

■ **PROCEDURAL BASIS**

Appeal from judgment in action for damages.

■ **FACTS**

Walker Rogge, Inc. (P) bought a tract of land from Alexander Kosa, who had acquired the land from Aiello. Before purchase, Kosa showed John Rogge, the company president, a 1975 survey by Price Walker which sized the tract at 18.33 acres. The sale contract referred to this Price Walker survey and indicated the tract was "19 acres more or less." The tract was priced at $16,000 per acre plus the cost of an existing house, with the total price being $363,000. The contract was signed on December 12, 1979, and closed on December 31. Rogge had the title work done by Chelsea Title and Guaranty Co. (D), which had issued two earlier title policies on the property. Chelsea's files contained the deed from Aiello to Kosa, which stated that the property contained only 12.486 acres. Both the deed from Kosa to Rogge and the title insurance policy by Chelsea referred to the Price Walker survey, but did not state the tract's acreage. The policy also stated, in part, that Chelsea (D) would insure against loss or damage which would result if the title were vested differently from what was stated in the policy; if any defect on the title existed, and if the title was unmarketable. An exception to this policy was that it would not insure against loss or damage which "could be disclosed by an accurate survey and inspection of the premises." In 1985, Walker Rogge (P) hired a surveyor to examine neighboring lots. This survey indicated the Walker Rogge (P) tract was 12.43 acres. Walker Rogge (P) then filed this action, saying the loss of acreage was insurable and that Chelsea (D) was negligent in failing to disclose the size of the property. The trial court found that the policy covered the shortage in acreage, that it was a defect in title, and that the title was unmarketable. It also found the survey exception to be meaningless, and awarded damages. The Appellate Division affirmed, but remanded for damages.

■ **ISSUE**

Can a title company be held liable under its policy for not disclosing the results of its title examination to the insured?

■ **DECISION AND RATIONALE**

(Pollock, J.) Yes. If a title company fails to conduct a reasonable title examination, or having conducted such an examination, fails to disclose the results to the insured, then it runs the risk

---

of liability under the terms of the insurance policy. As a preliminary issue, the survey exception outlined by Chelsea (D) is a pretty standard one, and not vague or meaningless. Like other insurance policies, title policies are liberally construed in favor of the insured, against the insurer. Title insurance policies are also inherently complex, however, and any buyer of real estate runs the risk of not receiving all the land he or she pays for without a surveyor's help. Title insurance is no substitute for a survey. A title insurance company does not insure the quantity of land if it makes no recitals of acreage. An insured should provide the title company with an acceptable survey. Here, such a survey would have revealed the shortage. With regard to liability, the rule in this state has been that a title company is only liable under the policy and not for negligence in searching records. The premise for that rule is that the duty of the title company depends on the agreement between insurer and insured. The evidence supports the trial court's finding that Chelsea (D) was only asked to prepare a title insurance policy. The title search performed by Chelsea was simply an internal procedure done for Chelsea's (D) own benefit. Courts and commentators have split over whether a title company should be liable under negligence and under its policy if it does not disclose information that would be of interest to the insured. This court believes the relationship between the two parties is essentially contractual, with the result being the insurance policy. An insured expects that, in exchange for its premium, it will be insured against certain risks subject to the terms of the policy. Thus, a title company that fails to make, or fails to disclose the results of, a reasonable title examination runs the risk of liability under the policy. Most states make such conduct a breach of the policy, as well. Chelsea (D) could be held liable if it assumed duties in addition to the mere insurance policy and damages resulted. The trial court did not determine whether Chelsea (D) assumed a duty to assure the acreage of the tract as a result of its earlier policies on the property. This court remands to the trial court on those issues. Judgment of Appellate Division affirmed in part, reversed in part, and remanded.

Analysis:

At first glance, it may seem foolish for a title insurance company to issue a policy without conducting a careful search of the records beforehand. Such a practice would obviously lead to larger claims down the road. The fact is that most title binders and policies do not explicitly state that a title search has been performed. Despite this, potential insurance buyers treat the policy as the practical result of a search, and consider it to be a report on the defects of title. The *Walker Rogge* case seems to suggest that the insured has a right to be fully informed of any defects in title that the insurer finds in the official records of title. These defects are not limited to those that would be covered by the policy, but rather include all those that would be excepted from the policy or that the insurer believes only present an inconsequential risk. *Walker* and cases in other states represent a clear and recent trend to increase the rights of the insured.

Lick Mill Creek Apartments v. Chicago Title Insurance Co.

(Property Owner) v. (Title Insurance Company)

231 Cal.App.3d 1654, 283 Cal.Rptr. 231 (1991)

TITLE INSURANCE POLICIES ONLY COVER THE CONDITION OF TITLE, NOT THE
EFFECTS OF THE PHYSICAL CONDITION OF THE LAND ITSELF

■ **INSTANT FACTS** The apartment owners tried to have the title company indemnify them for the costs of cleaning up and removing the hazardous substances under their property.

■ **BLACK LETTER RULE** Title insurance policies are intended to protect the condition of an owner's title to land, and not provide coverage for the physical condition of the land itself.

■ **PROCEDURAL BASIS**

Appeal from judgment of dismissal after demurrer.

■ **FACTS**

Before 1979, various companies operated warehouses and chemical plants on the property in question. In addition, underground tanks, pumps, and pipelines were used in handling hazardous substances, which later contaminated the soil, subsoil and groundwater. In 1979, Kimball Small Investments (KSI) purchased the property. The California Department of Health Services ordered KSI to remedy the contamination problem, but KSI did not comply. In 1986, Lick Mill Creek Apartments (LMC) (P) bought lot 1 of the property from KSI, and also bought title insurance from Chicago Title Insurance Company (Chicago Title) (D). Before issuing the policy, Chicago Title (D) commissioned a survey and inspection of the property. LMC (P) then bought lots 2 and 3 from KSI and secured two additional policies from Chicago Title (D). The entire site was surveyed and inspected, and the inspection revealed the tanks, etc. on the property. When these policies were issued, the Department of Health Services and other state and county agencies kept records disclosing the presence of hazardous substances on the property. LMC (P) paid for the removal and cleanup of the materials after purchase, then sought indemnity from Chicago Title (D) for its (P) costs. LMC (P) claimed the hazardous substances impaired the property's marketability, and that their presence was an encumbrance on title because it would lead to cleanup costs. The policy would pay for loss sustained because of the marketability of title or any lien or encumbrance on the title. Chicago Title (D) denied coverage. The trial court sustained Chicago Title's (D) demurrer.

■ **ISSUE**

Does a title insurance policy provide coverage when physical conditions of the land result in a lowered market value and the possibility of added costs to the owner?

■ **DECISION AND RATIONALE**

(Agliano, J.) No. Title insurance policies are intended to protect the condition of an owner's title to land, and not provide coverage for the physical condition of the land itself. LMC's (P) position on the marketability of their title is unsupported. There is a distinction between the marketability of title to land and the market value of the land. An owner's inability to make economic use of the land due to an owner's earlier violations of the law does not render the title defective or

---

unmarketable under a standard insurance policy. Here, LMC (P) has only made complaints regarding conditions affecting the marketability of the land, and not the title. This distinction is recognized in other jurisdictions as well. LMC (P) thus cannot claim coverage under a title insurance policy for problems stemming from the physical condition of the property. Moreover, the fact that the property is contaminated, and as such will lead to added costs, does not constitute an encumbrance on the title. "Encumbrances" have traditionally been defined as liens, easements, restrictive covenants, and interests held by third persons. This court refuses to broaden the definition of encumbrances to include the presence of hazardous substances. The mere possibility that the government may impose a lien on the property at some future date is not enough to count as a defect in or lien or encumbrance on title. Judgment affirmed.

Analysis:

Title insurance policies are different from most other forms of insurance in that they cover only effects on title, which are often mere matters of recordation and documentation. Title policies do not come into play when the property itself suffers physical effects, either by hazardous substances as here, or by government regulations, natural changes in the land, etc. Title insurance also differs from other types of insurance in several other ways. Title insurance is, generally, paid for in a single premium. In addition, the policy coverage can last indefinitely, provided the owner and his or her heirs or devisees, or even corporate successors, continue to hold the land. However, defects that arise after the policy's date of issue cannot be the basis of a claim on the policy; the policy only covers the title as of the date it was issued.

■ **CASE VOCABULARY**

ENCUMBRANCES: Claims, liens, charges, or liabilities which are attached to and are binding on property.

GROUNDWATER: Water within the earth that is the source of wells and springs.

SUBSOIL: Weathered rock and earth beneath the surface soil.

CHAPTER NINE

Judicial Land Use Controls: The Law of Nuisance

Morgan v. High Penn Oil Co.

Instant Facts: Trailer park owner sued for injunction against operator of a nearby oil refinery which produced nauseating fumes.

Black Letter Rule: A private nuisance occurs when there is substantial interference with the use and enjoyment of land, and that interference is either intentional and unreasonable, or unintentional and the result of negligence, recklessness, or abnormally dangerous activity.

Estancias Dallas Corp. v. Schultz

Instant Facts: The Schultzes sued Estancias Dallas Corporation to permanently enjoin it from operating excessively loud equipment on a neighboring building.

Black Letter Rule: An injunction will be denied as a remedy for nuisance only if the necessity of others compels an injured party to seek damages in an action at law, and not because the party causing the nuisance has the right to work a hurt or injury to his or her neighbor.

Boomer v. Atlantic Cement Co.

Instant Facts: A court found that a cement plant constituted a nuisance to neighbors, but denied an injunction.

Black Letter Rule: Courts can grant an injunction conditioned on the payment of permanent damages to a complaining party in order to compensate him or her for the impairment of property rights caused by a nuisance.

Spur Industries, Inc. v. Del E. Webb Development Co.

Instant Facts: Spur owned a cattle feedlot well outside Phoenix for years, but when Webb's residential development grew to that area, Webb wanted the feedlot removed.

Black Letter Rule: An otherwise lawful activity can become a nuisance because others have entered the area of activity, and thus be enjoined; if the party requesting the injunction, however, is the one that creates the need for the injunction, that party can be required to provide compensation for the cost of moving or shutting down the activity.

Morgan v. High Penn Oil Co.

(Trailer Park Owner) v. (Refinery Operator)

238 N.C. 185, 77 S.E.2d 682 (1953)

THE TORT OF NUISANCE SEEKS TO PROTECT AGAINST INTERFERENCE WITH A LANDOWNER'S USE AND ENJOYMENT OF HIS PROPERTY

■ **INSTANT FACTS** Trailer park owner sued for injunction against operator of a nearby oil refinery which produced nauseating fumes.

■ **BLACK LETTER RULE** A private nuisance occurs when there is substantial interference with the use and enjoyment of land, and that interference is either intentional and unreasonable, or unintentional and the result of negligence, recklessness, or abnormally dangerous activity.

■ **FACTS**

Prior to August 1945, Morgan (P) acquired a composite tract of land which contained a dwelling-house. Immediately after purchasing the land. Morgan (P) built a restaurant and trailer park on it. Morgan (P) rented these improvements to third persons after their completion, and rented space in his (P's) home for additional income. Beginning in October 1950, High Penn Oil Company (D) operated an oil refinery approximately 1,000 feet from Morgan's (P's) property. In addition, a church, at least twenty-nine homes, a plant nursery, and various small businesses were located within a mile of the refinery. Two or three days a week, the refinery produced large amounts of nauseating gases and odors. People "of ordinary sensitiveness" within roughly two miles of the refinery were rendered uncomfortable or sick by these emissions, and thus substantially impaired the enjoyment and use of Morgan's (P's) land by himself (P) and his (P's) renters. Morgan (P) and others nearby demanded that High Penn (D) put an end to the pollution, but High Penn (D) failed to do so. High Penn (D) argued that because its (D's) use of an oil refinery is part of its (D's) occupation, it was a lawful enterprise and thus was not a nuisance at law. Also, High Penn (D) argued that the refinery can only be a nuisance if it is constructed or operated in a negligent manner. A jury found the refinery to be a nuisance, and awarded $2,500 in damages. The trial judge entered a judgment along those lines and also enjoined the High Penn Oil (D) from continuing to operate the refinery. High Penn (D) appealed.

■ **ISSUE**

Can an otherwise lawful enterprise constitute a nuisance *per accidens* or in fact if it is not constructed or operated in a negligent manner?

■ **DECISION AND RATIONALE**

(Ervin, J.) Yes. A nuisance *per accidens* or in fact may be created or maintained even without the presence of negligence. A private nuisance occurs when there is substantial interference with the use and enjoyment of land, and that interference is either intentional and unreasonable, or unintentional and the result of negligence, recklessness, or abnormally dangerous activity. The refinery is a lawful enterprise, and thus is not a nuisance *per se* [act or structure which is a nuisance at all times, regardless of circumstances]. It is nonetheless a nuisance *per accidens* [act or structure which is a nuisance by virtue of location or manner of operation]. Courts have awarded damages for such nuisances even when negligence has not been proved or alleged.

The key concept here is *sic utere tuo ut alienum non laedas* [every person should use his or her own property so as not to injure another]. Interference with a person's private use and enjoyment of land is intentional when the person whose conduct is in question acts for the purpose of causing the nuisance, knows the nuisance is a result of his or her conduct, or knows that a nuisance is substantially certain to result from his or her conduct. A person who intentionally creates or maintains a private nuisance is liable for the resulting injury to others regardless of the degree of skill exercised to avoid such injury. It is clear that High Penn (D) intentionally and unreasonably caused harmful gases and odors to escape and substantially impair Morgan's (P's) use and enjoyment of his (P's) land. Moreover, the evidence shows that High Penn (D) intends to continue operating the refinery in this same manner, and will continue to inflict irreparable injury on Morgan (P) and his (P's) use and enjoyment of his (P's) property. Morgan (P) is therefore entitled to temporary damages and injunctive relief. Judgment affirmed.

Analysis:

A nuisance per se is considered an "absolute" nuisance, one that renders a person liable no matter how reasonable his or her conduct may be. This label becomes problematic, however, in several situations, such as those involving facilities for highly flammable or explosive substances. Oil refineries, storage areas for explosives used in construction, chemical waste facilities, and other structures along these lines would seem to demand questions of reasonableness. Though these activities are abnormal and unduly hazardous, they still have legitimate purposes and fill important needs that may need to be addressed, perhaps when damages are set.

■ CASE VOCABULARY

NUISANCE *PER ACCIDENS*: Also nuisance in fact; an otherwise lawful act or structure which can become a nuisance by virtue of its location, surroundings, or the manner in which it is conducted or maintained.

NUISANCE *PER SE*: Also nuisance at law; an act or structure that is a nuisance at all times, regardless of its location, surroundings, or the manner in which it is conducted or maintained.

SIC UTERE TUO ALIENUM NON LAEDAS: Latin phrase meaning, in essence, that one should not use his or her property in a way that injures another.

TERMINUS: The end or finishing point of a transport route.

Estancias Dallas Corp. v. Schultz

(Loud Equipment Operator) v. (Neighbors)

500 S.W.2d 217 (Tex. Civ. App. 1973)

TEXAS COURT OF CIVIL APPEALS HOLDS THAT A PERMANENT INJUNCTION AGAINST THE OPERATOR OF AIR CONDITIONING EQUIPMENT WHICH CONSTITUTED A NUISANCE TO NEIGHBORING RESIDENTS WAS PROPER AFTER A BALANCING OF THE EQUITIES

■ **INSTANT FACTS** The Schultzes sued Estancias Dallas Corporation to permanently enjoin it from operating excessively loud equipment on a neighboring building.

■ **BLACK LETTER RULE** An injunction will be denied as a remedy for nuisance only if the necessity of others compels an injured party to seek damages in an action at law, and not because the party causing the nuisance has the right to work a hurt or injury to his or her neighbor.

■ **FACTS**

In March or April 1969, an eight-building apartment complex was completed next to the home of Thad Schultz and his wife (Ps) in the City of Houston. Shortly after this completion, Estancias Dallas Corporation (D) began operating a large, single air conditioning unit to serve the entire complex. The unit is located five and one-half feet from the Schultzes (Ps') property line, and roughly seventy feet from their (Ps') bedroom. This unit sounds very much like a jet engine or helicopter. This noise prevents the Schultzes (Ps) from carrying on normal conversations within their (Ps') home, and also interferes with their sleep at night. As a result of this noise, the value of the Schultzes' property went from $25,000 to $10,000. The original owner of the apartment complex claimed that this air conditioning system cost about $80,000 to construct. Separate units for each of the eight buildings would have cost $120,000, and changing to this latter system would cost between $150,000 to $200,000. According to the owner, these apartments could not be rented without air conditioning. At the time, there was no shortage of apartments in the city of Houston. The jury found that the noise from the air conditioning equipment constituted a permanent nuisance. The court granted the Schultzes (Ps) a permanent injunction against Estancias (D), as well as $10,000 in interim damages, considering material personal discomfort, inconvenience, annoyance, and impairment of health as elements of damages. Estancias (D) appealed, claiming in part that the court had erred in failing to balance the equities in their favor.

■ **ISSUE**

Can a court properly grant an injunction to a party complaining of a permanent nuisance if the harm the complaining party has suffered is less than the harm the party causing the nuisance would suffer from the injunction?

■ **DECISION AND RATIONALE**

(Stephenson, J.) Yes. In determining whether to grant an injunction, a court, according to the doctrine of balancing of equities, will consider both the potential harm to the defendant and to the public if an injunction is granted, and the harm to the plaintiff if the injunction is denied. The rule of law was clearly established by the Texas Supreme Court in *Storey v. Central Hide and Rendering Co.*, 148 Tex. 509, 226 S.W.2d 615 (1950) [even though a jury finds facts constituting a nuisance, there should be a balancing of equities to determine whether an injunction should be granted]. If an injunction is not to be granted, it will not be because the party causing the nuisance has the right "to work a hurt, or injury to his neighbor." Instead, an injunction will only be denied, thereby allowing a nuisance to exist, if the necessity of others compels an injured party to seek relief in the form of damages. The Supreme Court of Texas, in deciding *Storey,* placed great emphasis on the public interest. It said that an injunction could be granted if it would cause only slight injury to the public and the nuisance-causing party compared to the injury suffered by the complaining party. Here, there is no evidence that there is a shortage of apartments in the City of Houston. Because of this, there is no indication that the public would suffer or have no place to live if the apartment complex had to go without this noisy air conditioning system. Further, there is no evidence that the 'necessity of others' compels the Schultzes (Ps) to seek relief through a suit for damages rather than one for an injunction. Judgment affirmed.

Analysis:

On the surface, this may seem to be a very unfair decision. The Schultzes (Ps) suffered, at most, $15,000 in loss of property value and $10,000 in various personal damages. Estancias (D) stands to lose up to $200,000 in dismantling the old air conditioning system and installing a new, quieter one in the eight separate units. There may be, however, other equities the court considered in its balancing test. The Schultzes (Ps) possibly had only one major asset, their home, while Estancias (D) was, presumably, a larger corporation, with more resources at its disposal. In addition, emotional costs may have been a factor if the Schultzes (Ps) needed to move to a new home. Moreover, court costs should probably be balanced as well. The court seems to have placed weight on the fact that the Schultzes (Ps) were in that area first, mentioning that the area was "a quiet neighborhood before these apartments were constructed." Estancias (D), arguably, should have known that its equipment was going to be excessively noisy, and that litigation could result from its actions.

■ CASE VOCABULARY

INJUNCTION: Judicial remedy requiring a party to refrain from doing or continuing to do a particular act or activity.

Boomer v. Atlantic Cement Co.

(Neighbor) v. (Cement Plant Operator)

26 N.Y.2d 219, 257 N.E.2d 870, 309 N.Y.S.2d 312 (1970)

COURT OF APPEALS OF NEW YORK HOLDS THAT AN INJUNCTION AGAINST THE OPERATOR OF A CEMENT PLANT WHICH CONSTITUTES A NUISANCE WILL REMAIN IN EFFECT UNLESS THE PLANT OPERATOR PAYS PERMANENT DAMAGES TO THE NEIGHBORING LANDOWNERS

■ **INSTANT FACTS** A court found that a cement plant constituted a nuisance to neighbors, but denied an injunction.

■ **BLACK LETTER RULE** Courts can grant an injunction conditioned on the payment of permanent damages to a complaining party in order to compensate him or her for the impairment of property rights caused by a nuisance.

■ **PROCEDURAL BASIS**

Appeal from judgment in actions for injunction and damages.

■ **FACTS**

Atlantic Cement Company (D), or ACC (D), runs a large cement plant near Albany. Boomer (P) and other neighboring land owners (Ps) claimed that their property interests were injured because of the high levels of dirt, smoke, and vibration that the plant produced. The trial court found this constituted a nuisance, and temporary damages were allowed in various specific amounts up to the time of trial to the respective neighbors. An injunction, however, was denied on the grounds that the total damages to Boomer and the other neighbors (Ps) was small compared to the value of ACC's (D's) operations and the damage that an injunction would inflict upon ACC (D). Boomer and the other neighbors (Ps) were also awarded $185,000 in permanent damages.

■ **ISSUE**

Can the courts grant an injunction as a remedy for a nuisance when such an injunction would have greater economic consequences for the nuisance-causing party than the nuisance itself has for the complaining party?

■ **DECISION AND RATIONALE**

(Bergan, J.) Yes. Courts can grant an injunction conditioned on the payment of permanent damages to a complaining party in order to compensate him or her for the harm caused by a nuisance. The trial court denied an injunction because of the large disparity in economic consequences between imposing the injunction and allowing the nuisance to continue. This reasoning, however, contradicts the longstanding doctrine that an injunction should be granted where a nuisance has been found and the complaining party has sustained substantial damage. Granted, following this rule literally would result in the closing of the plant. The trial court's awarding of damages, however, violates this longstanding rule. One option would be to grant the injunction, but postpone its effect until after a specified period of time. This way, technological advances would allow ACC (D) to eliminate the nuisance without shutting down its (D's) plant. There is no guarantee, however, that ACC could even make such advances on its

---

own. Further, any such advances in eliminating dust and pollution by cement plants would likely result from industry-wide efforts, and the rate of research and development by the entire cement industry is clearly out of ACC's (D's) control. For these reasons, the best option is to grant the injunction on condition that ACC (D) pays Boomer and the other neighbors (Ps) a level of permanent damages as may be fixed by the court. This court undoubtedly has the power to grant such an injunction on these conditional grounds. Also, permanent damages are allowable when the loss a complaining party could recover would be smaller than the cost of completely removing the nuisance. In essence, ACC (D) would be purchasing a servitude on the neighbors' (Ps') land. This action would preclude future recovery by Boomer and the other neighbors (Ps) or their grantees. Judgment reversed.

■ DISSENT

(Jasen, J.) Though a reversal is required here, an award of permanent damages should not be allowed in place of an injunction where substantial property rights have been impaired by the creation of a nuisance. The majority essentially allows ACC (D) to continue causing harm to the surrounding community for a fee set by the court. Moreover, once all those who complain about the nuisance are paid off, there will no longer be any incentive to correct the nuisance, and the air pollution and blasting noise will simply continue.

Analysis:

This case reflects an almost classic conflict between environmental and economic interests. In addition to the dirt, smoke, and vibration mentioned by the court, ACC also owned a quarry less than a mile away. Blasting operations there had frightened the neighborhood children and cracked the walls and ceilings of many of the nearby homes. This practice also contributed heavily to the level of air pollution. Moreover, the blasting conducted by ACC was arguably unnecessary, as it only served to completely shatter the stones in the quarry. This step could have been easily bypassed in the production of cement in favor of less explosive and violent means. At the same time, however, ACC's plant undoubtedly provided hundreds of jobs to the local population. Those same employees certainly stimulated the local economy, and contributed to the property tax base of the community—hence the conflict.

■ CASE VOCABULARY

METALLURGICAL: Having to do with the science of metals.

Spur Industries, Inc. v. Del E. Webb Development Co.

(Cattle Feeders) v. (Residential Developer)

108 Ariz. 178, 494 P.2d 700 (1972)

WHERE A COMPLAINING PARTY MOVES TO THE AREA OF A NUISANCE, AN INJUNCTION MAY BE ISSUED CONDITIONAL UPON THE COMPLAINING PARTY PAYING DAMAGES CAUSED BY ISSUANCE OF THE INJUNCTION

■ **INSTANT FACTS** Spur owned a cattle feedlot well outside Phoenix for years, but when Webb's residential development grew to that area, Webb wanted the feedlot removed.

■ **BLACK LETTER RULE** An otherwise lawful activity can become a nuisance because others have entered the area of activity, and thus be enjoined; if the party requesting the injunction, however, is the one that creates the need for the injunction, that party can be required to provide compensation for the cost of moving or shutting down the activity.

■ **PROCEDURAL BASIS**

Appeal from judgment in action for permanent injunction.

■ **FACTS**

This case centers on an area of land located along Grand Avenue, roughly 15 miles west of the urban area of Phoenix. Roughly two miles of Grand Avenue, running east to west, is Olive Avenue. This area was first put to agricultural use in 1911, and was used primarily for that purpose until 1959. In 1954, Youngtown, a retirement community for senior citizens, was established in this area. In 1956, a separate company developed feedlots about one-half mile south of Olive Avenue. In April and May of 1959, between 7,500 and 8,500 head of cattle were being fed. In May 1959, Del E. Webb Development Company (P) began work on a residential development later known as Sun City. Webb (P) purchased about 20,000 acres of farmland, land that was less expensive than land closer to Phoenix, for this purpose. In 1960, Spur Industries, Inc. (D) bought the feedlots and began expanding them. In January 1960, Webb (P) began offering homes two and one-half miles north of the Spur lots. By May 1960, roughly 500 houses were completed or being built. At this time, Webb (P) did not consider odors from Spur's (D's) lots to be a problem and continued its southward expansion. By 1962, the feedlots had expanded from 35 to 114 acres. By December 1967, Webb's (P's) property reached Olive Avenue and Spur's (D's) lots were within 500 feet of Olive Avenue, on its southern side. Webb (P), but neither the citizens of Sun City nor Youngtown, filed an action to enjoin Spur's (D's) operation of the feedlots, claiming it was a public nuisance because of the flies and odor blown from the lots to Sun City. At the time of Webb's (P's) complaint, Spur (D) was feeding between 20,000 and 30,000 head of cattle. In addition, the cattle produced over a million pounds of wet manure per day. Although Spur (D) practiced good management of the lots, the odor and flies nonetheless created an annoying if not unhealthy situation. Citizens of Sun City expressed several complaints about this situation, and Webb (P) had difficulty in selling new homes in the area.

■ ISSUE

(1) Can an otherwise lawful activity become a nuisance because others have entered the area of the activity, and thus be subject to injunction? (2) If such an activity can be enjoined, should the party requesting the injunction be required to provide compensation for the cost of ending the activity?

■ DECISION AND RATIONALE

(Cameron, J.) (1) Yes. An otherwise lawful activity can become a nuisance because others have entered the area of activity, and so the party causing the nuisance may be enjoined. A public nuisance affects the rights enjoyed by citizens as members of the general public. Here, it is clear that the feedlots amounted to both a public and a private nuisance as far as the southern residents of Sun City were concerned. Section 36–601 of Arizona state law lists public nuisances dangerous to public health, and includes "Any condition or place in populous areas which constitutes a breeding place for flies . . . which are capable of carrying and transmitting disease-causing organisms to any person or persons." The Sun City development satisfies the populous area requirement of the law. Moreover, as Webb (P) suffered an injury in the form of loss of sales, it (P) had standing to enjoin the nuisance. (2) Yes. The party requesting the injunction can be required to provide compensation for the cost of moving or shutting down the activity. Courts of equity must protect not only the public interest, but also the operators of lawful businesses whose activities become nuisances because of the encroachment of others. In such "coming to the nuisance cases," courts have held that parties may not obtain relief for injuries after they knowingly came into an area reserved for industrial or agricultural use. The law of nuisance, however, is elastic, not rigid. The goal should be to promote what is fair and reasonable under all the circumstances. Here, Spur (D) and its predecessors had no idea when they began their feedlot efforts that a new city would spring up and force their relocation. Spur (D) must move because of a proper regard for the public interest. Likewise, Webb (P) is entitled to relief because of the damage to people who bought homes in Sun City. Nonetheless, it would be unfair to allow a developer who has taken advantage of lower land prices in a rural area to develop a new city to use that city as a means of chasing a nuisance away without compensating the one who has to move. This kind of relief is limited to a case where a developer has introduced the very population which renders the lawful activity a nuisance. Judgment affirmed in part, reversed in part, and remanded.

Analysis:

The court calls Spur's (D's) operation of the feedlot both a public and a private nuisance. Courts usually hold that impairment of a person's use and enjoyment of his or her land, as was the case here, constitutes a private nuisance, regardless of how many people are hurt by the nuisance. Such an action can also be a public nuisance if it interferes with a more general public right, again as in *Spur*. Because a private nuisance is created when the use and enjoyment of land is interfered with, only an owner of land, or of an interest in land, can file a suit. With a public nuisance, any member of the public can sue. Generally, though, only a person who can show he or she has sustained injury or damage that is different from that suffered by the rest of the public can actually file a claim.

■ CASE VOCABULARY

CONFLUENCE: The place where two rivers flow into each other and form one river.

CHAPTER TEN

Private Land Use Controls: The Law of Servitudes

Willard v. First Church of Christ, Scientist

Instant Facts: McGuigan sold Petersen a lot with an easement allowing nearby churchgoers to park on it, but Petersen sold it to Willard without mentioning the easement.

Black Letter Rule: A grantor can reserve an easement in property for a person other than the grantee.

Holbrook v. Taylor

Instant Facts: Holbrook tried to block off a road on his property after Taylor used it extensively while building a tenant house for himself.

Black Letter Rule: A license cannot be revoked after the licensee has erected improvements on the land at considerable expense while relying on the license.

Van Sandt v. Royster

Instant Facts: Van Sandt claimed he never granted an easement for a sewer drain which connected his house to two others and flooded his basement.

Black Letter Rule: The implication of an easement will depend on the circumstances under which the conveyance of land was made, including the extent to which the manner of prior use was or might have been known by the parties; each party will be assumed to know about reasonably necessary uses which are apparent upon reasonably prudent investigation; an easement may be implied for a grantor or grantee on the basis of necessity alone.

Othen v. Rosier

Instant Facts: Othen used a roadway on Rosier's property to access the public highway, but Rosier later built a levee which made the road impassable for Othen.

Black Letter Rule: An easement can be created by implied reservation only when it is shown that there was unity of ownership between the alleged dominant and servient estates, that the easement is a necessity and not a convenience, and that the necessity existed at the time the two estates were severed; an easement by prescription can only be acquired if the use of the easement was adverse.

Matthews v. Bay Head Improvement Association

Instant Facts: The public sued the Bay Head Improvement Association (D) for access to a beach in the Borough of Bay Head on the Atlantic Ocean.

Black Letter Rule: The public's ability to exercise its rights under the public trust doctrine includes the right to pass across the upland beach; without some means of access, the public's right to use the shore is meaningless.

Miller v. Lutheran Conference and Camp Association

Instant Facts: Rufus Miller's executors licensed the Association to use the lake without referring to Frank Miller, who owned three-fourths of the interests in such rights.

Black Letter Rule: When two or more persons own an easement in gross, the easement must be used as "one stock," meaning that any actions involving the easement must be made with common consent of all the owners.

Brown v. Voss

Instant Facts: Voss (D) blocked off a private road easement for parcel B after Brown (P) started building a house that would sit on both parcels B and C.

Black Letter Rule: If an easement benefits its owner in the use of a particular parcel of land, any extension of the easement to other parcels is a misuse of the easement.

Preseault v. United States

Instant Facts: Property owners sued the Government for an unauthorized taking after the Government authorized the conversion of an abandoned railroad easement into a nature trail across the owners' property.

Black Letter Rule: An easement is terminated by abandonment when nonuse is coupled with an act manifesting either a present intent to relinquish the easement or a purpose inconsistent with its future existence.

Tulk v. Moxhay

Instant Facts: Tulk had a covenant which required maintenance of a garden on some land, but Moxhay later tried to put buildings on it after buying it.

Black Letter Rule: A covenant will be enforceable in equity against a person who purchases land with notice of the covenant.

Sanborn v. McLean

Instant Facts: The McLeans tried to build a gas station on their lot in a residential district, but were enjoined from doing so by their neighbors.

Black Letter Rule: An equitable servitude can be implied on a lot, even when the servitude is not created by a written instrument, if there is a scheme for development of a residential subdivision and the purchaser of the lot has notice of it.

Neponsit Property Owners' Association, Inc. v. Emigrant Industrial Savings Bank

Instant Facts: Emigrant Bank took title to land previously deeded by Neponsit Realty, and the Neponsit Association tried to foreclose a lien contained in the earlier deed.

Black Letter Rule: An affirmative covenant to pay money for improvements or maintenance done in connection with, but not upon the land which is to be subject to the burden of the covenant does touch and concern the land, and a homeowners' association, as the agent of the actual owners of the property, can rightfully enforce the covenant.

Shelley v. Kraemer

Instant Facts: A black couple were buying a house while unaware of a racially based restrictive covenant on that street; the white homeowners tried to stop them.

Black Letter Rule: Judicial enforcement of a restrictive covenant based on race constitutes discriminatory state action, and is thus forbidden by the equal protection clause of the Fourteenth Amendment of the Constitution.

Western Land Co. v. Truskolaski

Instant Facts: Homeowners want to prevent a shopping center from being built in their subdivision, even though the surrounding area has become more crowded and more commercialized.

Black Letter Rule: A restrictive covenant establishing a residential subdivision cannot be terminated as long as the residential character of the subdivision has not been adversely affected by the surrounding area, and it is of real and substantial value to the landowners within the subdivision.

Rick v. West

Instant Facts: West bought land from Rick under a restrictive covenant, and refused to release the covenant when Rick attempted to sell similar land to a hospital.

Black Letter Rule: A landowner in a subdivision under a restrictive covenant has the right to insist upon adherence to the covenant even when the other owners consent to its release.

Nahrstedt v. Lakeside Village Condominium Association, Inc.

Instant Facts: Nahrstedt wants to continue living with her three cats in her condominium, in violation of the recorded covenants, conditions and restrictions governing the condominium.

Black Letter Rule: The enforceability of restrictions on the ownership and possession of pets should be decided in a trial court after evidence is heard as to whether the restriction was reasonable as applied to the particular facts of a case.

40 West 67th Street Corp. v. Pullman

Instant Facts: After a shareholder-tenant moved into his cooperative apartment, he began engaging in outrageous conduct directed particularly at his upstairs neighbors, and the cooperative board ultimately terminated his tenancy; he sued, and the courts disagreed as to whether the business judgment rule applied to the board's action.

Black Letter Rule: *Levandusky* established a standard of review analogous to the corporate business judgment rule for a shareholder-tenant challenge to a decision of a residential cooperative corporation.

Willard v. First Church of Christ, Scientist

(Realtor) v. (Church)

7 Cal.3d 473, 102 Cal.Rptr. 739, 498 P.2d 987 (1972)

CALIFORNIA SUPREME COURT HOLDS THAT AN EASEMENT CAN BE CREATED IN FAVOR A THIRD PERSON BY RESERVATION

■ **INSTANT FACTS** McGuigan sold Petersen a lot with an easement allowing nearby churchgoers to park on it, but Petersen sold it to Willard without mentioning the easement.

■ **BLACK LETTER RULE** A grantor can reserve an easement in property for a person other than the grantee.

■ PROCEDURAL BASIS

Appeal from judgment in action to quiet title.

■ FACTS

Genevieve McGuigan owned two lots, numbered 19 and 20, in Pacifica, California. These lots were located across the street from the First Church of Christ, Scientist (D). McGuigan was a member of this church (D), and she allowed lot 20, which was vacant, to be used as a parking lot during church (D) services. She sold lot 19 to Petersen, who used the building on that lot for office space. Wishing to resell the lot, Petersen listed it with Donald E. Willard (P), a Realtor. At the time, Petersen did not own lot 20. He did approach McGuigan with an offer to buy it. McGuigan would only sell the lot if the church (D) could continue to use it for parking space. She then had the church's (D) attorney draw up a provision for the deed to the lot stating that the change of ownership was "subject to an easement for automobile parking during church hours . . . such easement to run with the land only so long as the property for whose benefit the easement is given is used for church purposes." After this clause was inserted in the deed, McGuigan sold the property to Petersen, and he recorded the deed. Willard (P) paid Petersen the agreed purchase price and received Petersen's deed ten days later. Willard (P) recorded this deed, which did not mention an easement for parking by the church (D). Apparently, Petersen did mention that the church (D) would want to use lot 20 for parking, but did not tell him of the easement clause in his deed from McGuigan. Willard (P) became aware of this clause several months after he bought the lot, and then began an action to quiet title against the church (D). McGuigan testified in court that she had bought lot 20 to provide parking for the church (D). She also stated she would not have sold it unless she was sure the church (D) could use it for parking. While the trial court found that both McGuigan and Petersen intended to convey an easement for the church (D), the easement clause in the deed was invalid because a person cannot reserve an interest in property to a stranger to the title.

■ ISSUE

Can a property owner, in granting his or her property to a second person, reserve an easement in the property for a third person?

■ **DECISION AND RATIONALE**

(Peters, J.) Yes. An owner who is granting property to a second person can reserve an easement in that property for a third person. The old common law rule stated that such a reservation of an interest was not possible. This rule was based on the feudal concept of reservation from a grant. In that time, a grantor could pass his whole interest in property to a grantee, but a new interest was created in the grantor. Early common law courts opposed the possibility of vesting an interest in a third party. While California used to follow this rule very closely, today's courts should not feel so restrained by feudal methods. The main objective should be carrying out the intent of the grantor. Thus, property grants are to be treated in the same way as contracts. Dealing with grants under the more rigid feudal approach would lead to unfair results. This is because the original grantee has likely paid a reduced price on the property in exchange for allowing a certain use of the property to continue. Willard (P) has not presented any evidence that he (P) or any others have relied on the common law rule when purchasing the property. Neither can Willard (P) claim he was prejudiced because the lot had not been used by the church (D) for an extended period of time. Indeed, the church (D) used lot 20 for parking throughout the period when Willard (P) was trying to buy it. Here, the interests of the grantors outweigh the interests the grantees may have if the old rule is followed. Looking at the clause as a whole, it is clear that McGuigan and Petersen intended to convey the easement for parking to the church (D). Judgment reversed.

Analysis:

There used to be serious questions in early English and American law as to whether a grantor, particularly one who owned a neighboring parcel of land, could maintain an easement on the granted property after its conveyance. Over the years, these concerns have been eased, and it is generally settled that such an easement can be reserved in the instrument of conveyance (*e.g.*, a deed). Likewise, most jurisdictions today hold that an easement of this kind cannot be held in favor of a third person, as was done in *Willard*, generally because a third party would have no interest in the land being conveyed from which the third party could reserve an easement in the first place. Many legal commentators are critical of the predominant ban on third party easements, which the Third Restatement of Property also refused to adopt. While the question is by no means completely resolved, grantors may avoid this problem of reservation by simply making explicit grants of the given property and of the desired easement in one deed.

■ **CASE VOCABULARY**

ABUTTING: Bordering on; sharing a boundary.

ESCROW: A legal document, money, or some other property of value delivered from one person to a third person and held by that person until some agreed upon condition or event occurs, at which point the third person then delivers the held property to the second person as intended.

[handwritten margin notes: "treated like a K"; "important"; "permissible to reserve an easement in favor of 3rd parties —but this is a minority rule —look to see what jurisdiction you're in"]

Holbrook v. Taylor

(Landowner) v. (House Builder)

532 S.W.2d 763 (Ky. 1976)

A LICENSE IS IRREVOCABLE ONCE THE LICENSEE HAS RELIED ON THE LICENSE TO HIS OR HER EXPENSE OR DETRIMENT

- ■ **INSTANT FACTS** Holbrook tried to block off a road on his property after Taylor used it extensively while building a tenant house for himself.

- ■ **BLACK LETTER RULE** A license cannot be revoked after the licensee has erected improvements on the land at considerable expense while relying on the license.

■ PROCEDURAL BASIS

Appeal from judgment in action for declaratory and injunctive relief.

■ FACTS

Mr. and Mrs. Holbrook (D) purchased the property in question in 1942. Two years later, they (D) allowed a mining road to be cut on the property. The road was used for that purpose until 1949, and the Holbrooks (D) received a royalty for use of the road during that period. In 1965, the Taylors (P) bought a three-acre building site next to the Holbrooks' (D) property. The Taylors (P) built a house on that site the following year. During the preparation for and the actual building of the house, the Taylors (P) were permitted to use the roadway for access for workmen, for transporting equipment and materials, and for the construction and improvement of the house. The Taylors' (P) home was completed at a cost of $25,000. After it was completed, the Taylors (P) continued to use the road on a regular basis. At trial, Mr. Holbrook (D) testified that he (D) allowed the Taylors (P) to use and repair the road so they (P) could reach their (P) home. This was the only location where a road could be created to provide an access route. The Taylors (P) widened the road and graveled part of it at a cost of roughly $100. The Holbrooks (D) and Taylors (P) had no disagreement over the use of the road until 1970. Then, according to Mr. Holbrook (D), he (D) wanted the Taylors (P) to give him (D) a writing which would relieve him (D) of any responsibility in case someone were injured or otherwise damaged on the old mining road. The Taylors (P) testified that the writing was an attempt to make them (P) buy the land the road was situated on for $500. The disagreement continued, and the Holbrooks (D) later raised a steel cable across the road to block passage, and set up "no trespassing" signs. The Taylors (P) then filed suit to remove the obstructions and to declare their (P) right to use the road without interference.

■ ISSUE

Can an easement be established by estoppel, or reliance?

■ DECISION AND RATIONALE

(Stemberg, J.) Yes. An easement can be established by estoppel, even when the person making use of the property does not do so adversely, but with the permission of the property owner. It has long been recognized that a right to the use of a roadway over another person's land may be established by estoppel. The established rule in this state was set forth by this court in *Lashley Telephone Co. v. Durbin,* 190 Ky. 792, 228 S.W. 423 (1921). As stated in that case, a licensor may not revoke a license which includes the right to erect structures and acquire an interest in the land similar to an easement after the licensee has exercised the privilege of the license and erected improvements on the land at considerable expense. Here, it is clear that the Taylors (P) used the road with the consent, or at least the tacit approval, of the Holbrooks (D). Moreover, the Taylors (P) used the road to build and improve their $25,000 home, and widened and maintained the road at their own additional expense. These facts satisfy the requirements of the Lashey rule. Thus, the Taylors' (P) license to use the road may not be revoked, and their (P) right to use the road has been established by estoppel. Judgment affirmed.

Analysis:

Essentially, the Court here took a presumably oral agreement for a use of land out of the realm of the Statute of Frauds. The estoppel theory, as explained here, is one of the most widely used methods of avoiding the Statute. Some courts, particularly those in California and Illinois, have used even stronger terms to back estoppel in the past. These decisions have stated that allowing a grantor to revoke a license in such circumstances would work a "fraud" against the grantee. Several experts, most notably Judge Clark, have dismissed the use of the fraud theory as overkill, saying that the use of estoppel is sufficient to protect the license. The doctrine of equitable part performance is also demonstrated in this case. Basically, the idea is that the act of improving the property is tangible evidence that the license, or "oral easement," actually exists. Thus, one would not need to rely on the oral statements of the licensor and licensee alone, but rather the improvements themselves would attest to the presence of the easement.

■ CASE VOCABULARY

EGRESS: Exit; the path for, or the act of, going out.

ESTOPPEL: Term which denotes that one person is prevented from claiming a particular right because another person was entitled to rely on such conduct and has acted on that reliance.

INGRESS: Entrance; the path for, or the act of, entering.

PROBATIVE: Tending or able to prove an issue or fact.

SERVIENT: Denotes that which is burdened with or subject to a servitude; the estate that benefits from an easement, by contrast, is called the "dominant" estate.

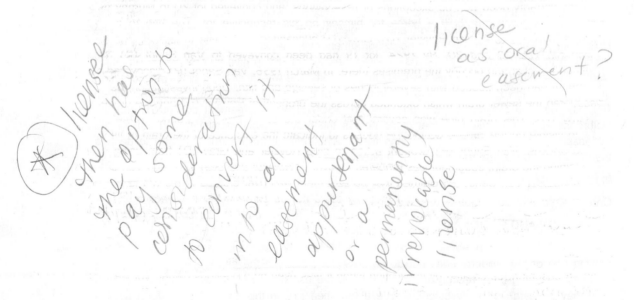

Van Sandt v. Royster

(Flooded West Neighbor) v. *(Center Neighbor)*

148 Kan. 495, 83 P.2d 698 (1938)

AN EASEMENT CAN BE IMPLIED FROM THE CIRCUMSTANCES SURROUNDING THE CONVEYANCE OF THE LAND, INCLUDING THE PRIOR USE OF THE LAND

■ **INSTANT FACTS** Van Sandt claimed he never granted an easement for a sewer drain which connected his house to two others and flooded his basement.

■ **BLACK LETTER RULE** The implication of an easement will depend on the circumstances under which the conveyance of land was made, including the extent to which the manner of prior use was or might have been known by the parties; each party will be assumed to know about reasonably necessary uses which are apparent upon reasonably prudent investigation; an easement may be implied for a grantor or grantee on the basis of necessity alone.

■ **PROCEDURAL BASIS**

Appeal from judgment in action for injunctive relief.

■ **FACTS**

In 1904, Laura Bailey owned a plot of land lying directly south of Tenth Street and east of Highland Avenue in Chanute, Kansas. This plot was divided into three lots numbered, from east to west, as lots 19, 20, and 4. Bailey's home was on lot 4, the eastern part of her land. Early that year, the city of Chanute built a public sewer on Highland Avenue. At roughly the same time, a private, lateral drain was built, running from the Bailey home on lot 4, across lots 20 and 19, and to the public sewer. Also that year, Bailey conveyed lot 19 to John Jones by a general warranty deed with no exceptions or reservations, and conveyed lot 20 to Murphy by a similar deed. Each one built a home for himself on his respective lot. The title to lot 20 eventually passed to Louise Royster (D). Gray (D) succeeded to the title to lot 4 by the time Bailey sold lots 19 and 20. By 1924, lot 19 had been conveyed to Van Sandt (P), who continued to own and occupy the premises there. In March 1936, Van Sandt (P) discovered his basement had been flooded with several inches of sewage and filth. Upon investigation, he (P) discovered the sewer drain which extended across the property of Royster (D) and the property of Gray (D). This drain pipe was several feet under the surface of the ground. There was nothing visible on the ground behind the houses to indicate the existence of the drain or its link to the houses. Van Sandt (P) brought action to stop Royster and Gray (D) from using and maintaining the drain. Judgment was rendered in favor of Royster and Gray (D), and Van Sandt (P) appealed. Van Sandt (P) claimed that no easement was ever created in his (P) land, and that even if one was created, his (P) property could not be burdened with it because he (P) had no notice. Royster and Gray (D) argued that an easement was created by implied reservation when lot 19 was severed from Bailey's lot as a result of the sale to Jones.

■ **ISSUE**

Can an easement be created by implication when it was used by a previous owner, yet was not readily visible to a party to the conveyance of the property?

■ **DECISION AND RATIONALE**

(Allen, J.) Yes. The implication of an easement will depend on the circumstances under which the conveyance of land was made, including the extent to which the manner of prior use was or might have been known by the parties; each party will be assumed to know about reasonably necessary uses which are apparent upon reasonably prudent investigation. An easement is an interest which a person has in another person's land. While this means an owner cannot have an easement in his or her own land, an owner can nonetheless use one part of his or her land to the benefit of another part of the land. This arrangement is generally known as a quasi-easement. Accordingly, the part of the land that benefits from this use is a quasi-dominant tenement, while the part of the land burdened with the particular use is a quasi-servient tenement. Early cases held that when the owner of the overall property transferred the quasi-servient tenement to a new owner, an implied reservation of an easement was made in favor of the conveyor of the property. Here, this factor, that the grantor of property is the one who claims the easement, is but one of many to consider in determining whether an easement can be implied. An implied easement arises as an inference of the intentions of the parties to a conveyance of land, and such an inference is to be drawn from the circumstances, not the language, of the conveyance. Under the Restatement, those circumstances should include the extent to which the manner or prior use was or might have been known by the parties. Thus, the parties will be assumed to know and to contemplate the continuance of reasonably necessary uses which would be apparent upon reasonably prudent investigation. When Jones bought lot 19, he was aware of the lateral sewer drain, and knew that it was built for the benefit of Bailey. The easement for the drain was necessary for the comfortable enjoyment of her property, and an easement can be implied on the basis of necessity alone. Moreover, Van Sandt (P) cannot claim that he (P) had no notice when he (P) bought the property. Van Sandt (P) and his (P) wife made a careful inspection of the property, and knew the house had modern plumbing and that the plumbing had to drain into a sewer. Thus, Van Sandt (P) had notice of the lateral sewer, and the easement was apparent. Judgment affirmed.

Analysis:

Note that there is no Statute of Frauds problem regarding the easement in this case because the easement does not stem from any of the language of the conveyance, but rather the circumstances of the conveyance. Of course, the Statute could very well apply to the conveyance itself. Also, note the requirement that the easement implied from the prior use be "reasonably necessary." This part of the rule has led to much litigation. While some courts still believe that the prior use must be strictly necessary to the use and enjoyment of the dominant parcel of land, most courts follow the relaxed standard of *Van Sandt*. This rule of necessity has often been interpreted to mean whatever will be convenient to the enjoyment of the dominant land. Usually, the courts have found the rule is violated if the owner of the dominant land would be put to appreciable expense to provide an alternative to the claimed easement.

■ **CASE VOCABULARY**

APPURTENANT: Essentially, connected to; an easement is appurtenant to a given parcel of land when the easement is used to the benefit of that parcel of land.

MESNE CONVEYANCES: Intermediate conveyances; those that occurred after the initial grantee and before the present holder in the whole chain of title.

Have an implied easement to tap into the drain valve based on pre-existing use

why?
1) the previous use was apparent
2) + Its continuing use is reasonably necessary for dominant land's use + enjoyment

Othen v. Rosier

(Landlocked Neighbor) v. (Neighbor with Roadway)

148 Tex. 485, 226 S.W.2d 622 (1950)

reasonable necessity is the majority rule

strict necessity is the minority rule

AN EASEMENT CAN BE IMPLIED FROM NECESSITY BASED ON THE CIRCUMSTANCES, OR BY PRESCRIPTION IF THE USE WAS ADVERSE

→ but this case was neither

■ **INSTANT FACTS** Othen used a roadway on Rosier's property to access the public highway, but Rosier later built a levee which made the road impassable for Othen.

■ **BLACK LETTER RULE** An easement can be created by implied reservation only when it is shown that there was unity of ownership between the alleged dominant and servient estates, that the easement is a necessity and not a convenience, and that the necessity existed at the time the two estates were severed; an easement by prescription can only be acquired if the use of the easement was adverse.

easement implied by strict necessity or easement created by prescription if use was adverse

■ **PROCEDURAL BASIS**

Appeal from judgment in action for injunctive relief and damages.

■ **FACTS**

Hill once owned the entire 2493-acre Tone Survey. On August 26, 1896, Hill conveyed a 100-acre tract just west of Belt Line Road, a public highway running north and south. This tract was eventually conveyed to Estella Rosier (D) and others in 1924. In 1897, Hill conveyed a 60-acre tract just southeast of, and contiguous to, the 100-acre tract to others. Albert Othen (P) acquired this tract in 1904. By this point, Hill owned a 53-acre tract just east of the 100-acre tract, and a 16.31 acre tract just west of the 60-acre tract. On January 26, 1899, Hill conveyed the 53- and 16.31- acre tracts to separate buyers. These buyers later conveyed the larger tract to Othen (P) in 1913, and the smaller tract to Rosier (D) in 1924. Othen's (P) 113 acres are not contiguous with Belt Line Road or with either of the highways that border the Tone Survey to the north and south. Before this case, Othen (P) would reach the Belt Line Road by going through a gate on the west line of his 60-acre tract and the east line of Rosier's (D) 16.31-acre tract, then into a fenced lane which runs along the south side of Rosier's (D) 100 acres. This lane went to a gate which opened out onto the Belt Line Road. The south fence was built in 1895, while the north fence and the outside gate were built in 1906. Near this exit gate was the Rosiers' (D) home, orchard, and barns. They (D) used it to haul wood and to permit their livestock to go to the pasture on the 16.31-acre tract. The Rosiers' (D) tenants on the smaller tract have also used the roadway in the same way Othen (P) has. The Rosiers (D) made all necessary repairs to the lane, and no one else recognized any obligation to maintain it. Surface waters threatened to make the road impassable and erode the Rosiers' (D) farmland. To prevent this, the Rosiers (D) built a 300-foot-long levee along the southern fence of the road. This levee made the lane so muddy that the lane was impassable, except by horseback, for several weeks at a time. Othen (P) filed suit claiming this act of the Rosiers (D) deprived him of access between the highway and his (P) home. Othen (P) wanted a temporary writ of injunction to keep the Rosiers (D) from maintaining the levee and a mandatory writ of injunction to keep the Rosiers (D) from interfering with his (P) use of the roadway. The trial court found that Othen (P) had an easement of necessity along the roadway, and ordered the Rosiers (D) to ensure that it would be in a usable condition. The Court of Civil Appeals initially affirmed the judgment but reversed the injunction because it was too vague. On rehearing, the appellate court concluded that Othen (P) has no easement either of necessity or by prescription.

■ ISSUE

Can an easement to use a roadway on a neighbor's property be implied when the owner seeking the easement has not proven the use of the roadway is a necessity, or that the use was not done with the permission of the neighboring property owner?

■ DECISION AND RATIONALE

(Brewster, J.) No. This court has held previously that an easement can be created by implied reservation only when it is shown that there was unity of ownership between the alleged dominant and servient estates, that the easement is a necessity and not a convenience, and that the necessity existed at the time the two estates were severed. As previously stated, the entire Tone Survey had been owned by Hill. Unity of ownership is satisfied. There is no evidence, however, that the roadway was a necessity when Hill conveyed the 100-acre tract on August 26, 1896 and still retained the 60-acre tract which Othen (P) now owns. At the time, it appears the roadway was merely a convenience. Hill may easily have been able to cross the 53-acre tract and go around the 100-acre tract, or be able to go around the small 16.31-acre tract, to get to the Belt Line Road. Obviously, no such easement over the 16.31 acre tract existed, as Hill still held title to that land in 1896, and thus an easement could not be created over his own land. The mere fact that Othen's (P) land is completely surrounded by other people's land does not automatically mean that Othen (P) has a way of necessity over other property. No easement by necessity can be implied here. Moreover, an easement by prescription can only be acquired if the use of the easement was adverse. If one owner's property is put to use by another by virtue of permission or license, then the non-owner cannot claim he or she has a separate right to use the property. Here, the roadway has been fenced on both north and south sides since 1906. The Rosiers (D) and their (D) tenants have used it for general farm purposes as well as to haul wood and move livestock. In light of those facts, it appears that Othen's (P) use of the roadway has been merely with the permission of the Rosiers (D). Thus, his (P) use could not develop into a prescriptive right. Othen's (P) evidence of his (P) use of the roadway prior to 1906, when the fences and gate were completed, is also too vague to establish a prescriptive right to the road. Judgment affirmed.

Analysis:

Most litigation involving easements implied from necessity stems from questions of what is "necessary." Undoubtedly, if a parcel of land is left without access to the public roads and highways—in other words, landlocked—the easement that would grant such access would meet the strictest definitions of "necessary." Most courts recognize a degree of flexibility, allowing a claimant an easement if it is necessary to make effective use of his or her land. This does not mean that the necessity requirement for prior use easements and other implied easements is to be treated synonymously. Such a treatment would be extreme, as elements of pre-existing and apparent use would be essentially meaningless. In addition, it should be noted that the requirements for use by prescription, often known as adverse use, are not identical to those for adverse possession. While both require that the possession or use must be actual, open, notorious, and hostile (or non-permissive), the adverse possession requirements that the possession be "continuous" and "exclusive" are somewhat different for prescriptive uses. For easements, the particular use is treated as being "continuous" if the claimant engages in it as often as is normal for an easement of that kind.

■ **CASE VOCABULARY**

CONTIGUOUS: Coming into contact with; adjacent.

LEVEE: A continuous ridge used to control irrigation and prevent flooding.

If landlocked, then a necessity

Matthews v. Bay Head Improvement Association

(Public Representative) v. (Beachfront Property Owners Group)

471 A.2d 355 (N.J.), *cert. denied*, 469 U.S. 821 (1984)

IN ORDER FOR THE PUBLIC TO EXERCISE ITS RIGHT TO ENJOY PUBLIC WATERS, IT MUST HAVE A WAY TO GET TO THEM

My enjoyment of the beach is increased by my ability to get to it.

stus.com

■ **INSTANT FACTS** The public sued the Bay Head Improvement Association (D) for access to a beach in the Borough of Bay Head on the Atlantic Ocean.

■ **BLACK LETTER RULE** The public's ability to exercise its rights under the public trust doctrine includes the right to pass across the upland beach; without some means of access, the public's right to use the shore is meaningless.

■ **PROCEDURAL BASIS** ·

State supreme court review of an intermediate appellate court decision.

■ **FACTS**

The Borough of Bay Head borders the Atlantic Ocean. Nine of Bay Head's streets end at the dry sand of the ocean's beach. The Bay Head Improvement Association (D) controls and supervises its beach property during the summer. Only members of the Association (D) may use the beach during the summer daytime hours. Membership in the Association (D) is generally limited to property owners in the borough. The Public Advocate (P), who stepped in after the original plaintiff, the Borough of Point Pleasant, was dismissed, asserted that the Borough of Bay Head had wrongfully denied the general public its right of access during the summer bathing season to public trust lands along the beaches in Bay Head.

■ **ISSUE**

Does the public trust doctrine include the right to gain access through and to use the dry sand area not owned by a municipality but by a quasi-public body?

■ **DECISION AND RATIONALE**

(Schreiber, J.) Yes. The public's ability to exercise its rights under the public trust doctrine includes the right to pass across the upland beach; without some means of access, the public's right to use the shore is meaningless. The public's reasonable enjoyment of the public lands and the sea cannot be realized unless some enjoyment of the dry sand area is also allowed. Under the public trust doctrine, ownership of and sovereignty over land flowed by tidal waters, which extend to the mean high water mark, is vested in the state in trust for the people. The public's right to use tidal lands and waters encompasses navigation, fishing, and recreational uses such as bathing, swimming, and other shore activities. The Bay Head Improvement Association owns the street-wide strip of dry sand at the foot of seven public streets that extends to the mean high water line. The question we must address here is whether the dry sand area that the Association owns or leases should be open to the public to satisfy the public's rights under the public trust doctrine. Our analysis turns on whether the Association may restrict its membership to Bay Head residents and thereby preclude public use of the dry sand area. We hold that membership in the association must be open to the public at large. The members, and thereby the public, will be assured access to the common beach property during the summer daytime hours and may exercise their right to swim and bathe and use the sandy

---

area. We need not go further than this, as the Public Advocate would have us do, and hold that all privately owned beachfront property must be opened to the public. Opening Association membership to the public is enough to ensure reasonable compliance with the public trust doctrine. Judgment is entered for the plaintiff against the Association. The individual property owners are dismissed.

Analysis:

Note that there is no public beach in Bay Head. If the residents of all boroughs on the Jersey Shore adopted the same policy that Bay Head did, the public would be prevented from exercising its right to enjoy the foreshore. The court would not allow the Bay Head residents to frustrate the public's rights in this manner. By limiting membership to residents, the Association was acting in conflict with the public good and contrary to the strong public policy of encouraging and expanding public access to shoreline areas. Accordingly, in order to avoid undermining the public's right under the public trust doctrine, membership in the Association had to be open to the public at large.

Miller v. Lutheran Conference and Camp Association

(Surviving Brother) v. (Dead Brother's Executors Licensee)

331 Pa. 241, 200 A. 646, 130 A.L.R. 1245 (1938)

AN EASEMENT IN GROSS CAN ONLY BE USED OR TRANSFERRED AS "ONE STOCK," WITH THE CONSENT OF ALL COMMON OWNERS

■ **INSTANT FACTS** Rufus Miller's executors licensed the Association to use the lake without referring to Frank Miller, who owned three-fourths of the interests in such rights.

■ **BLACK LETTER RULE** When two or more persons own an easement in gross, the easement must be used as "one stock," meaning that any actions involving the easement must be made with common consent of all the owners.

■ **PROCEDURAL BASIS**

Appeal from decree in action for injunctive relief.

■ **FACTS**

Frank Miller (P), his brother, Rufus Miller, and others created the Pocono Spring Water Ice Company in September 1895 to create Lake Naomi. The Company would have "the exclusive use of the water and its privileges," and was created for the purpose of "erecting a dam . . . , for pleasure boating, skating, fishing, and the cutting, storing and selling of ice." This Company built a 14-foot dam across Tunkhannock Creek in Monroe County which formed Lake Naomi. This lake was about a mile long and one-third of a mile wide. The Company granted to Frank Miller (P) and "his heirs and assigns forever, the exclusive right to fish and boat in all the waters of [the Company]" by a deed dated March 20, 1899. On February 17, 1900, Frank Miller (P) granted to Rufus Miller, his heirs and assigns forever, "all the one-fourth interest in and to the fishing, boating, and bathing rights and privileges at, in, upon and about Lake Naomi . . ." that had been conferred to him (P) by the Company in March of 1899. On the same day, Frank (P) and Rufus entered a business partnership which operated and rented boats and houses on the lake. Three-fourths of all interests were allocated to Frank (P) and one-fourth were allocated to Rufus. They exercised their privileges without interruption until Rufus' death on October 11, 1925. On July 13, 1929, the executors of Rufus Miller's estate granted a year's license to the Lutheran Conference and Camp Association (D). This license allowed the Association (D) members to boat, bathe, and fish in the lake, with a percentage of their receipts to be paid to Rufus' estate. This led Frank Miller (P) to file a suit in equity, claiming that the Association (D) was threatening to license its own guests to bathe, boat, and fish in the lake. Frank Miller (P) requested an injunction to prevent the Association (D) from trespassing, and the trial court issued the injunction. He (P) claims that the Company never conveyed bathing rights to him (P) in its 1899 grant, and thus he (P) could not and did not vest them to Rufus. Moreover, if such bathing rights were vested in him (P), Frank (P) claims all of the bathing, boating and fishing privileges were easements in gross and as such were inalienable and indivisible. The Association (D) argues that the 1899 deed to Frank (P) transferred the bathing privileges along with the others, or alternatively that he (P) and Rufus acquired the bathing privileges by prescription, thus rendering the privileges alienable and divisible.

■ ISSUE

Can one of two owners of an easement in gross grant a license to another party independently of the other owner?

■ DECISION AND RATIONALE

(Stern, J.) No. When two or more persons own an easement in gross, the easement must be used as "one stock," meaning that any actions involving the easement must be made with the common consent of all the owners. The 1899 deed cannot be construed as conveying bathing privileges to Frank Miller (P). It clearly states the grant of exclusive rights to fish and boat; bathing rights are not mentioned at all. There is evidence, however, that Frank Miller (P) acquired these bathing rights by prescription. No principle of law forbids an adverse enjoyment of an easement in gross form becoming a title by prescription. Indeed, Lake Naomi has grown into a popular summer resort, with bathing and boating facilities having particular importance. Bathing uses are listed among the purposes for which the Company was chartered. From 1900 to at least 1925, both Frank (P) and Rufus Miller systematically exercised the bathing rights in pursuit of their business partnership. It would be highly unjust, therefore, to hold that the Miller brothers did not hold a title to the bathing rights by prescription that was just as valid as the boating and fishing rights conveyed by express grant. While there is disagreement over the assignability of easements in gross such as the fishing, boating and bathing privileges involved here, the important issue to consider is their divisibility. If these easements are to be divided between the owners, the easements must be used or exercised as an entirety. In other words, one user alone cannot convey a share in the common right; such action must occur with the consent of all the owners. Here, it appears clear that Frank (P) did not wish to grant Rufus a separate right to subdivide and sublicense their lake privileges. Instead, it is clear Frank (P) intended for them to use the rights together for their business, with one-fourth of the proceeds going to Rufus and three-fourths going to himself (P). This further demonstrates that these easements should be treated as "one stock," and not by two owners separately. Decree affirmed, and costs to be paid by defendant.

Analysis:

An easement in gross is an easement that gives a property owner the right to use a servient property and does not benefit its owner in the use and enjoyment of his or her land. Transfers of these easements are different than those for easements appurtenant. As the latter kind are created to benefit a particular parcel, any transfer of title of that dominant parcel will carry the easement along with it. Of course, easements in gross for commercial purposes, as demonstrated by *Miller*, are transferable. By contrast, legal experts have speculated that "personal" easements in gross, namely those held for personal recreation and not for economic benefit, are probably not alienable. This distinction rests on the idea of grantor's intent. The belief is that a grantor would not intend the holder of an easement to transfer it when the easement was intended for the narrow purpose of benefiting the holder. The Restatement has proposed making the alienability of easements in gross depend on "the manner or the terms if their creation."

■ CASE VOCABULARY

FI. FA.: An abbreviation for the Latin phrase 'fieri facias,' which means that you "cause it to be done"; in essence, denotes a writ of execution.

RIPARIAN: Relating to the bank of a river or stream.

Brown v. Voss

(B and C Owners) v. (A Owners)

105 Wash.2d 366, 715 P.2d 514 (1986)

the scope of an easement

AN EASEMENT WHICH IS APPURTENANT TO ONE PARCEL OF LAND CANNOT BE EXTENDED TO BENEFIT ANOTHER PARCEL

■ **INSTANT FACTS** Voss (D) blocked off a private road easement for parcel B after Brown (P) started building a house that would sit on both parcels B and C.

■ **BLACK LETTER RULE** If an easement benefits its owner in the use of a particular parcel of land, any extension of the easement to other parcels is a misuse of the easement.

■ **PROCEDURAL BASIS**

Appeal from judgment in action for injunctive relief and damages.

owner of A granted easement for access to + from B only, not B+c

■ **FACTS**

In 1952, the then-owners of parcel A granted a private road easement across their property to the then-owners of parcel B for "ingress to and egress from" parcel B. The Vosses (D) acquired parcel A in 1973. The Browns (P) bought parcel B from one owner on April 1, 1977, and then parcel C from another owner on July 31, 1977. The previous owners of parcel C were not parties to the easement grant. The Browns (P) planned to build a single home that would straddle the boundary line between parcels B and C. The Browns (P) began clearing both parcels in November 1977. The Vosses (D) began trying to stop the Browns (P) from using the easement in April 1979, by which time the Browns (P) had spent over $11,000 in developing the properties. At this point, the Vosses (D) placed logs, a concrete pit, and a chain link fence within the easement. The Browns (P) sued for removal of the obstructions, an injunction against further interference with the use of the easement and damages. The Vosses (D) counterclaimed for damages and an injunction against the Browns (P) using the easement for parcel C. The trial court awarded each party $1 in damages, with the award against the Browns (P) being for a minor inadvertent trespass. The trial court also found that the Browns (P) made no unreasonable use of the easement while developing their (P) property, nor had they (P) acted unreasonably in making these developments. Also, if the Vosses' (D) injunction were granted, parcel C would be landlocked and the Browns (P) would not be able to make use of their property. The trial court also found that the Vosses (Ds) would suffer no appreciable hardship or damage their (D) requested injunction were denied. Moreover, the trial court held that framing and enforcing such an injunction would be impractical. Based on these and other findings of fact, the Vosses (D) were denied their injunction and the Browns (P) were allowed to use the easement as long as their properties were used solely for a single family residence.

■ **ISSUE**

Can the holder of a private easement use it to access a parcel of land that is not the dominant estate when there will be no increased burden on the servient estate? *NO*

■ DECISION AND RATIONALE

(Brachtenbach, J.) No. The easement in this case resulted from an express grant made in 1952. Thus, the scope of this right acquired through the easement is to be determined from the terms of the grant and the way they give effect to the intention of the parties. By the express terms of the 1952 grant, the previous owners of parcel B acquired a private easement across parcel A and the right to use it to enter and exit parcel B. While the Browns (P) acquired these same rights to enter and exit parcel B, they (P) have no such easement rights with regard to parcel C. Parcel C was not a part of the original dominant estate under the terms of the 1952 grant. If an easement benefits its owner in the use of a particular parcel of land, any extension of the easement to other parcels is a misuse of the easement. Even though, as the Browns (P) contend, their (P) use of the easement to gain access to a home located partially on parcel B and partially on parcel C is at most a mere technical misuse of the easement, it is nonetheless a misuse. This does not automatically mean that the Vosses (D) are entitled to injunctive relief. As the proceeding for determining the validity of an injunction is an equitable one, deference should be paid to the findings of the trial court unless an abuse of discretion is shown. No such abuse is demonstrated in this case. Judgment of Court of Appeals is reversed and judgment of trial court is affirmed.

■ DISSENT

(Dore, J.) While the extension of this easement to nondominant property did constitute a misuse of the easement, the Vosses (D) should be entitled to injunctive relief. Misuse of an easement is a trespass. Consequently, the Browns' (P) continued misuse of the easement in building and residing in the home they (P) have proposed would result in a continuing trespass. Damages on such a prolonged trespass would be too difficult to measure; thus, injunctive relief would be the appropriate remedy under such circumstances. The Browns (P) should have known from public records that the easement was not connected to parcel C. If an injunction were granted for the Vosses (D), the Browns (P) could still acquire access to parcel C through other means, either by renegotiating the easement or some other statutory means.

Analysis:

While damages were awarded in this case, courts have also granted injunctive relief when easements were improperly extended to other properties. *Brown* demonstrates the courts' opposition to the use of an easement for inseparable activities situated on both dominant and nondominant property simultaneously. This rule, however, does not entirely block changes in the easement over the course of time. The permitted purposes behind an easement can change and expand to a certain degree. Specifically, changes in the dominant parcel that can be reasonably anticipated can be accommodated by the easement. Similar principles control the scope of easements stemming from prescription, implication, prior use, and necessity.

■ CASE VOCABULARY

SUMP: A pit or reservoir, often used for drainage.

Preseault v. United States

(Landowner) v. (Government)

100 F.3d 1525 (Fed. Cir. 1996)

CONVERSION OF ABANDONED RAILROAD EASEMENT INTO PUBLIC NATURE TRAIL
CONSTITUTES UNAUTHORIZED TAKING OF SERVIENT ESTATE

■ **INSTANT FACTS** Property owners sued the Government for an unauthorized taking after the Government authorized the conversion of an abandoned railroad easement into a nature trail across the owners' property.

■ **BLACK LETTER RULE** An easement is terminated by abandonment when nonuse is coupled with an act manifesting either a present intent to relinquish the easement or a purpose inconsistent with its future existence.

■ **PROCEDURAL BASIS**

Appeal from judgment for defendant in action for damages for unauthorized taking of land by government.

■ **FACTS**

The Preseaults (P) owned a fee simple interest in a tract of land along Lake Champlain in Burlington, Vermont. A right-of-way ran across the land. The right-of-way had been acquired in 1899 by a railroad company which laid rails and operated a railroad on the strip. In the 1960's the State of Vermont acquired all assets of the railroad and leased the right to use the right-of-way to the Vermont Railway. The Vermont Railway operated trains over the land until 1970. In 1975 the tracks and all railroad equipment were removed from the portion of the right-of-way running over the Preseaults' (P) tract. Eight years later, Congress approved the Rails-to-Trails Act in order to preserve discontinued railroad corridors for future railroad use and to permit public recreational use of the rights-of-way. The Act empowered the Interstate Commerce Commission ("ICC") to permit discontinuance of rail services and transfer the rights-of-way to public or private groups willing to maintain the strip as a public trail. In 1986 the ICC approved an agreement between the Virginia Railway and the state of Vermont and city of Burlington to discontinue rail service over the Preseaults' (P) land and to maintain the former railroad strip as a public trail. The Preseaults (P) sued the ICC, claiming the Rails-to-Trails Act was unconstitutional. The Supreme Court held that the Act was constitutional but that the Preseaults (P) may have a remedy under the Fifth Amendment Takings Clause. The Preseaults (P) then sued the United States (D), claiming that the Government (D), through the ICC, took the Preseaults' (P) property when it authorized the conversion of the former railroad right-of-way to public trail use. The Preseaults (P) argued that the right-of-way was originally an easement, that the use for public trail purposes was beyond the scope of the easement, and that the easement had terminated by abandonment in 1970. The trial court disagreed, ruling for the Government (D). The Preseaults (P) appeal.

■ **ISSUE**

(1) Does governmental use of land that goes beyond the scope of an easement constitute a "taking" of the servient estate? (2) Is an easement terminated by mere nonuse?

■ DECISION AND RATIONALE

(Plager, J.) (1) Yes. Governmental use of land that goes beyond the scope of an easement constitutes a "taking" of the servient tenement owner's property. In the instant action, we agree with the trial court that the right-of-way was (at least for a time) an easement. When a railroad acquires an estate in land for laying track and operating railroad equipment thereon, the estate acquired is no more than that needed for the purpose, and that typically means an easement, not a fee simple estate. Assuming for the sake of argument that the easement still existed in 1986, we find that the Government's (D) use of the land for a recreational trail is not within the scope of the easement. The scope of the original easement was specifically for the transportation of goods and persons via railroad. The scope of an easement may be adjusted over time only if the change is consistent with the terms of the original grant. We agree with the majority of courts in holding that the change to a public recreational trail is not consistent with the original terms of a railroad easement. There are significant differences in the degree of the burden imposed on the Preseaults' (P) servient estate between railroad and public usage. Although railroad usage is noisy, it is far less frequent and more controlled than public pedestrians and bicyclists. (2) No. An easement is not terminated by mere nonuse. In order to terminate an easement by abandonment, there must also be acts by the owner of the dominant tenement conclusively and unequivocally manifesting either a present intent to relinquish the easement or a purpose inconsistent with its future existence. In the case at hand, we agree with the trial court in holding that the removal of the rails and all railroad equipment in 1975 constituted an abandonment. It is inconsequential that it remains *possible* to restore the railway service over the right-of-way. In addition, the actions taken by the Vermont Railway in collecting various license and crossing fees from persons crossing the track is not persuasive evidence of a purpose or intent not to abandon the use of the right-of-way for actual railroad purposes. Furthermore, in the years since 1975, neither the State nor the Railroad has made any attempt to reinstate railroad service on the right-of-way. Our determination of abandonment provides an alternative ground for concluding that a governmental taking occurred. The Government has chosen to impose upon the Preseaults' (P) property interests, and the Fifth Amendment compels compensation. Reversed and remanded.

■ DISSENT

(Justice Not Stated). We feel that the Railroad did not abandon its easement. Even though the tracks were removed, there was no clear and unequivocal signal of intent to abandon. To the contrary, the Railroad continued to enter into crossing and license agreements after 1975. On the issue of scope, a railroad easement can be used as a public trail. This merely shifts the use from one public use to another and imposes no greater burden on the servient tenement.

Analysis:

This case touches on a number of important topics related to easements, including the creation, scope, and termination of easements. The holdings are fundamental and straightforward. First, when railroads acquire estates in land for laying track and operating a railroad, the estates are typically easements. Second, the scope of easements may change over time; however, a railroad easement is limited to railroad (and possibly other transportation) uses. Third, the easements may terminate by abandonment where nonuse is coupled with an act evidencing an intent to abandon the property. In the railroad context, the act of removing all rails and equipment evidences an intent to abandon. Fourth, governmental use of an easement that goes beyond the scope of the easement, or that occurs after the easement is terminated, entitles the servient estate owner to compensation. The dissent raises some good points with respect to the scope and abandonment issues. Is it really inconsistent with the scope of a railroad easement to allow pedestrians and bicycles to use the land? This is a difficult question that depends on whether easements should be narrowly or broadly interpreted.

■ **CASE VOCABULARY**

HABENDUM CLAUSE: A clause in a deed which typically begins with "to have and to hold" and which defines the extent of ownership.

Court of equity -
The purpose is
for fairness

Tulk v. Moxhay

(Garden Seller) v. (Garden Buyer)

2 Phillips 774, 41 Eng.Rep. 1143 (1848)

[handwritten: equitable servitude]

ENGLAND COURT OF CHANCERY HOLDS THAT IT WOULD BE INEQUITABLE FOR A COVENANT THAT IS ENFORCEABLE AGAINST A SELLER OF LAND TO BE UNENFORCEABLE AGAINST A PERSON WHO PURCHASES THE LAND WITH NOTICE OF THE COVENANT

[handwritten margin: SKHa p.100-102]

■ **INSTANT FACTS** Tulk had a covenant which required maintenance of a garden on some land, but Moxhay later tried to put buildings on it after buying it.

[handwritten: really an equitable servitude]

■ **BLACK LETTER RULE** A covenant will be enforceable in equity against a person who purchases land with notice of the covenant.

[handwritten: really appears to be an equitable servitude b/c a true desire for an injunction]

■ **PROCEDURAL BASIS**

Appeal from injunction granted by Master of the Rolls.

■ **FACTS**

[handwritten: T → E → M]

In 1808, Tulk (P) sold a vacant piece of land in Leicester Square to Elms. Tulk (P) also owned several of the houses that formed the Square. The deed of conveyance contained a covenant by which Elms, his heirs, and assigns would keep and maintain the property as a pleasure ground and square garden, enclosed by an iron railing. The covenant also stated that the property was to be "uncovered with any buildings." This property passed by various mesne conveyances [intermediate conveyances between the first grantee and the current holder of title] from Elms to Moxhay (D). Moxhay's (D) purchase deed contained no similar covenant against building on the Square. Moxhay (D) did admit, however, that he (D) purchased the land with notice of the original covenant in the 1808 deed. Moxhay (D) tried to assert the right to build structures on the garden as he (D) saw fit, and Tulk (P) filed for an injunction to prevent Moxhay (D) from using the pleasure ground and garden for any purpose other than as an open area, uncovered with buildings.

■ **ISSUE**

Is a covenant enforceable against a purchaser of land when that purchaser acquired the land with knowledge of the covenant?

■ **DECISION AND RATIONALE**

(Cottenham, J.) Yes. Here, there was a clear contract between Tulk (P) and Elms, by which Elms promised not to use the land adjoining Tulk's (P) houses in the Square for anything other than a square garden. If Moxhay (D) were allowed to purchase this land from Elms and violate this contract, then any owner of land who tried to sell part of his land, like Tulk (P), would risk having his remaining land be rendered worthless. This is because the sale price of the land in question would be affected by the covenant. Moxhay (D) likely paid less for the land than he would have had to pay for land unburdened by such a covenant. If Moxhay (D) were allowed to build on the land, he (D) would have effectively received unburdened land for the lower price of burdened land. Nothing could be more inequitable than allowing this, for Moxhay (D) could then resell the unburdened land at a higher price, and thus would be unjustly enriched. If a covenant is attached to property by its original owner, no one with notice of that covenant can purchase that property and not be bound by the covenant. Decision affirmed.

Analysis:

This case created the equitable servitude. An equitable servitude is a covenant regarding the use of land that is enforceable in equity against subsequent possessors, even if the covenant itself is not enforceable at law. The traditional difference between this and a real covenant relates to the available remedies. When a real covenant is breached, the remedy is damages in a suit a law. When an equitable servitude is breached, however, the remedy is either an injunction or enforcement of a consensual lien, which secures a promise to pay money, in a suit in equity.

■ CASE VOCABULARY

ASSIGNEE: Person to whom one's property is transferred to.

ASSIGNS: Another name for assignees.

DIVERS: Various.

MASTER OF THE ROLLS: An assistant judge of the English court of equity (known as court of chancery).

MESNE CONVEYANCE: A conveyance which is between the first grantee and the present holder in the chain of title.

[Handwritten margin notes: "Yes! important"]

[Handwritten notes at bottom of page:]

Tulk owns several lots. He sells one to Elms, extracting from Elms the promise that Elms maintain the common garden

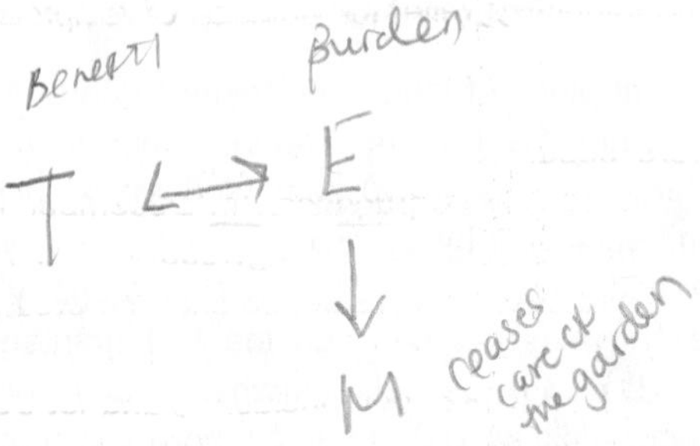

Benefit   Burden

T ⟶ E
↓
M ceases care of the garden

T sues M to enforce the promise

E burdened, T benefited

only need to ask whether the burden runs, not the benefit b/c T stays put

(even though don't need it, T + E are in a grantor-grantee relationship, so horizontal privity)

Sanborn v. McLean

(Neighbor) v. (Gas Station Builder)

233 Mich. 227, 206 N.W. 496, 60 A.L.R. 1212 (1925)

[handwritten: implied equitable servitude]

[handwritten: SHG p. 100, 102]

MICHIGAN SUPREME COURT HOLDS THAT WHERE A PROPERTY OWNER SELLS OFF LOTS BY DEEDS CONTAINING COVENANTS MEANT TO CARRY OUT A SCHEME OF A RESIDENTIAL DISTRICT, AND A LOT PURCHASER HAS NOTICE OF THOSE COVENANTS, THAT PURCHASER IS BARRED FROM BUILDING A GAS STATION ON HIS LOT BY AN IMPLIED COVENANT

■ **INSTANT FACTS** The McLeans tried to build a gas station on their lot in a residential district, but were enjoined from doing so by their neighbors.

■ **BLACK LETTER RULE** An equitable servitude can be implied on a lot, even when the servitude is not created by a written instrument, if there is a scheme for development of a residential subdivision and the purchaser of the lot has notice of it.

[handwritten: really an equitable servitude]

[handwritten: implied equitable service notice of the restriction]

■ **PROCEDURAL BASIS**

Appeal from decree providing injunctive relief for violation of reciprocal negative easement.

■ **FACTS**

In 1891, ninety-one lots were subdivided along Collingwood Avenue in Detroit. Each lot was designed for and sold solely for residence purposes. In December 1892, Robert J. and Joseph R. McLaughlin, then the owners of the lots on Collingwood, deeded lots 37 to 41 and 58 to 62, inclusive, with restrictions that provided "No residence shall be erected . . . which shall cost less than $2,500, and nothing but residences shall be erected upon said premises." In July 1893, they conveyed lots 17 to 21 and 78 to 82, both inclusive, and lot 98 with the same restrictions. On September 7, 1893, the McLaughlins sold lot 86 to the McLeans (D) by a deed which did not contain these restrictions. The McLeans (D) occupied a house on the lot. They (D) later started to erect a gasoline filling station at the rear of their (D) lot. Sanborn (P), who owned the neighboring lot, filed for an injunction. The McLeans (D) were enjoined by decree, and appealed.

[handwritten: common scheme doctrine/ reciprocal negative servitude p. 101-102]

■ **ISSUE**

Can a restriction on the use of property be implied on a lot purchased in a subdivision when the restriction is not contained in the deed, but is contained in the deeds of other lots in the subdivision that were previously sold? *[handwritten: p. 101 SHG]*

■ **DECISION AND RATIONALE**

(Wiest, J.) Yes. A negative servitude, such as a covenant restricting a lot to residential use, can be implied on a lot if a developer has set up a scheme for a residential subdivision and if the purchaser of the lot has notice of the covenants used to set up the scheme. Here, the McLaughlins imposed the restrictions on the Collingwood lots for the benefit of the lands they retained, namely to carry out the scheme of a residential district. Because they sold these lots with restrictions in order to benefit themselves, the servitude became a mutual one, and so the McLaughlins were bound by the same restrictions as their buyers. This restriction is thus considered a reciprocal negative easement, and this reciprocal negative easement attached to

---

lot 86 before the McLeans (D) acquired the land. Such an easement was still attached to lot 86 after the sale to the McLeans (D) and can still be enforced by Sanborn (P) if the McLeans (D) had actual or constructive knowledge of it. Because the abstract of title to lot 86 showed that lot 86 was part of a much larger subdivision, and because the deeds resulting in reciprocal negative easements were on record, the McLeans (D) were bound by constructive notice to follow that easement. Furthermore, the general plan for the residential district had been observed by all lot purchasers, whether explicitly restricted or not, for over thirty years. The McLeans (D) could not have avoided noticing the strictly uniform residential use of the neighboring lots, and therefore were on inquiry notice to learn why all the lots conformed with each other. The least inquiry by the McLeans (D) would have revealed the easement on lot 86. Decree affirmed.

Analysis:

Most jurisdictions imply negative restrictions from a common scheme. A few, however, strictly apply the Statute of Frauds in such matters. Courts in these jurisdictions say that an equitable servitude will not be implied from the presence of restrictions on other lots in a subdivision, from a developer's oral promise to impose such restrictions, or from a general scheme not included in the deed to the lot in question.

■ CASE VOCABULARY

NUISANCE PER SE: An act that would produce public annoyance and inconvenience regardless of the circumstances surrounding it.

PLAT: A map of a specific area of land, such as a subdivision.

RECIPROCAL NEGATIVE EASEMENT: An easement created when the owner of two or more lots sells one with restrictions on it that benefit the land retained by the owner. This sale creates a mutual servitude, and while it is in effect, the original owner cannot use his or her retained land in any way that is forbidden to the buyer of the other lot.

Neponsit Property Owners' Association, Inc. v. Emigrant Industrial Savings Bank

(Property Owners' Assn.) v. (Mortgage Bank)

278 N.Y. 248, 15 N.E.2d 793 (1938)

NEW YORK COURT OF APPEALS HOLDS THAT A COVENANT REQUIRING MEMBERS OF A RESIDENTIAL COMMUNITY TO PAY A MAXIMUM FOUR-DOLLAR-PER-YEAR CHARGE FOR MAINTENANCE OF PUBLIC AREAS IS ONE THAT TOUCHES AND CONCERNS THE LAND, AND THEIR PROPERTY OWNERS' ASSOCIATION HAS THE RIGHT TO ENFORCE THE COVENANT

■ **INSTANT FACTS** Emigrant Bank took title to land previously deeded by Neponsit Realty, and the Neponsit Association tried to foreclose a lien contained in the earlier deed.

■ **BLACK LETTER RULE** An affirmative covenant to pay money for improvements or maintenance done in connection with, but not upon the land which is to be subject to the burden of the covenant does touch and concern the land, and a homeowners' association, as the agent of the actual owners of the property, can rightfully enforce the covenant.

■ **PROCEDURAL BASIS**

Appeal from order denying motion for judgment on pleadings in action to foreclose lien on land.

■ **FACTS**

In January 1911, Neponsit Realty Company, owner of a tract of land in Queens County, caused a map of the land to be filed in the office of the clerk of the county. This tract was developed for a strictly residential community. Neponsit Realty sold lots in the tract to purchasers. In 1917, Neponsit Realty deeded a lot to Mr. and Mrs. Deyer. The deed contained a covenant which provided that the property would be "subject to an annual charge . . . (not) exceeding in any year the sum of four dollars," and the charge was to be used for the "maintenance of the roads, paths, parks, beach, sewers, and such other public purposes." The covenant also stated that the charges would be payable to a Neponsit Property Owners' Association (P), as an assignee of Neponsit Realty, and the Association (D) would be responsible for the use of the charges. In addition, the covenant stated that owners would be required to pay the charge on the first of May every year, and that failure to do so would result in a lien on the land until the fully paid. Emigrant Industrial Savings Bank (D) later acquired title to the Deyers' land at a judicial sale. The deed from the referee of the sale to Emigrant Bank (D) and every deed in the chain of title since the conveyance by Neponsit Realty claims to convey the property subject to the original covenant. The Association (P) brought this action to foreclose the lien and enforce the covenant for the annual maintenance charge. Emigrant Bank (D) filed a motion for judgment on the pleadings, and the motion was denied. Emigrant Bank (D) appealed.

■ **ISSUE**

Does a covenant to pay money for maintenance done in connection with, but not actually on, an area of land touch and concern the land and thus become enforceable against subsequent purchasers?

■ DECISION AND RATIONALE

(Lehman, J.) Yes. The terms are not defined by statute, as they are meant to be determined by the court based on the facts of a given case. The key question to consider is to what degree the covenant substantially affects the legal rights of the parties to the covenant. This distinguishes a covenant that runs with the land from a mere agreement between a promisor and promisee. Here, by paying the annual charge, an owner in the tract acquired an easement, or right of common enjoyment, with other property owners in roads, beaches, public spaces and improvements in those areas. To fully enjoy these areas, the owners must help pay for their maintenance. Thus, the burden was inseparably attached to the land, held by the various owners, which enjoys the benefit, and so the covenant clearly touches and concerns the land. There was also concern over a possible lack of privity of estate between the Association (P) and Emigrant Bank (D). The Association (P) never owned the roads or other public places mentioned in the covenant, and was created solely as the assignee of the property owners. However, looking beyond the corporate nature of the Association (P), it is clear that the Association (P) was formed as a convenient means of advancing the common interests of the property owners. It would be almost impossible to separate the interests of the Association (P) and the individual owners. There is essentially privity of estate between the Association (P) and Emigrant Bank (D). An affirmative covenant to pay money for improvements or maintenance done in connection with, but not upon, the land does touch and concern the land, and a homeowners' association, as the agent of the property owners, can rightfully enforce the covenant.

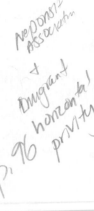

Analysis:

Courts have almost always held that covenants that restrict the use of land do touch and concern the land, because such negative covenants substantially affect the value of the land. By contrast, courts have been hesitant to enforce affirmative covenants against successors for three reasons. First, courts do not like to compel parties to perform a series of acts that require long-term supervision. Second, an affirmative obligation that requires a party to maintain property or pay money may leave a successor with a sizable personal liability. Finally, such a covenant, with an unlimited duration, is similar to perpetual rent or some other feudal device.

Shelley v. Kraemer

(Black Home Buyers) v. (White Homeowners)

334 U.S. 1, 68 S.Ct. 836 (1948)

[handwritten: restrictive covenant based on race is unenforceable]

THE UNITED STATES SUPREME COURT HOLDS THAT WHERE MISSOURI SUPREME COURT ENFORCED A RESTRICTIVE COVENANT WHICH BARRED NON-WHITES FROM OCCUPYING PROPERTY, ITS ACT CONSTITUTED DISCRIMINATORY STATE ACTION AND WAS BARRED BY THE FOURTEENTH AMENDMENT OF THE CONSTITUTION

■ **INSTANT FACTS** A black couple was buying a house while unaware of a racially based restrictive covenant on that street; the white homeowners tried to stop them.

[handwritten: restrictive/negative]

■ **BLACK LETTER RULE** Judicial enforcement of a restrictive covenant based on race constitutes discriminatory state action, and is thus forbidden by the equal protection clause of the Fourteenth Amendment of the Constitution.

■ **PROCEDURAL BASIS**

Appeal from action to enforce covenant through divesting and revesting of title.

■ **FACTS**

On February 16, 1911, thirty out of thirty-nine owners of property along both sides of Labadie Avenue between Cora and Taylor Avenues in St. Louis entered into an covenant relating to the use and occupancy of the property. This covenant provided that, for the next fifty years after the date of signing, no part of any of the property was to be used or occupied "by any person not of the Caucasian race, it being intended hereby to restrict the use of said property for said period of time against the occupancy . . . by people of the Negro or Mongolian race." These thirty owners held title to forty-seven out of the total fifty-seven parcels of land in that district. On August 11, 1945, the Shelleys (P) (who were African-American) received a warranty deed to one of these forty-seven parcels from one Fitzgerald. The Shelleys (P) had no actual knowledge of the restrictive covenant at the time of purchase. On October 9, 1945, Kraemer and other owners of property subject to the covenant (Ds) brought suit to restrain the Shelleys (P) from taking possession of the parcel they bought. They (Ds) also requested that judgment be entered divesting title out of the Shelleys (P) and revesting title in Shackleford or some other person the court saw fit. The Missouri Supreme Court directed the trial court to grant relief for Kraemer (P) and the other owners (P).

■ **ISSUE**

Can a restrictive covenant based on race be judicially enforced?

■ **DECISION AND RATIONALE**

(Vinson, J.) No. The equal protection clause of the Fourteenth Amendment prohibits judicial enforcement by state courts of restrictive covenants based on race. There is no question that the civil rights meant to be protected from discriminatory state action by the Fourteenth Amendment included the rights to acquire, own, enjoy, and dispose of property. These rights are essential to the enjoyment of other civil rights and liberties. If the restrictions imposed by the covenant on the Labadie Avenue property had been imposed by statute or ordinance, they would be clearly unconstitutional. Because it is the product of private, not state, action,

---

however, the covenant by itself does not violate the Fourteenth Amendment. So long as the covenant is put into effect through voluntary action, it remains constitutional. Here, by contrast, the purposes of the covenant were secured through judicial enforcement by the state courts. It has long been established that the official action by state courts and judicial officers constitute action of the State, and this proposition applies to action regarding the Fourteenth Amendment as well. The undisputed facts clearly indicate that the Shelleys (P) were willing buyers of a parcel of property on Labadie Avenue, and that Fitzgerald was a willing seller. The Shelleys (P) would have been free to occupy the property if not for the intervention of the Missouri state courts. Though the racial restriction was initially defined by a private agreement, the State nonetheless has the responsibility of complying with the Fourteenth Amendment, and its action in judicially enforcing the covenant violated that Amendment. Judgment reversed.

Analysis:

In addition to the Fourteenth Amendment, a covenant that has a racially discriminatory effect may also violate the federal Fair Housing Act. This Act, passed as Title VIII of the Civil Rights Act of 1968, 42 U.S.C.A. §§ 3601-3631, prohibits anyone from refusing to sell or rent, or otherwise make a dwelling unavailable, to another person on the basis of race, color, sex, religion, national origin, handicap, or familial status. In addition, § 3604(c) of the Fair Housing Act makes it unlawful to print or publish any statement, like a deed, that indicates a racial, religious, or ethnic preference with respect to the purchaser of a dwelling.

■ CASE VOCABULARY

IMPRIMATUR: "Let it be printed." License or permission.

a consolidation of two cases

Western Land Co. v. Truskolaski

(Shopping Center Builder) v. *(Homeowners in Subdivision)*

88 Nev. 200, 495 P.2d 624 (1972)

NEVADA SUPREME COURT HOLDS THAT WHERE A COMPANY WISHED TO BUILD A SHOPPING CENTER IN A RESIDENTIAL SUBDIVISION AFTER THE SURROUNDING AREA BECAME INCREASINGLY COMMERCIAL, THE RESIDENTIAL COVENANT COULD BE ENFORCED BECAUSE IT WAS STILL OF SUBSTANTIAL VALUE TO THE HOMEOWNERS

■ **INSTANT FACTS** Homeowners want to prevent a shopping center from being built in their subdivision, even though the surrounding area has become more crowded and more commercialized.

■ **BLACK LETTER RULE** A restrictive covenant establishing a residential subdivision cannot be terminated as long as the residential character of the subdivision has not been adversely affected by the surrounding area, and it is of real and substantial value to the landowners within the subdivision.

[handwritten margin notes: SHQ p. 102-103 hard to show the character of area has changed]

■ PROCEDURAL BASIS

Appeal from action seeking injunctive relief to enforce covenant. *[handwritten: really a servitude b/c of the Injunction]*

■ FACTS

In 1941, the Western Land Company (P) subdivided a forty-acre development southwest of Reno, outside the city limits. Western Land (P) subjected the lots to restrictive covenants which restricted them to single-family dwellings and prohibited any stores, butcher shops, grocery or mercantile business of any kind. The land around the subdivision was put to mainly residential and agricultural use, with very little commercial development. At the time, Plumb Lane, which bordered the subdivision to the south, went only as far east as one Arlington Avenue, and Reno had a population of about 20,000 people. By 1961, Plumb Lane had extended further east to one Virginia Street, and had been extended by the city of Reno into a four lane arterial boulevard. Plumb Lane had become the major east-west artery through the southern part of Reno. By 1969, Reno's population jumped up to roughly 95,100 people. In addition, a major shopping center had been built across from the east end of the subdivision, along with two more even further east. Despite these changes, the amount of traffic within the subdivision remained low. The homeowners (D) stated that this low level of traffic resulted in a safe living and playing environment for their (D) children. The homes in the subdivision were also very well maintained. The homeowners (D) brought an action in district court to enjoin Western Land (P) from building a shopping center on a 3.5 acre parcel in the subdivision. The court there held that the restrictive covenants were still enforceable, and Western Land (P) appealed.

■ ISSUE

Can a restrictive covenant for a residential subdivision be terminated when the nature of the surrounding area has changed and the homeowners within the subdivision still value the residential nature of the subdivision?

■ DECISION AND RATIONALE

(Batjer, J.) No. A restrictive covenant establishing a residential subdivision cannot be terminated as long as the residential character of the subdivision has not been adversely affected by the surrounding area, and it is of real and substantial value to the landowners within the subdivision. There is enough evidence that the subdivision is still suitable for residential purposes despite the changed conditions of the area, and that the restrictions remain of substantial value to the landowners (D). The lower level of traffic has led to a safe environment for children which the landowners (D) value. This safety would likely be compromised if commercial traffic were allowed. Though Western Land (P) points to an intent by the Reno city council to rezone the area in question for commercial use, this intent does not prove that the property is more suited for commercial than residential use. A zoning ordinance does not override a private restriction, and a court cannot be forced to terminate a restrictive covenant merely because of a change in zoning. Even if the parcel in question would be more valuable if converted to commercial use, that does not permit Western Land (P) to escape its earlier restrictions. Other landowners (D) would still receive a substantial benefit from the enforcement of the restrictions. Moreover, though Western Land (P) points to violations by the landowners (Ds), including a nursery in one house and a contractor's office in another, the violations are too isolated to frustrate the purpose of the restrictions. Thus, they do not equal a waiver of the restrictions. Judgment affirmed.

Analysis:

Restatement (Third) of Property, Servitudes § 7.10 adopts this change of conditions doctrine, allowing courts to terminate or modify servitudes based on changed circumstances. The awarding of damages, instead of specific performance, as a remedy for breach of covenant has rarely been mentioned in cases denying an injunction. It does, however, have the backing of several commentators, who support a damages remedy when multiple parties benefit from a covenant, making voluntary release impracticable, if not impossible.

■ CASE VOCABULARY

ARTERIAL: A street or highway where the traffic going through is given preference.

MERCANTILE: Relating to trade.

ZONING ORDINANCE: A municipal law dividing a city or town into districts with specific regulations regarding building use and construction.

Rick v. West

(Land Developer) v. (Uncompromising Landowner)

34 Misc.2d 1002, 228 N.Y.S.2d 195 (1962)

NEW YORK SUPREME COURT HOLDS THAT WHERE NEIGHBORING LANDOWNERS ATTEMPTED TO SELL LAND IN THEIR RESIDENTIAL SUBDIVISION TO A HOSPITAL AND ONLY ONE LANDOWNER DID NOT WISH TO RELEASE THE RESTRICTIVE COVENANT, THE LOT OWNER HAS THE RIGHT TO INSIST UPON ADHERENCE TO THE COVENANT

■ **INSTANT FACTS** West bought land from Rick under a restrictive covenant, and refused to release the covenant when Rick attempted to sell similar land to a hospital.

■ **BLACK LETTER RULE** A landowner in a subdivision under a restrictive covenant has the right to insist upon adherence to the covenant even when the other owners consent to its release.

■ **PROCEDURAL BASIS**

Appeal from action to declare covenant unenforceable due to change of conditions.

■ **FACTS**

Chester Rick (P) subdivided sixty-two acres of vacant land in 1946. Covenants that restricted the land to single-family dwellings were filed. In 1956, Rick (P) sold a half-acre lot to Catherine West (D), and there she (D) built a house. In 1957, the land was zoned for residential use. Rick (P) later contracted for the sale of forty-five acres to an industrialist, with the sale being conditioned upon the tract being rezoned for industrial use. The forty-five acres was rezoned, but the sale fell through after West (D) refused to release the covenant. After selling only a few more lots, Rick (P) conveyed the remaining land to the other lot owners (P). In 1961, they (P) contracted to sell fifteen acres from the tract to Peekskill Hospital, but again West (D) refused to consent to the release of the covenant. The other owners (P) sued, claiming the covenant was no longer enforceable because of a change in conditions. The trial court held for West (D) and the other owners (P) appealed.

■ **ISSUE**

Is a restrictive covenant still enforceable when only one landowner in a subdivision refuses to consent to the release of the covenant?

■ **DECISION AND RATIONALE**

(Hoyt, J.) Yes. A landowner in a subdivision under a restrictive covenant has the right to insist upon adherence to the covenant even when the other owners consent to its release. In 1946, Rick (P) owned the land free and clear of all restrictions, and had the right to do what he felt was best for the property. Rick (P) chose to turn it into a residential development, and to encourage purchase of the resulting lots, he (P) imposed the residential restrictions. West (D) relied upon those restrictions when she (D) purchased the property and she (D) has the right to continue relying on them. The balancing of equities and the potential advantages of having a hospital on the property are irrelevant. The fact that West (D) is the only person opposed to releasing the covenant does not make her (D) right to have the covenant enforced any less deserving of this court's protection. She (D) has done nothing but insist upon adherence to a covenant which is just as binding as it was when she (D) and the other owners (P) entered it. Her (D) refusal to release the covenant, resulting from her satisfaction with the covenant as it stands, must be protected. Judgment affirmed.

Analysis:

Rick demonstrates the same issue as *Western Land*, only to a greater degree. In *Western Land*, a small minority blocked development; in *Rick*, a *single* holdout stands in the way of commercial progress. The argument against these decisions is utilitarian; allowing a few holdouts to prevent commercial efficiency seemingly violates the utilitarian ideal of "the greatest good for the greatest number." Economists might argue that the person resisting change should be forced to pay damages for the value that cannot be created because of him. But courts generally recognize holdouts' reliance interests. Note that the latest Restatement gives courts considerable leeway to terminate servitudes or modify them because of changed conditions. Restatement (Third) of Property, Servitudes § 7.10.

■ CASE VOCABULARY

PECUNIARY DAMAGES: Any damages which can be compensated for with money.

Nahrstedt v. Lakeside Village Condominium Association, Inc.

(Cat Owner) v. (Condominium Association)

11 Cal.Rptr.2d 299 (Ct. App. 1992), hearing granted by Calif. Sup. Ct

CALIFORNIA COURT OF APPEAL, SECOND DISTRICT, HOLDS THAT WHERE A CONDOMINIUM ASSOCIATION LEVIED FINES AGAINST A UNIT OWNER FOR VIOLATING A RESTRICTION AGAINST ANIMALS IN HER UNIT, SUCH A BLANKET PET RESTRICTION WAS OVERLY BROAD AND THUS WAS UNREASONABLE

■ **INSTANT FACTS** Nahrstedt wants to continue living with her three cats in her condominium, in violation of the recorded covenants, conditions and restrictions governing the condominium.

■ **BLACK LETTER RULE** The enforceability of restrictions on the ownership and possession of pets should be decided in a trial court after evidence is heard as to whether the restriction was reasonable as applied to the particular facts of a case.

■ **PROCEDURAL BASIS**

Appeal from sustaining of demurrers without leave to amend in action for declaratory relief, invasion of privacy, negligent and intentional infliction of emotional distress, and invalidation of levied fines.

■ **FACTS**

Natore Nahrstedt (P) lives in a condominium at the Lakeside Village complex. Article VII, section 11 of the recorded covenants, conditions, and restrictions (CC & Rs) on the condominium provides that "no animals (which shall mean dogs and cats) . . . shall be kept in any unit" and that "the Association (D) shall have the right to prohibit maintenance of any pet which constitutes, in the opinion of the Board [of Directors of the homeowners association], a nuisance to any other owner." She (P) owns three pet cats, which she (P) claims make no noise and are not a nuisance. The Association (D) has allegedly harassed her (P) by imposing increasingly large fines as a penalty for the cats. Nahrstedt (P) filed this action to obtain, among other things, a declaration that she (P) is entitled to keep the cats, in spite of the CC & Rs, and that she (P) has no legal obligation to pay the fines. Nahrstedt (P) argues that the restriction was unreasonable under Civil Code section 1354 [restrictions in the declaration of CC & Rs shall be enforceable equitable servitudes unless unreasonable]. The trial court sustained, without leave to amend, demurrers on all five causes of action in Nahrstedt's (P) original complaint.

■ **ISSUE**

Can a condominium association's enforcement of a restriction on pets be considered reasonable by a court without hearing evidence on the circumstances of the homeowner challenging the restriction?

■ **DECISION AND RATIONALE**

(Croskey, J.) No. The enforceability of restrictions on the ownership and possession of pets should be decided in a trial court, after evidence is heard as to whether the restriction was reasonable as applied to the particular facts of the homeowner challenging them. The Association (D) claims the pet restriction was reasonable and enforceable because it protects the Association (D) from always needing to litigate against homeowners whose pets are causing problems. This argument goes against the logic of the court in *Bernardo Villas Management Corp. v. Black* (1987) 190 Cal.App.3d 153, 235 Cal.Rptr. 509 [provision allowing parking of trucks only for loading and unloading held unreasonable when applied to clean noncommercial pickup trucks] and the court in *Portola Hills Community Assn. v. James* (1992) 4 Cal.App.4th 289, 5 Cal.Rptr.2d 580 [ban on satellite dishes in planned community held unreasonable when dish not visible to other community residents], which is to judge situations on their own specific facts. Nahrstedt's (P) home is her castle, and she should enjoy it by the least restrictive means possible. The Association's (D) argument could be extended to support all-inclusive bans on anything from stereo equipment to visitors under eighteen years of age. Blanket restrictions against such things likely would not be reasonable, and it is certainly possible that a trial court would consider Nahrstedt's (P) three cats to be less of a threat to the peace and quiet in the complex. The trial court should hear evidence on the circumstances surrounding Nahrstedt's (P) ownership of the cats. Judgment of dismissal reversed, and cause remanded.

■ **DISSENT**

(Hinz, J.) Courts should have the power to rule on these matters at the demurrer stage, because an association has a duty to its members to enforce restrictions. If an association were forced to litigate every matter, such litigation, paid for by the mandatory fees of each property owner, would become very expensive. The majority's ruling only encourages prolonged litigation, which would burden both the courts and the parties involved. Condominium living involves increased density and intensified use of common areas, and so it necessarily requires that individual unit owners relinquish some of the freedoms they would enjoy if they lived in separate property. The other residents at Lakeside Village apparently desired pet-free conditions, and Nahrstedt (P) consented to those conditions. The restriction is reasonable, and should be enforced. The demurrer should be sustained.

Analysis:

Recent cases involving homeowners associations demonstrate that there is far more litigation with condominium homeowners associations than there is for associations of owners of detached, single-family homes. Most cases involve faulty construction suits against the builder of the condominium, tort suits by an individual owner against the association, or suits by the association against a unit owner for improper activity. Such activity has included everything from unauthorized fences to repairing a car in the project's driveway.

■ **CASE VOCABULARY**

DEMURRER: A claim by a defendant that, even if all the plaintiff's allegations in the complaint are true, the plaintiff has not successfully raised a cause of action to force the defendant to respond.

FIDUCIARY: Describes a person who has a special duty involving the good faith or trust of another.

40 West 67th Street Corp. v. Pullman

(Cooperative) v. (Tenant)

790 N.E.2d 1174 (N.Y. 2003)

COOPERATIVE TENANTS MUST LIVE BY THE COOPERATIVE'S RULES OR LIVE ELSEHWERE

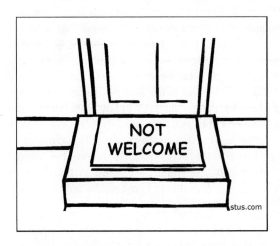

■ **INSTANT FACTS** After a shareholder-tenant moved into his cooperative apartment, he began engaging in outrageous conduct directed particularly at his upstairs neighbors, and the cooperative board ultimately terminated his tenancy; he sued, and the courts disagreed as to whether the business judgment rule applied to the board's action.

■ **BLACK LETTER RULE** *Levandusky* established a standard of review analogous to the corporate business judgment rule for a shareholder-tenant challenge to a decision of a residential cooperative corporation.

■ **PROCEDURAL BASIS**

State high court review of an appellate court decision reversing the trial court's judgment for the tenant.

■ **FACTS**

The plaintiff owned an apartment building at 40 West 67th Street in Manhattan. Pullman (D) bought into the building's cooperative and acquired stock therein appurtenant to his proprietary lease of one of the apartments in the building. Soon after moving in, Pullman (D) engaged in conduct that was, per the cooperative, intolerable, including making bizarre accusations about another tenant, becoming involved in a physical altercation with the other tenant, distributing flyers referring to the tenant as a psychopath and alleging the cooperative board's president and the tenant's wife were intimately involved with each other, and ultimately initiating four lawsuits against the tenant. Pullman (D) also made unauthorized alterations to his apartment. The cooperative called a special meeting to consider the Pullman (D) situation pursuant to the lease agreement's terms, which allowed for termination of a tenancy by a two-thirds vote when the lessee's objectionable conduct rendered continuing tenancy undesirable. Owners of more than three-fourths of the shares were in attendance, and they voted unanimously to terminate Pullman's (D) proprietary lease and cancel his shares. The board sent Pullman (D) a notice of termination, but he remained in the apartment nonetheless, prompting the cooperative to bring suit for possession and ejectment, as well as for a declaratory judgment cancelling Pullman's (D) stock, and a money judgment for use and occupancy of the apartment. The state court declined to apply the business judgment rule to sustain the board's action, holding that to terminate a tenancy, a cooperative must prove its claim of objectionable conduct by competent evidence to the court's satisfaction. The appellate court disagreed, holding that the *Levandusky* decision prohibited judicial scrutiny of actions of cooperative boards taken in good faith and in the exercise of honest judgment in the lawful furtherance of corporate purposes. The plaintiff appealed to the state's highest court.

■ **ISSUE**

Is a court's review of a cooperative board's action subject to the business judgment rule?

■ DECISION AND RATIONALE

(Rosenblatt, J.) Yes. *Levandusky* established a standard of review analogous to the corporate business judgment rule for a shareholder-tenant challenge to a decision of a residential cooperative corporation. In the context of cooperative dwellings, the business judgment rule provides that a court should defer to a cooperative board's determination so long as the board acts for the purposes of the cooperative, within the scope of its authority and in good faith. The defendant argues that the application of the business judgment rule conflicts with New York law, but we see no such conflict. RPAPL 711(1) requires competent evidence to show that a tenant was objectionable before his tenancy may be terminated, but that rule was intended to prevent arbitrary and punitive landlord actions, which concern is not present in the cooperative context, where a board vote is required. Indeed, in the context of a cooperative board, the competent evidence standard is satisfied by the business judgment rule, so there is really no conflict. When a tenant buys into a cooperative, he agrees to abide by certain rules or forfeit his tenancy, and that is what occurred here. Cooperative living assumes the voluntary assumption of a shared code of conduct, to which Pullman (D) failed to adhere. The board acted within the scope of its authority in terminating Pullman's (D) tenancy. The board's action was to further the overall welfare of the cooperative, and there was no indication that the board acted in bad faith or arbitrarily, or that it engaged in malice, favoritism, or discrimination. The board's action passes the *Levandusky* test. Affirmed.

Analysis:

The defendant argued that the court should apply RPAPL 711(1), which provides that "[a] proceeding seeking to recover possession of real property by reason of the termination of the term fixed in the lease pursuant to a provision contained therein giving the landlord the right to terminate the time fixed for occupancy under such agreement if he deem the tenant objectionable, shall not be maintainable unless the landlord shall by competent evidence establish to the satisfaction of the court that the tenant is objectionable." The court held that the standard set forth in that rule does not conflict with, and is satisfied by applying, the rule set forth in *Levandusky v. One Fifth Ave. Corp.*, 553 N.E.2d 1317 (N.Y. 1990). In *Levandusky*, the court held that a standard of review analogous to the business judgment rule applies to challenges to decisions of the board of directors of a residential cooperative corporation; thus, where, as here, the board acted for purposes of the cooperative, within the scope of its authority, and in good faith, courts will not substitute their judgment for board's.

■ CASE VOCABULARY

DECLARATORY JUDGMENT: A binding adjudication that establishes the rights and other legal relations of the parties without providing for or ordering enforcement. Declaratory judgments are often sought, for example, by insurance companies in determining whether a policy covers a given insured or peril.

EJECTMENT: The ejection of an owner or occupier from property; a legal action by which a person wrongfully ejected from property seeks to recover possession, damages, and costs; the writ by which such an action is begun. The essential allegations in an action for ejectment are that (1) the plaintiff has title to the land, (2) the plaintiff has been wrongfully dispossessed or ousted, and (3) the plaintiff has suffered damages.

CHAPTER ELEVEN

Legislative Land Use Controls: The Law of Zoning

Village of Euclid v. Ambler Realty Co.

Instant Facts: A realty company challenged a municipal ordinance which established a zoning plan restricting the use and size of buildings in various districts.

Black Letter Rule: Zoning ordinances are a valid exercise of the police power and thus do not violate the constitutional protection of property rights.

PA Northwestern Distributors, Inc. v. Zoning Hearing Board

Instant Facts: After an adult bookstore was opened, a local zoning board enacted an adult business ordinance which gave the bookstore operator only ninety days to comply.

Black Letter Rule: If a zoning law or regulation has the effect of depriving a property owner of the lawful pre-existing nonconforming use of his or her property, it amounts to a taking for which the owner must be justly compensated.

State ex rel. Stoyanoff v. Berkeley

Instant Facts: Stoyanoff wanted to build a pyramid-shaped house in a neighborhood with more traditional-looking houses, but Stoyanoff refused to issue a building permit.

Black Letter Rule: An architectural review board may deny a permit for a structure if it would be unsuitable in appearance with reference to the character of the surrounding neighborhood and thus adversely affect the general welfare and property values of the community.

Anderson v. City of Issaquah

Instant Facts: An architect appealed the denial of a construction permit, arguing that the subjective aesthetic standards used by the city building commission were unconstitutionally vague.

Black Letter Rule: Local building ordinances that impose aesthetic conditions must provide sufficiently clear guidance to all interested parties.

City of Ladue v. Gilleo

Instant Facts: A resident challenges a city ordinance that prohibits the displaying of signs, such as an antiwar protest sign, on front yards.

Black Letter Rule: A city may not constitutionally adopt ordinances that prohibit nearly all signs on residential property.

Guru Nanak Sikh Society of Yuba City v. County of Sutter

Instant Facts: After religious group's application for a conditional use permit to construct a Sikh temple at one location was denied by the county, it sought a permit for another location, which was also denied.

Black Letter Rule: Local land use regulations that require individualized assessments of the proposed uses of the property and impose substantial burdens on religious exercise without a compelling governmental reason violate the Federal Religious Land Use and Institutionalized Persons Act of 2000.

Fisher v. Giuliani

Instant Facts: City residents challenged zoning amendments affecting Manhattan Theater District on the grounds that an environmental impact statement was required before the changes could be implemented.

Black Letter Rule: Review of an agency determination of whether a zoning amendment will have a significant environmental impact is limited to deciding whether the agency took a hard look at identified relevant areas of environmental concern and made a reasoned statement of the basis for its determination.

Village of Belle Terre v. Boraas

Instant Facts: Boraas and five others challenged a Belle Terre ordinance which restricted land use to one-family dwellings and excluded households with over two unrelated persons.

Black Letter Rule: The legislature may define what counts as a "family" for zoning purposes if the definition is rationally related to legitimate objectives, such as creating zones where family values, youth values, and the blessings of quiet seclusion and clean air are preserved.

City of Edmonds v. Oxford House, Inc.

Instant Facts: A city sued to enforce its residential single-family zoning restrictions against a group home for recovering alcoholics and drug addicts.

Black Letter Rule: A single-family zoning regulation is not automatically exempt from FHA scrutiny, even if it indirectly limits the maximum number of occupants in a house.

Southern Burlington County NAACP v. Township of Mount Laurel

Instant Facts: Mount Laurel enacted a general zoning ordinance which effectively prevented low and middle income persons from acquiring affordable homes within the township.

Black Letter Rule: A developing municipality must, by its land use regulations, make realistically possible the opportunity for an appropriate variety and choice of housing for all categories of people who may desire to live there, including those of low and moderate income.

Village of Euclid v. Ambler Realty Co.

(Suburb) v. (Landowner)

272 U.S. 365, 47 S.Ct. 114 (1926)

UNITED STATES SUPREME COURT HOLDS THAT A MUNICIPAL ZONING ORDINANCE WHICH CREATES AND MAINTAINS DIFFERENT TYPES OF RESIDENTIAL DISTRICTS, WHILE EXCLUDING BUSINESSES FROM SUCH DISTRICTS, IS CONSTITUTIONAL

■ **INSTANT FACTS** A realty company challenged a municipal ordinance which established a zoning plan restricting the use and size of buildings in various districts.

■ **BLACK LETTER RULE** Zoning ordinances are a valid exercise of the police power and thus do not violate the constitutional protection of property rights.

[handwritten margin notes: municipal zoning ordinances are valid; excludes businesses from the residential districts; SHG p.125, general info about zoning]

■ **PROCEDURAL BASIS**

Appeal from order granting injunction against enforcement of ordinance.

■ **FACTS**

The Village of Euclid (D) is essentially a suburb of the City of Cleveland. Most of this land is used for farms or undeveloped. Ambler Realty Co. (P) owns a 68-acre tract of land in the western end of the village. This tract is bordered by a principal highway, Euclid Avenue, to the south, and by a major railroad, the Nickel Plate, to the north. There are residential lots with buildings to the east and west of Ambler Realty's (P) land. In 1922, the Village Council (D) adopted a comprehensive zoning plan to regulate and restrict the use of land, as well as the size of the lots and the heights of buildings. This ordinance divided the village into six use districts, U–1 to U–6. Each higher-numbered district included the uses of the district below it. Thus, U–1 districts allowed only single-family dwellings, while U–2 districts were extended to include two-family dwellings along with U–1 uses; U–3 districts were extended to include public buildings like churches, schools, hospitals with U–2 uses, and so on. U–6 districts could be used for sewage plants and junkyards, as well as for all residential and industrial operations below this level. The ordinance also divides the village into three height districts, H–1 to H–3, and four area districts, A–1 to A–4. The zone map attached to this ordinance shows that the use, area, and height districts are all allowed to overlap one another. The ordinance is enforced by the inspector of buildings under the board of zoning appeals. This board is authorized to make rules in order to implement the ordinance, as well as impose penalties for violations. The board can also interpret the ordinance in harmony with its general purpose and intent, so that the public health, safety, and general welfare may be protected. Ambler Realty's (P) land itself falls under the U–2, U–3, and U–6 districts. Ambler Realty (P) claims this land is vacant and that it has been held in order to sell and develop it for industrial uses. If Ambler Realty's (P) land is used for industrial purposes, it is worth about $10,000 per acre, but if it is kept for residential use, it is only worth roughly $2,500 per acre. The records indicate the normal and reasonably expected use of the land facing Euclid Avenue is for industrial and trade purposes. Ambler Realty (P) claims the ordinance violates its (P) constitutional rights, at both the state and federal levels, against deprivation of property and liberty without due process of law and denies it (P) the equal protection of the law.

■ ISSUE

Is it unconstitutional to enact an ordinance which establishes a comprehensive zoning plan regulating the use of property?

■ DECISION AND RATIONALE

(Sutherland, J.) No. Zoning ordinances are a valid exercise of the police power and thus do not violate the constitutional protection of property rights. It is not necessary to decide separately if this ordinance violates the Ohio Constitution, as the question is substantively the same. Building zone laws are relatively new, yet are clearly necessary and valid. The increasing urbanization of modern life has required the use of regulations which, fifty years ago, would have been considered arbitrary or oppressive. While the meaning behind constitutional guarantees is constant, they must be applied in ways to meet the new conditions of life. The ordinance under review, then, must be justified through some aspect of the police power. This line is not a clear one, but must vary with circumstances and conditions. As with the law of nuisances, the maxim *sic utere tuo ut alienum non laedas* can serve as a guide. The building of a structure should be considered after the building itself is looked at in connection with the circumstances and its surroundings. No one has doubted the validity of regulations regarding the height of buildings within reasonable limits, the materials used in construction, the exclusion of certain trades from residential areas, etc. The Village (D), though essentially a suburb of Cleveland, is nonetheless a separate political body. As such, it has the power to govern itself as it sees fit within the limits of the Ohio and Federal Constitutions. Here, the serious question is over the exclusion of apartment houses, stores and shops, and other similar establishments from residential areas. The state courts that deny or narrow this power are greatly outnumbered by the state courts that sustain it. Various commissions and experts have reported for the separation of residential, business, and industrial buildings. They have pointed to the ease of providing appropriate firefighting measures in each section; increased safety, especially for children, by reducing traffic in residential areas; and increased home security. Also, the distracting of apartment houses helps preserve the quiet, open character of single-family neighborhoods, while preventing heavy traffic, overcrowding, and excessive noise. If nothing else, these reasons are enough to counter any arguments that the ordinance is arbitrary, unreasonable, or not substantially related to the public health, safety, morals, or general welfare. Unless such arbitrariness and unreasonableness is proven, the ordinance cannot be declared unconstitutional. Granted, it is entirely possible that the provisions set forth in a zoning ordinance may be found to be clearly arbitrary or unreasonable in a specific situation. When an injunction is sought, however, because the mere existence or threat of enforcement of the ordinance may cause an injury, the court will not go over the ordinance, sentence by sentence, to find which parts are constitutional and which parts are not. Without a specific complaint of actual injury, a land owner cannot challenge the constitutionality of such an ordinance. Decree reversed.

Analysis:

The seeds of four dominant themes in legislative zoning are planted in this opinion. First, there is the idea that a city or municipality is allowed to exclude some uses of property in certain circumstances. Second, the court essentially allows the same government body to control the economic markets, in a way, by designating where areas of trade can be set up. Third, the court places emphasis on local control in zoning measures, particularly when it establishes early in its opinion that Euclid is a separate governing entity. Finally, the court places some emphasis on aesthetic values, and how these can be a valid basis for a zoning ordinance in the appropriate context. This concept can be found in the discussion on separating apartment buildings from other residences.

■ CASE VOCABULARY

CLEW: Old English spelling of "clue."

DEROGATION: Act of discrediting or belittling.

MUNICIPALITY: A legally incorporated association of residents in a relatively small area for governmental or other public purposes; another term for town, village or city.

PARALLELOGRAM: A geometric figure with two pairs of parallel and equal sides, such as a rectangle or square.

SANITARIUM: A medical institution for the care of invalids or convalescing patients.

Commulative, cookie-cutter zoning

Commulative zoning
- graded + ranked uses
from most to least desirable
U-1 single family home
U-2 two family home
U-3 apartment building
U-4 - infrastructure uses
(hospitals, schools, etc,
U-5 - commercial of a modest size
U-6 - commercial of a large size
(factory)
U-7 - commercial that included toxins/dangers
(factory emitting poison)

Ⓧ Takes as a premise a more desirable use is always allowed into a less desirable use district, but not vice versa, can put a U-1 in a U-3, but not a U-3 into a U-1

commercial uses

this created a ghettoization of housing

PA Northwestern Distributors, Inc. v. Zoning Hearing Board

(Adult Bookstore Owner) v. (Local Zoning Board)

526 Pa. 186, 584 A.2d 1372 (1991)

PENNSYLVANIA SUPREME COURT HOLDS THAT A ZONING ORDINANCE THAT REGULATED ADULT BUSINESSES AND GAVE AN ADULT BOOKSTORE OWNER A NINETY-DAY AMORTIZATION PERIOD IN WHICH TO COMPLY WITH THE ORDINANCE WAS AN UNCONSTITUTIONAL TAKING OF PROPERTY WITHOUT JUST COMPENSATION

■ **INSTANT FACTS** After an adult bookstore was opened, a local zoning board enacted an adult business ordinance which gave the bookstore operator only ninety days to comply.

■ **BLACK LETTER RULE** If a zoning law or regulation has the effect of depriving a property owner of the lawful pre-existing nonconforming use of his or her property, it amounts to a taking for which the owner must be justly compensated.

■ **PROCEDURAL BASIS**

Appeal from order denying appeal to zoning board.

■ **FACTS**

On May 4, 1985, PA Northwestern Distributors, Inc. (P), or PAND (P), opened an adult bookstore in Moon Township, Pennsylvania. Four days later, the local Board of Supervisors published a notice of its intention to amend the Moon Township Zoning Ordinance to regulate "adult commercial enterprises." A public hearing followed, and on May 23, 1985, the Board of Supervisors adopted Ordinance No. 243, effective May 28, 1985. This ordinance imposes extensive restrictions on the location and operation of adult commercial enterprises. It also includes an amortization provision which gave all those who operated pre-existing businesses in conflict with this ordinance a period of ninety days to comply. PAND's (P's) bookstore, by definition, is an adult commercial enterprise under Ordinance No. 243, and it does not fall into any of the areas designated for such businesses by the ordinance. The Zoning Officer of Moon Township informed PAND (P) that the bookstore did not comply with the ordinance. PAND (P) then filed an appeal to the Zoning Hearing Board of Moon Township (D), challenging the validity of this ninety-day provision. After a hearing, the Board (D) upheld the validity of the ordinance as applied. PAND (P) then filed an appeal to the Court of Common Pleas of Allegheny County. No further evidence was taken, and the appeal was dismissed. This decision was appealed, and the Commonwealth Court affirmed, citing *Sullivan v. Zoning Board of Adjustment*, 83 Pa.Commw. 228, 478 A.2d 912 (1984) [provisions for the amortization of nonconforming uses are constitutional exercises of the police power so long as they are reasonable.]. The Commonwealth Court held that the "real and substantial benefits to the Township of elimination of the nonconforming use from this location . . . more than offset the losses to the affected landowner," and ruled against PAND (P). PAND (P) then appealed to the Pennsylvania Supreme Court.

■ **ISSUE**

Is an ordinance which has the effect of depriving a property owner of a nonconforming use of his or her property constitutional when such use was pre-existing and lawful?

■ DECISION AND RATIONALE

(Larsen, J.) No. Sullivan is not a correct statement of the law regarding amortization provisions. Amortization is not a reasonable means of zoning regulation. In Pennsylvania, all property is held subject to the right of reasonable regulation by the government that is necessary to preserve the health, safety, morals, or general welfare of the people. A zoning ordinance is generally presumed to be valid. That presumption, however must be balanced by an individual's constitutionally guaranteed right to use property without government restrictions, except when his or her use creates a nuisance or violates a covenant, restriction, or easement. It has long been the law of this Commonwealth that local governments cannot compel a change in the nature of an existing lawful use of property. A lawful nonconforming use establishes a vested property right in its owner that cannot be infringed upon unless it is a nuisance, it is abandoned, or it is extinguished by eminent domain. If a zoning law or regulation has the effect of depriving a property owner of the lawful pre-existing nonconforming use of his or her property, it amounts to a taking for which the owner must be justly compensated. Here, the amortization provision deprives PAND (P) of the lawful use of its property by forcing it to cease its business operations there within ninety days. The Pennsylvania Constitution protects the right of a property owner to use his or her property in any lawful way that he or she chooses. This ordinance restricts future uses and extinguishes a present lawful nonconforming use against the owner's wishes. If municipalities were allowed to amortize nonconforming uses out of existence, economic development could be seriously compromised, with investors afraid of changes in the zoning laws. Further, any use could be subsequently amortized out of existence without just compensation to the property owner. No use and no property owner would be safe. Judgment reversed.

■ CONCURRENCE

(Nix, J.) The Sullivan decision should be upheld, because a reasonable amortization provision is valid if it reflects the consideration of several factors. Any blanket rule against amortization provisions would prevent effective zoning, unnecessarily restrict a state's police power, and prevent the elimination of nonconforming uses to further the public interest. Several factors have been used to determine the reasonableness of amortization, including the duration of the investment in the property use; the length of the amortization period in relation to the nonconforming use; and the degree of offensiveness of the nonconforming use to the character of the surrounding neighborhood. A community should have the right to change its character without being locked into outdated definitions of what is or is not offensive. Here, the amortization provision is not a reasonable one as it does not provide adequate time for the nonconforming use to be eliminated. Ninety days is not enough time to allow a merchant to close a business and settle contractual obligations. Moreover, such a period is not enough for PAND (P) to find an alternative means of income or obtain a reasonable return on its (P) investment. Commonwealth Court order reversed.

Analysis:

This protection of a nonconforming use "runs with the land," and not with the owner. Thus, as long as the use is maintained, it can survive a change of ownership. If, however, a landowner abandons that nonconforming use, the right to continue that use may be terminated. In addition, expanding the scope of the use (bigger stores, increased business, etc.) can also lead to a termination of the right. Occasionally, communities attempt to discourage undesirable businesses from entering their areas by enacting ordinances that set limits on expansion and renovation, or prevent owners from repairing nonconforming structures when damaged.

■ CASE VOCABULARY

AMORTIZATION: As used in zoning matters, provisions in zoning ordinances that require the termination of nonconformities—where land does not conform to new zoning ordinances—within a certain specified time.

ATTRITION: Wearing away or erosion.

State ex rel. Stoyanoff v. Berkeley

(Building Commissioner) v. (Architect)

458 S.W.2d 305 (Mo. 1970)

[handwritten: regulating aesthetic appeal]

BUILDING PERMIT DENIED BECAUSE THE PROPOSED HOUSE DESIGN WOULD DESTABILIZE PROPERTY VALUES IN THE AREA

■ **INSTANT FACTS** Stoyanoff wanted to build a pyramid-shaped house in a neighborhood with more traditional-looking houses, but Stoyanoff refused to issue a building permit.

■ **BLACK LETTER RULE** An architectural review board may deny a permit for a structure if it would be unsuitable in appearance with reference to the character of the surrounding neighborhood and thus adversely affect the general welfare and property values of the community.

[handwritten right margin: Stff P.126 must not adversely affect surrounding property values]

■ **PROCEDURAL BASIS**

Appeal from summary judgment for a peremptory writ of mandamus to compel the issuance of a residential building permit.

■ **FACTS**

The City of Ladue is one of the finer residential suburbs of St. Louis, Missouri. There, the homes are considerably larger and more expensive than those in cities of comparable size. The average market value of these homes ranged from $60,000 to $85,000 each. Most of the residences were built in Colonial, French Provincial and English Tudor styles. Stoyanoff (P) and others (P) applied to Berkeley (D), the Ladue Building Commissioner, for a building permit that would allow them (P) to construct a single family residence in Ladue. This residence, however, would be of ultramodern design, with a pyramid shape, a flat top, and triangular shaped windows and doors at the corners. Stoyanoff (P) argued this design, though unusual, would nonetheless comply with all existing zoning regulations and ordinances. The permit application was not approved by the Architectural Board of the City of Ladue. A zoning ordinance was in effect in Ladue to promote a comprehensive plan "designed to promote the health and general welfare of the residents of the City of Ladue." The Architectural Board, established by Ordinance 131, as amended by Ordinance 281, is composed of three architects. It was created to ensure that new buildings would "conform to certain minimum architectural standards of appearance and conformity with surrounding structures." Those structures that were "detrimental to the stability of value and the welfare of surrounding property" were not permitted in Ladue under the Ordinances. According to another developer, a house built to Stoyanoff's (P) design would have a substantial adverse effect upon the market values of other residential property in the neighborhood. Stoyanoff (P) filed a motion for summary judgment to compel Berkeley (D) to issue a residential building permit for the proposed house. The trial court held that the ordinances deprived Stoyanoff (P) of the use of the property without due process of law.

[handwritten right margin: P. 126-127 spot zoning; P. 125 two-prong test, area variance vs. use variance p. 126]

■ **ISSUE**

Can a zoning ordinance be considered valid if it prohibits the building of property because it would not conform in appearance with neighboring structures?

■ DECISION AND RATIONALE

(Pritchard, J.) Yes. An architectural review board may deny a permit for a structure if it would be unsuitable in appearance with reference to the character of the surrounding neighborhood and thus adversely affect the general welfare and property values of the community. There is an existing, comprehensive plan of zoning intended to maintain the general character of buildings in the City of Ladue. The concerns regarding architectural appearance and stability of value are directly related to the general welfare of the community. Indeed, the assured preservation of property values is one of the most pressing reasons to have zoning ordinances in the first place. Neighboring owners are not the only ones threatened by property uses which may offend others' sensibilities and debase market values. The public also suffers, as lowered property values also affect the tax base of the community as a whole. While Stoyanoff (P) may argue that these zoning restrictions are unreasonable and arbitrary because they are based solely on aesthetic concerns, in fact, the aesthetic factor is not the sole one considered. The effect on property values in the area must also be considered. The building permit for Stoyanoff (P) was denied for the basic purpose of serving the general welfare of the community. Judgment reversed.

Analysis:

Architectural design regulations, like Ordinances 131 and 281 here, rarely come up for review in appellate courts. When they do, they have usually resulted from disputes in suburban communities. In a few of these cases regulations were invalidated because the promotion of aesthetic values was not considered a proper purpose of zoning. More recent cases, like *Stoyanoff* have relied on the protection of property values in their rationale rather than purely aesthetic justification. Some states, like California and Florida, have accepted the use of purely aesthetic considerations in deciding cases involving the regulation of signs and billboards. There is the possibility that architects or other individuals may challenge these sorts of design regulations on First Amendment grounds in the future.

■ CASE VOCABULARY

AESTHETIC: Having to do with beauty and art.

COGENT: Compelling, convincing.

PEREMPTORY: Blocking or precluding a course of action.

PREAMBLE: An introduction.

RELATOR: One who is permitted to bring a suit on behalf of the People or the Attorney General.

Anderson v. City of Issaquah

(Architect) v. (Municipality)

70 Wash.App. 64, 851 P.2d 744 (1993)

COURT STRIKES MUNICIPAL BUILDING ORDINANCES AS UNCONSTITUTIONALLY VAGUE

■ **INSTANT FACTS** An architect appealed the denial of a construction permit, arguing that the subjective aesthetic standards used by the city building commission were unconstitutionally vague.

■ **BLACK LETTER RULE** Local building ordinances that impose aesthetic conditions must provide sufficiently clear guidance to all interested parties.

■ **PROCEDURAL BASIS**

Appeal of verdict dismissing action seeking approval of certification of building plans.

■ **FACTS**

In 1988, Bruce Anderson (P) applied to the City of Issaquah (D) for certification to build a 6800-square-foot commercial building to be used for retail space. The application stalled when it was reviewed by the Issaquah Development Commission. The Development Commission was required to enforce various provisions of the Issaquah Municipal Code regarding building design and the relationship between the proposed building and the adjoining area. Among other things, the Code required that buildings be interesting and harmonious with the surrounding valley and mountains. The Development Commission informed Anderson (P) that his proposed building did not fit with the concept of the surrounding area. Specifically, the Commission did not like the building color, the design of either the front or rear facade, or the full-length glass windows. On three separate occasions, Anderson (P) modified his designs and returned to the Commission for approval. After nine months of this, the Commission finally denied his application, noting that Anderson (P) was unwilling to make the required changes to protect and enhance the aesthetic values of the City (D). Anderson (P), who had spent approximately $250,000 by this point, appealed to the Issaquah City Council. When the City Council denied his appeal, Anderson (P) filed suit in state court, arguing that the Code provisions were unconstitutionally vague. The trial court dismissed Anderson's (P) complaint, and he appeals.

■ **ISSUE**

Must aesthetic building standards provide clear guidance to all concerned parties?

■ **DECISION AND RATIONALE**

(Kennedy, J.) Yes. Aesthetic building standards must provide clear guidance to all concerned parties. Aesthetic standards are an appropriate and important component of land use governance. However, the Issaquah Code sections do not give effective or meaningful guidance to applicants, to design professionals, or to the public officials of Issaquah who are responsible for enforcing the Code. The words employed are not technical words which are commonly understood within the professional building design industry. Rather, the Code uses such subjective terms as "appropriate proportions" and harmony with "the natural setting of the valley," and it states that "monotony should be avoided." As a result, the commissioners were left to their own individual, subjective feelings about the "image of Issaquah" in reviewing

Anderson's (P) application. We hold that the Code sections at issue are unconstitutionally void, both on their face and as applied to Anderson (P). We order that Anderson's (P) land use certification be issued, provided that the changes to which Anderson agreed be imposed.

Analysis:

This case presents the interesting issue of local zoning ordinances designed to promote aesthetic values. The opinion demonstrates how difficult it is to effectively draft such an ordinance, which necessarily is based upon subjective evaluations. The City of Issaquah (D) certainly had a laudable goal in drafting the building design regulations. The City (D) should be entitled to maintain its beautiful character by imposing reasonable restrictions. On the other hand, architects working on projects in Issaquah (D) must have a clear and understandable set of regulations to follow. Note that if the regulations had been imposed by a private architectural control committee, such as a homeowners association, Anderson (P) would probably have lost. Specific standards are not required when private architectural restrictions are involved; rather, the committee is only required to act reasonably and in good faith.

■ **CASE VOCABULARY**

AD HOC: For a special purpose.

City of Ladue v. Gilleo

(Municipality) v. (Resident)

512 U.S. 43, 114 S.Ct. 2038 (1994)

SUPREME COURT INVALIDATES ORDINANCE THAT RESTRICTS SIGNS ON RESIDENTIAL PROPERTY

■ **INSTANT FACTS** A resident challenges a city ordinance that prohibits the displaying of signs, such as an antiwar protest sign, on front yards.

■ **BLACK LETTER RULE** A city may not constitutionally adopt ordinances that prohibit nearly all signs on residential property.

■ **PROCEDURAL BASIS**

Writ of certiorari reviewing order affirming judgment holding city ordinance unconstitutional.

■ **FACTS**

Margaret Gilleo (P) owned a home in the City of Ladue (D). A city ordinance prohibited homeowners from displaying any signs except residence identification signs, for sale signs, or signs warning of safety hazards. In December 1990, Gilleo (P) erected on her front lawn a 24- by 36-inch sign printed with the words "Say No to War in the Persian Gulf, Call Congress Now." Gilleo's (P) sign was removed, and when she reported it to the police they instructed her that such signs were prohibited in Ladue (D). After the City Council denied her petition for a variance, Gilleo (P) sued the City in federal court, arguing that Ladue's (D) sign ordinance violated her First Amendment right of free speech. The District Court issued a preliminary injunction against enforcement of the ordinance. Ladue (P) then placed a 8.5- by 11-inch sign in her window stating "For Peace in the Gulf." The City responded by amending its ordinance to include a Declaration of Findings, which stated that the ordinance was aimed at preventing ugliness, visual blight and clutter, among other things. The District Court held the new ordinance unconstitutional. The Court of Appeals affirmed, holding that the ordinance was a content-based regulation and that the City's (D) interests were not sufficiently compelling to support the restriction. The Supreme Court granted certiorari.

■ **ISSUE**

Is a city ordinance that prohibits homeowners from displaying virtually any signs on their property constitutional?

■ **DECISION AND RATIONALE**

(Stevens, J.) No. A city ordinance that prohibits homeowners from displaying virtually any signs on their property is not constitutional. Our past decisions identify two analytically distinct grounds for challenging the constitutionality of a municipal ordinance regulating the display of signs. First, the measure may restrict too little speech because its exemptions discriminate on the basis of the signs' messages. Second, the measure may prohibit too much protected speech. The City of Ladue (D) argues that its ordinance was content-neutral and that the City's (D) regulatory purposes justified the comprehensiveness of the sign regulation. We disagree. Ladue's (D) sign ordinance is based on the desire to minimize the visual clutter associated with signs. This is a valid interest, but it is not sufficient to overcome the ordinances chilling effects on free speech. Signs such as Gilleo's (P), protesting an imminent governmental decision to go to war, are absolutely pivotal in our society. Ladue (D) has almost completely foreclosed a venerable means of communication that is both unique and important. Indeed, Gilleo (P) could have communicated her message through other means, such as pamphlets or bumper stickers, but a much stronger statement is made by having the sign on your front lawn. Ladue's (D) restrictions foreclose an entire media (lawn signs) and thus suppress too much speech. We feel that more temperate measures could satisfy Ladue's (D) regulatory needs without harm to the First Amendment rights of its citizens. Affirmed.

Analysis:

Cities have a legitimate interest in keeping their neighborhoods free from visual clutter. But does an 8.5- by 11-inch sign in a window really cause visual clutter? In all likelihood, the City (D) ordinance was in fact aimed at suppressing the content of speech. The City (D) and its police force may have selectively chosen to enforce the ordinance against Gilleo (P) only because they did not like her antiwar message. According to the Court, even if the City had a benign, content-neutral goal, the indirect suppression of free speech was unconstitutional. Indeed, as Justice Stevens notes, most Americans would be dismayed by an ordinance that prohibited a small window sign that expressed political views.

■ CASE VOCABULARY

CONTENT-NEUTRAL: A regulation that restricts the time, place, or manner of some form of speech rather than restricting the content of the speech itself.

Guru Nanak Sikh Society of Yuba City v. County of Sutter

(Sikh Religious Group) v. (Governmental Entity)

456 F.3d 978 (9th Cir. 2006)

DENIAL OF A CONDITIONAL USE PERMIT MAY CONSTITUTE A SUBSTANTIAL BURDEN ON THE EXERCISE OF RELIGION

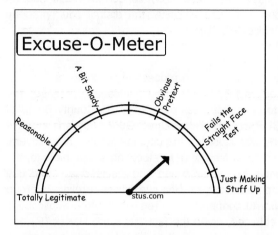

■ **INSTANT FACTS** After religious group's application for a conditional use permit to construct a Sikh temple at one location was denied by the county, it sought a permit for another location, which was also denied.

■ **BLACK LETTER RULE** Local land use regulations that require individualized assessments of the proposed uses of the property and impose substantial burdens on religious exercise without a compelling governmental reason violate the Federal Religious Land Use and Institutionalized Persons Act of 2000.

■ **PROCEDURAL BASIS**

Review of the district court's summary judgment in favor of the plaintiff.

■ **FACTS**

Guru Nanak (P) applied for conditional use permit (CUP) to construct a Sikh temple on a parcel of land zoned for low-density residential use. When citizens voiced concerns about noise and traffic interfering with the existing neighborhood, the county planning commission denied the CUP. Guru Nanak (P) subsequently purchased a larger parcel in an area zoned as a general agricultural district and again applied for a CUP to build a temple there. When the county planning commission approved the CUP, several neighbors appealed to the county board of supervisors. The board rejected the project mainly on the ground that the temple site was so separated from existing infrastructure as to constitute leapfrog development that did not promote orderly growth. The district court invalidated the County's (D) denial of the CUP, holding that it violated the Federal Religious Land Use and Institutionalized Persons Act of 2000 (RLUIPA).

■ **ISSUE**

Did the trial court err when it ruled that the County violated the RLUIPA by denying the religious group's conditional use permit?

■ **DECISION AND RATIONALE**

(Bell, J.) No. Local land use regulations that require individualized assessments of the proposed uses of the property and impose substantial burdens on religious exercise without a compelling governmental reason violate the Federal Religious Land Use and Institutionalized Persons Act of 2000. The RLUIPA prohibits the government from imposing a substantial burden on religious exercise in the absence of a compelling governmental interest. While the RLUIPA does not apply directly to land use regulations written in general and neutral terms, such as the county zoning code, it does apply when individualized assessments of the proposed land use to particular pieces of property are made, which is what happened in the case of both of the CUP applications submitted by Guru Nanak (P). The principal issue here was whether under the RLUIPA denial of the second CUP constituted a substantial burden on Guru Nanak's (P) religious exercise. Looking at the totality of the history behind the two CUP applications, we find that a substantial burden was imposed in light of the fact that the broad reasons given by the

---

County (D) for the two denials could readily apply to any future applications by Guru Nanak (P). Moreover, Guru Nanak (P) had agreed to every condition suggested by the planning division to obtain CUP approval, but the County (D) had, without explanation, found that cooperation insufficient. The effect of the two denials was to shrink the potentially available land for temple construction under the zoning code to a few scattered sites that may or may not ultimately be approved by the County (D). Since the County (D) conceded that it had no compelling interest that might permit its actions under the RLUIPA, the district court properly invalidated the County's (D) denial of Guru Nanak's (P) CUP.

Analysis:

The court emphasized the entire history of the CUP application process in reaching its decision that the County's (D) actions, including its reasons for the denials, significantly decreased the chances of Guru Nanak (P) ever being able to construct a temple. While the County Board of Supervisors, in connection with the second CUP denial, had assured Guru Nanak (P) that it would support a future application if the property was closer to the city and located near several other churches, and that it would cooperate with Guru Nanak (P) in locating a suitable site, the court observed that the RLUIPA does not permit the use of broad and discretionary land use rationales as leverage for a local government to select the specific site where a religious group can worship. Furthermore, the County's (D) offer to cooperate with regard to future applications was not any assurance that a CUP would be obtained, given the fact that Guru Nanak (P) had precisely followed the suggestions of various County (D) entities on how to obtain a permit to no avail the first two times around.

■ CASE VOCABULARY

CONDITIONAL USE PERMIT: A zoning board's authorization to use property in a way that is identified as a special exception in a zoning ordinance. • Unlike a variance, which is an authorized violation of a zoning ordinance, a special-use permit is a permitted exception.

Fisher v. Giuliani

(City Residents) v. (City)

720 N.Y.S.2d 50 (App. Div. 2001)

ENVIRONMENTAL IMPACT OF ZONING CODE AMENDMENTS MUST BE CONSIDERED AT TIME THEY ARE ENACTED

■ **INSTANT FACTS** City residents challenged zoning amendments affecting Manhattan Theater District on the grounds that an environmental impact statement was required before the changes could be implemented.

■ **BLACK LETTER RULE** Review of an agency determination of whether a zoning amendment will have a significant environmental impact is limited to deciding whether the agency took a hard look at identified relevant areas of environmental concern and made a reasoned statement of the basis for its determination.

■ **PROCEDURAL BASIS**

Appeal from trial court judgment in favor of plaintiffs.

■ **FACTS**

The City (D) proposed amending its zoning resolution with respect to the as-of-right transfer of developmental rights from designated theaters to receiving sites in the Theater Subdistrict. In addition the amendments established a mechanism for obtaining greater transfer rights via a special permit or discretionary authorization. As required by law, a City (D) agency, the Department of City Planning, performed an environmental assessment of the impact of the proposed as-of-right amendments, and after finding no significant impact issued a "negative declaration," which meant that no environmental impact statement needed to be prepared. No assessment was made as to the impact of the discretionary transfer amendments. Following city council approval of the amendments, residents of a neighboring city district (P) challenged the adequacy of the environmental review and resulting negative declaration. Trial court agreed with the challengers and annulled the amendments in their entirety and ordered an environmental impact statement be done, based on its conclusion, contrary to the agency's assessment, that the amendments would stimulate development. The City (D) appealed.

■ **ISSUE**

Did the trial court err in annulling the zoning amendments and ordering preparation of an environmental impact statement.

■ **DECISION AND RATIONALE**

(Friedman, J.) Yes, in part. Review of an agency determination of whether a zoning amendment will have a significant environmental impact is limited to deciding whether the agency took a hard look at identified relevant areas of environmental concern and made a reasoned statement of the basis for its determination. We will not consider the desirability of amendments, resolve expert disputes, choose among alternatives or substitute our judgment for that of the agency. If the agency's determination was not based on an error of law or arbitrary and capricious or an abuse of discretion it must stand. With respect to the as-of-right transfer mechanism zoning amendments, the agency's detailed analysis in the environmental assessment statement was entirely rational and supported its determination of no significant environmental impact, thereby obviating the need for an environmental impact statement. Those provisions of the zoning resolution not have been annulled by the trial court. However, the agency's failure to perform any environmental review at all of the discretionary transfer mechanism amendments prior to their enactment was error. It could not defer such analysis until an owner applied for a special permit to do so. Those provisions only must be severed from the zoning resolution and annulled

Analysis:

Among the assessment deficiencies identified by the residents were claims that the agency underestimated future demand in the Theater Subdistrict, that the as-of-right amendments will stimulate development and that it failed to look beyond ten years when it considered the long-term impact of those amendments. The agency's environmental assessment statement established, however, that it projected growth in excess of historic levels and that market demand and consequent development will remain stable. Furthermore, it was obligated to examine environmental consequences only into the foreseeable future, not the theoretical possibilities grounded in mere speculation asserted by the petitioners.

Village of Belle Terre v. Boraas

(Long Island Village) v. (College Student)

416 U.S. 1, 94 S.Ct. 1536 (1974)

UNITED STATES SUPREME COURT UPHOLDS A ZONING ORDINANCE'S ATTEMPT TO PROMOTE FAMIILY VALUES

■ **INSTANT FACTS** Boraas and five others challenged a Belle Terre ordinance which restricted land use to one-family dwellings and excluded households with over two unrelated persons.

■ **BLACK LETTER RULE** The legislature may define what counts as a "family" for zoning purposes if the definition is rationally related to legitimate objectives, such as creating zones where family values, youth values, and the blessings of quiet seclusion and clean air are preserved.

very interesting but seems to be a minority opinion ✱

■ **PROCEDURAL BASIS**

Appeal from action for injunction and judgment declaring ordinance constitutional.

■ **FACTS**

The Village of Belle Terre (D) is located on the north shore of Long Island. Though less than one square mile in area, it (D) is inhabited by 700 people in about 220 homes. Belle Terre (D) has restricted land use to single-family dwellings, excluding boarding houses, fraternity houses, and other multiple-dwelling houses. "Family" is defined as "[o]ne or more persons related by blood, adoption or marriage, living and cooking together as a single housekeeping unit." Households with more than two unrelated persons are explicitly excluded from the allowed definition of "family." Bruce Boraas (P), a student at nearby State University at Stony Brook, entered into a lease for a house in the village owned by the Dickmans (P). Another student was already leasing the house at this point. Later, four more students moved into the house. None of the students is related to the other by blood, adoption, or marriage. The Dickmans (Ps), Boraas (P), and two other tenants (P) filed suit for an injunction and a judgment to declare the Belle Terre ordinance unconstitutional. They (P) challenge the statute as arbitrary and unreasonable on several grounds, including that the restriction violates their right of privacy, that it is of no rightful concern to villagers whether the residents are married or not, and that having the neighborhood conform to one type of family is not a legitimate governmental interest. The District Court held the ordinance unconstitutional, but the Court of Appeals reversed.

■ **ISSUE**

Can a zoning ordinance which restricts land use according to what it defines as a family be constitutional?

■ **DECISION AND RATIONALE**

(Douglas, J.) Yes. The legislature may define what counts as a "family" for zoning purposes if the definition is rationally related to legitimate objectives, such as creating zones where family values and the blessings of quiet seclusion and clean air are preserved. The concept of public welfare, which is usually the goal of zoning regulations, is a broad and inclusive one. The legislature may determine what is involved in maintaining standards to protect the public welfare. The reasons offered by Boraas (P) and the others (P) for challenging the ordinance are invalid in this case. No fundamental right of the Constitution, including the right of privacy, is

Zoning generally P. 125

at stake in this case. Numerous cases in the past have involved the drawing of lines by the legislature between two different classifications of people. The distinctions here are not made on lines that are inherently suspect, like those based on race. Economic and social legislation such as this should withstand charges of violating the Equal Protection Clause if it is reasonable, not arbitrary, and if it bears a rational relationship to a permissible state objective. Here, a line is drawn between two unrelated people and three or more unrelated people in the definition of "family." The discretion in setting this line belongs with the legislature, not the courts. Moreover, boarding houses, fraternity houses, and other similar living arrangements present legitimate concerns for the Village (D). Increased population density, higher traffic flow, higher numbers of cars parked at each property, and greater noise levels can all result without the single-family restriction. These are all legitimate guidelines in a land-use project directed at filling family needs. The police power includes the ability to establish zones where "family values, youth values, and the blessings of quiet seclusion and clean air make the area a sanctuary for people."

■ DISSENT

(Marshall, J.) The classification imposed by the Belle Terre (D) ordinance burdens the students' fundamental rights of association and privacy as guaranteed by the First and Fourteenth Amendments. Although deference should be given to legislatures in areas of zoning, this Court still has the duty of protecting fundamental rights. People have the freedom to choose their associates, not only in the political sense, but also in areas that are of economic and social benefit. This concept is tied to the individual's right to privacy in his or her home. Surely, the choice of one's household companions falls within this right. Here, the ordinance essentially singles out those people who choose to live their lives in a manner that differs from that of current residents. The concerns of population density and traffic are legitimate ones. The ordinance does not, however, impose any occupancy limitations whatsoever on people who are related by blood, adoption, or marriage. It is even more underinclusive in that it does not restrict the number of automobiles owned by members of one household. The ordinance is also overinclusive in that it can exclude a large number of unrelated persons who may live together even if they had only one income and no vehicles contributing to traffic and space problems. It goes beyond restricting land use and attempts to regulate the people's particular means of association. Because such fundamental rights are at stake, the ordinance should only pass constitutional scrutiny if the burden imposed is necessary to protect a compelling and substantial governmental interest.

Analysis:

The Court makes particular note here of "family values . . . and clean air" in its listing of legitimate purposes for zoning ordinances. It is certainly possible that in addition to the more "urban" problems, the residents of Belle Terre (D) were afraid that their quiet little village would be overrun by "hippies" from the State University looking to establish co-ops and communes in the area. Since then, more and more state courts have invalidated the kind of restrictive definition of "family" that was sustained here, on either state statutory or constitutional grounds. For example, the New Jersey Supreme Court believes its state constitution prohibits zoning regulations that limit the number of people in a given household, saying that "such regulations are insufficiently related to the perceived social ills" that they are meant to address [*State v. Baker*, 81 N.J. 99, 405 A.2d 368 (1979)]. The highest courts in Michigan, New York and Pennsylvania have all made similar rulings. The California Supreme Court, as well, has held that a zoning ordinance that sets out a definition of a "family" violates state constitutional protections of "privacy."

■ CASE VOCABULARY

ANIMOSITY: Resentment.

CAPRICE: A sudden, unmotivated impulse.

DOGMA: An established opinion, taken as authority.

PHILANTHROPIC: Characterized by goodwill and generosity.

TRANSIENT: One who passes through a place and stays only briefly.

City of Edmonds v. Oxford House, Inc.

(Municipality) v. (Group Home)

514 U.S. 725, 115 S.Ct. 1776 (1995)

SINGLE-FAMILY ZONING RESTRICTION IS NOT EXEMPT FROM FEDERAL HOUSING ACT SCRUTINY

■ **INSTANT FACTS** A city sued to enforce its residential single-family zoning restrictions against a group home for recovering alcoholics and drug addicts.

■ **BLACK LETTER RULE** A single-family zoning regulation is not automatically exempt from FHA scrutiny, even if it indirectly limits the maximum number of occupants in a house.

■ **PROCEDURAL BASIS**

Writ of certiorari reviewing order reversing judgment exempting city housing ordinance from FHA.

■ **FACTS**

The City of Edmonds' (P) zoning code restricted the composition of households in single-family areas, defining "family" as any number of persons related by genetics, adoption, or marriage, or a group of five or fewer unrelated persons. Oxford House (D) opened a group home in Edmonds (P) for 10 to 12 unrelated adults recovering from alcoholism and drug addiction in a neighborhood zoned for single-family residences. The City (P) issued criminal citations to the owner and a resident of the Oxford House (D) for violating the zoning code. The City (P) then sued Oxford House (D) in federal district court for a declaration that the Fair Housing Act ("FHA") did not prohibit Edmonds' (P) ordinance. Oxford House (D) counterclaimed based on the FHA, claiming that the City failed to make reasonable accommodations for handicapped persons. The City (P) conceded that the residents of Oxford House (D) were "handicapped" for purposes of the FHA, but the City (P) relied on an FHA exception which exempts any reasonable restrictions regarding the maximum number of occupants permitted to occupy a dwelling. The District Court held that the Edmonds' (P) ordinance was exempt from FHA scrutiny, but the Ninth Circuit reversed. The Supreme Court granted certiorari.

■ **ISSUE**

Does a city's single-family zoning ordinance, requiring households to be related or fewer than five people, qualify for an exemption to the FHA as a restriction of the maximum number of occupants permitted to occupy a dwelling?

■ **DECISION AND RATIONALE**

(Ginsburg, J.) No. A city's single-family zoning ordinance, requiring households to be related or house fewer than five people, does not qualify for an exemption to the FHA as a restriction of the maximum number of occupants permitted to occupy a dwelling. The broad purpose of the FHA is to provide, within constitutional limitations, for fair housing throughout the United States. We feel that the FHA's exception to this general policy statement should be read narrowly in order to preserve the primary purpose of achieving fair housing. In contrast to single-family restrictions, which are aimed at preserving the character of neighborhoods, maximum

---

occupancy restrictions cap the number of occupants in relation to floor space in order to protect health and safety. Single-family restrictions do not fall within the FHA's maximum-occupancy exemption. The City of Edmonds' (P) restriction is a classic example of a use restriction and family composition rule. This rule does not cap the number of people who may live in a dwelling for health reasons. Rather, a separate provision in the city code provides for maximum occupancy limitations. The single-family restriction does not answer the question, "What is the maximum number of occupants permitted to occupy a house?" Any number of genetically-related individuals could live in a house and be in conformity with the single-family restriction. We thus hold that Edmonds' (P) single-family occupancy restriction does not qualify for the FHA exemption. It remains for the lower court to determine whether the restriction violates the FHA. Affirmed.

Analysis:

The Court's analysis in this case makes clear that the purpose of the FHA exemption was to allow maximum-occupancy restrictions for the purposes of health and safety. Health and safety is arguably a more important goal than preserving the single-family character of neighborhoods. Nevertheless, it is important to note that single-family restrictions are not necessarily invalid; they just are not automatically exempt from the FHA. On remand, Oxford House (D) would probably stress the importance of allowing recovering addicts to live in a community environment, and it would argue that it would be financially prohibitive to limit the number of residents to five or fewer. The City (P) probably would cite the increased traffic and noise resulting from the occupants. But would this group of people create any more noise or traffic than a large family with lots of children?

■ CASE VOCABULARY

EUCLIDEAN ZONING: A typical general zoning plan that separates a city into different districts based on use restrictions.

Southern Burlington County NAACP v. Township of Mount Laurel

(Minority and Poor Representatives) v. (Town)

67 N.J. 151, 336 A.2d 713 (1975), appeal dismissed and cert. denied, 423 U.S. 808, 96 S.Ct. 18

A MUNICIPALITY CANNOT ESTABLISH REGULATIONS WHICH MAKE IT IMPOSSIBLE FOR LOW AND MODERATE INCOME FAMILIES TO RESIDE THERE

■ **INSTANT FACTS** Mount Laurel enacted a general zoning ordinance which effectively prevented low and middle income persons from acquiring affordable homes within the township.

■ **BLACK LETTER RULE** A developing municipality must, by its land use regulations, make realistically possible the opportunity for an appropriate variety and choice of housing for all categories of people who may desire to live there, including those of low and moderate income.

■ **PROCEDURAL BASIS**

Appeal from judgment in action for declaratory and injunctive relief.

■ **FACTS**

The Township of Mount Laurel (D) is roughly 22 square miles, or 14,000 acres, in area. In 1950, Mount Laurel had a population of only 2817. By 1970, the population had grown to 11,221. The general zoning ordinance for the township (D) was enacted in 1964. About 10,000 acres is divided into four residential zones, designated R−1, R−1D, R−2, and R−3. All of these zones allow only single-family, detached dwellings, with only one house per lot. While this development arrangement did result in the quadrupling of the population, it has also resulted in intensive development of only the R−1 and R−2 sections, and at a low density. These homes were worth a substantial $32,500 in 1971 and are worth more today. The general zoning ordinance also establishes large minimum lot areas (9,375 square feet) and large minimum floor areas for houses (1,100 to 1,300 square feet) in the R−1 and R−2 zones. The R−1D district was created by ordinance amendment in 1968 as a cluster zone, and contains dwellings that are comparable in character and cost to those in the R−1 and R−2 zones. Between 1967 and 1971, Mount Laurel approved four planned unit developments (PUDs). These projects involve at least 10,000 sale and rental housing units of various types to be built over several years. None of these units, however, will be within the financial reach of low and middle-income families, especially those with young children. Indeed, the number of apartments having more than one bedroom are limited, and the number of children that can live in each unit are more strictly regulated. Also, rents are pushed higher as a result of required amenities, such as central air conditioning, and developer contributions to the township, such as contributions to schools, fire departments, and other public services. Further, a 1972 supplement to the general zoning ordinance created a new zone, R−4, Planned Adult Retirement Community (PARC). The supplement restricted the number of occupants in each unit and ensured that they would be too costly for many retirees. While an official report in 1969 recognized the lack of decent housing for citizens living in substandard conditions, the government has responded by waiting for rundown buildings to be vacated and then forbidding people to occupy them. When a private non-profit group attempted to construct subsidized, multi-family housing in the R−3 zone in 1968, the township (D) held the corporation to the strict zoning requirements for single-family dwellings on 20,000 square foot lots. Such requirements blocked this attempt at low-cost housing. The Southern Burlington County NAACP (P) represent the minority group poor, predominantly black and Hispanic, who have sought low and moderate-cost housing in Mount Laurel (D).

■ ISSUE

Can a municipality validly, through its land use regulations, make it physically and economically impossible to provide low and moderate income housing in the municipality for the various categories of persons who may need it or want it?

■ DECISION AND RATIONALE

(Hall, J.) No. A developing municipality must, by its land use regulations, make realistically possible the opportunity for an appropriate variety and choice of housing for all categories of people who may desire to live there, including those of low and moderate income. This obligation must be met unless the municipality in question can sustain the heavy burden of showing that particular circumstances prevent it from fulfilling the obligation. Land use regulation is part of the police power of the state, and any zoning provision that goes against the general welfare is invalid. Granted, determining what is valid or invalid in the area of land use regulation is not always easy to determine. Nonetheless, a fundamental concept to be aware of is that when regulation has a substantial impact outside its original municipality, the welfare of the citizens of the state as a whole cannot be disregarded and must be recognized and served. Proper provision for adequate housing for all categories of people is critical in promoting this general welfare required in all local land use regulation. In this case, while single-family dwellings are readily provided by Mount Laurel (D), this housing option is certainly the most expensive one possible. Such housing is out of the economic reach of low and middle income families, most young people and many retired persons. The minimum lot area and house area requirements also clearly increase the size and cost of housing in the township (D). The inescapable conclusion is that Mount Laurel (D) permits this zoning to continue in order to benefit from the high property taxes that will result from it. Thus, Mount Laurel's (D) zoning ordinance is facially invalid, and so the burden shifts to the township (D) to establish valid reasons for not fulfilling its obligation to provide a full range of housing. The township (D) argues that it has the right to encourage the presence of commerce and industry and their accompanying high rates of tax revenue. It (D) also argues for the right to limit the presence of school-age children, for such residents would then require costly services and facilities, yet would be unable to pay their own way taxwise. These arguments are invalid, and no municipality may exclude or limit categories of housing for such financial reasons or purposes. Relief from these tax burdens will have to be paid for by other branches of government, and not through the zoning process. There is no reason why growing areas like Mount Laurel (D) may not continue to be attractive and prosperous communities, providing good housing and services for all their different residents. The entire zoning ordinance should not be nullified, as the trial court has held. The township (D) is given 90 days to adopt amendments which will comply with the ruling of this court, and it (D) should first have the opportunity to act without judicial supervision. Judgment modified.

Analysis:

The New Jersey Supreme Court eventually decided a second Mount Laurel appeal, along with seven other cases. The court extended the first Mount Laurel with four major clarifications. First, all municipalities, developing and otherwise, must provide a realistic opportunity for low and middle income housing. Second, those challenging exclusionary zoning can establish a prima facie case that the zoning is invalid if they can prove the zoning substantially limits the building of low and middle income housing. Third, to counter this prima facie case, a municipality has to show "numerical" evidence of the number of units needed, both immediately and within a reasonable time in the future, and do more than show a "bona fide effort" to eliminate exclusionary zoning. Fourth, if removal of the invalid zoning regulations was insufficient, a municipality would have to take affirmative steps to provide a reasonable opportunity for low and middle income housing.

■ **CASE VOCABULARY**

RATABLE: A proportional value; something that can be apportioned according to changing values.

TOWNSHIP: Essentially, a town or parish.

In the aftermath, the legislature did nothing with this decision, so then leads to Mt. Laurel II

See the outline

Builders remedy - builder can challenge a town as non-compliant

She says that the Mt. Laurel mandate can work, but the legislature needs to do its job

She likes Mt. Laurel

CHAPTER TWELVE

Eminent Domain and the Problem of Regulatory Takings

Kelo v. City of New London

Instant Facts: The City of New London condemned private property to be used for commercial, residential, and recreational purposes as part of an economic revitalization project.

Black Letter Rule: Takings of private property for use by other private citizens pursuant to an economic development plan intended for a public purpose are valid under the Fifth Amendment.

Loretto v. Teleprompter Manhattan CATV Corp.

Instant Facts: A new building owner sued a cable company over the cable it was allowed to install on the building by a state statute.

Black Letter Rule: A permanent physical occupation of an owner's property authorized by the government constitutes a taking of property which requires just compensation, regardless of the public interests it may serve.

Hadacheck v. Sebastian

Instant Facts: Hadacheck built a brickyard outside city limits, but after the city grew and surrounded it, the city said Hadacheck violated an ordinance against brickyards.

Black Letter Rule: A regulation that deprives an owner of property for the purpose of prohibiting a nuisance is an exercise of the police power, and therefore does not result in a taking which requires compensation.

Pennsylvania Coal Co. v. Mahon

Instant Facts: A company sold surface rights to some land to Mahon, but retained the right to mine underneath, and such mining was prohibited by statute.

Black Letter Rule: While property may be regulated to a certain extent, if that regulation goes too far in diminishing the economic value of the property, it will be recognized as a taking.

Penn Central Transportation Co. v. City of New York

Instant Facts: Penn Central made plans to construct an office building over Grand Central Terminal, but was blocked by a Landmarks Preservation Law.

Black Letter Rule: A law which does not interfere with an owner's primary expectation concerning the use of the property, and allows the owners to receive a reasonable return on his or her investment, does not effect a taking which demands just compensation.

Lucas v. South Carolina Coastal Council

Instant Facts: Lucas claimed that a South Carolina statute which barred him from building on his barrier island property resulted in a taking without just compensation.

Black Letter Rule: A land-use regulation that deprives an owner of all economically valuable use of property by prohibiting uses that are permitted under background principles of property and nuisance law results in a taking, and thus requires compensation.

Palazzolo v. Rhode Island

Instant Facts: Rhode Island (D) found that regulations designating most of Palazzolo's (P) land as protected "coastal wetlands" did not effect of taking partly because the regulations predated Palazzolo's (P) title to the land.

Black Letter Rule: The acquisition of title after the enactment of a regulation does not bar a challenge to that regulation under the Takings Clause.

Tahoe-Sierra Preservation Council, Inc. v. Tahoe Regional Planning Agency

Instant Facts: Property owners in the Lake Tahoe area were prohibited from undertaking any development of their property for thirty-two months in order to get a handle on the development needs of the area to preserve its natural beauty.

Black Letter Rule: A regulation that prohibits economic use of land for an extended but finite period of time does not constitute a taking requiring that the owner of the property be compensated.

Stop the Beach Renourishment, Inc. v. Florida Department of Environmental Protection

Instant Facts: The state created an "erosion line" on the beach by adding dredged-up sand to the existing beach area and then claimed the land as public property, thereby decreasing the amount of beach owned by the littoral property owners.

Black Letter Rule: If an avulsion exposes land seaward of littoral property that had previously been submerged, that land belongs to the state even if it interrupts the littoral owner's contact with the water, and there is no exception when the state itself causes the avulsion.

Nollan v. California Coastal Commission

Instant Facts: The Commission granted Nollan a building permit on the condition that Nollan allow the public to pass across his property to access a public beach.

Black Letter Rule: If a regulatory condition is imposed on a development permit, that condition must substantially advance the same governmental purpose that refusing the permit would serve or else the action will constitute a taking and require just compensation.

Dolan v. City of Tigard

Instant Facts: In exchange for the approval of a building permit, a city attempted to force a business owner to dedicate a portion of her property to the city for floodplain and recreational easements.

Black Letter Rule: Exactions are constitutional provided the benefits achieved are reasonably related and roughly proportional, both in nature and extent, to the impact of the proposed development.

Koontz v. St. Johns River Water Management District

Instant Facts: Koontz (P) applied for a permit to develop a small part of a parcel he owned that was classified as wetlands, but the Water Management District conditioned the permit on either reducing the size of the development to one acre or paying for improvements to other public lands; Koontz (P) argued that the district's actions constituted a taking.

Black Letter Rule: The government may not deny a benefit to a person because he exercises a constitutional right.

Kelo v. City of New London

(Property Owner) v. *(Municipality)*

545 U.S. 469, 125 S.Ct. 2655 (2005)

ECONOMIC DEVELOPMENT IS A VALID PUBLIC PURPOSE FOR WHICH EMINENT DOMAIN MAY BE EXERCISED

You know the song, "This land is your land, this land is my land"? The Supreme Court says It's actually my land.

stus.com

- **■ INSTANT FACTS** The City of New London condemned private property to be used for commercial, residential, and recreational purposes as part of an economic revitalization project.

- **■ BLACK LETTER RULE** Takings of private property for use by other private citizens pursuant to an economic development plan intended for a public purpose are valid under the Fifth Amendment.

■ PROCEDURAL BASIS

Certiorari to review a decision of the Connecticut Supreme Court for the defendant.

■ FACTS

In 2000, the City of New London (D) proposed a development plan in an effort to revitalize the local economy. In total, the plan involved seven parcels of land, some of which was privately owned, intended to be used for a mixture of commercial, residential, and recreational purposes. The City of New London (D) appointed and authorized the New London Development Corporation, a private nonprofit entity, to negotiate and purchase the private property necessary to implement the plan. When negotiations with Kelo (P) and eight other property owners broke down, the City of New London (D) initiated condemnation proceedings under its eminent domain powers. The City (D) made no claim that the properties were in poor condition. The petitioners brought suit in superior court, challenging the City's (D) actions, claiming that the taking of their property was not for public use within the meaning of the Fifth Amendment. After trial, the superior court held that some of the takings were invalid, while others were permissible. Both parties appealed to the Connecticut Supreme Court, which held that all of the City's (D) takings were valid as part of a development plan intended for public use and in the public interest. The petitioners sought certiorari.

■ ISSUE

Is the taking of private property to be used for commercial, residential, and recreational purposes under an economic revitalization project for "public use"?

■ DECISION AND RATIONALE

(Stevens, J.) Yes. A sovereign may not take the private property of one person with the purpose to confer a benefit upon another. Yet, the mere fact that one's private property is taken and given to another private citizen does not render the taking invalid, so long as the taking is for future "use by the public." Here, the taking was effected pursuant to a "carefully considered" development plan, and neither court below found an illegitimate purpose. However, the taken land is not intended to be entirely opened to the public, nor are the lessees of the land compelled to entirely open the land to the public. Nonetheless, "public use" does not require that the property be intended only for "use by the public," but rather that that taking be for a "public purpose." Therefore, the takings are valid if the development plan authorizing the takings is intended for a public purpose. When considering whether a development plan is for a public purpose, considerable deference is given to legislative judgments. Plans are not considered piecemeal, lot by lot, but rather in their entirety to determine the overall intentions of the plan.

Here, the plan was carefully considered to promote the local economy and public welfare. Although the plan combines commercial, residential, and recreational purposes for the condemned land, transferring some private property from one individual to another, the plan's overall character furthers the public purposes of job growth, increased tax revenue, and economic development. Economic development is a longstanding function of government. Just as with the conversion of blighted areas into respectable communities, *Berman v. Parker*, 348 U.S. 26 (1954), and the breaking up of land oligopolies, *Hawaii Housing Authority v. Midkiff*, 467 U.S. 229 (1984), economic development constitutes a public purpose, even if the land itself is not entirely "used by the public." Affirmed.

Analysis:

In an omitted dissenting opinion, Justice O'Connor predicted that the Court's decision left the door open to governmental taking of any private property capable of improvement and resale under any economic development plan. But that prophecy has not proven true. Rather, since the *Kelo* decision, the most emphasized aspect of the case has been the court's deference to legislative decision-making in matters of eminent domain. That emphasis has prompted significant federal and state legislation limiting the right of eminent domain for purely economic development.

■ CASE VOCABULARY

EMINENT DOMAIN: The inherent power of a governmental entity to take privately owned property, especially land, and convert it to public use, subject to reasonable compensation for the taking.

JUST COMPENSATION: Under the Fifth Amendment, a fair payment by the government for property it has taken under eminent domain—usually the property's fair market value, so that the owner is no worse off after the taking.

PUBLIC PURPOSE: An action by or at the direction of the government for the benefit of the community as a whole.

TAKING: The government's actual or effective acquisition of private property either by ousting the owner and claiming title or by destroying the property or severely impairing its utility.

Loretto v. Teleprompter Manhattan CATV Corp.

(Building Owner) v. (Cable Company)

458 U.S. 419, 102 S.Ct. 3164 (1982)

UNITED STATES SUPREME COURT HOLDS THAT A NEW YORK STATUTE ALLOWING A CABLE TELEVISION COMPANY TO PERMANENTLY ATTACH ITS COMPONENTS TO AN APARTMENT BUILDING WITHOUT INTERFERENCE AMOUNTED TO A TAKING

■ **INSTANT FACTS** A new building owner sued a cable company over the cable it was allowed to install on the building by a state statute.

■ **BLACK LETTER RULE** A permanent physical occupation of an owner's property authorized by the government constitutes a taking of property which requires just compensation, regardless of the public interests it may serve.

■ **PROCEDURAL BASIS**

Appeal from summary judgment in class action for damages and injunctive relief.

■ **FACTS**

On June 1, 1970, Teleprompter Manhattan CATV Corporation (D) installed a cable on an apartment building located at 303 West 105th Street, New York City. The owner gave Teleprompter (D) the exclusive right to provide cable television (CATV) services to the tenants. The cable was about one-half inch in diameter, and about 30 feet long. It ran along the roof of the building, and was attached to two small directional taps, which allowed for future connections. These and other components were attached directly to the masonry. This cable served as a "crossover" line, helping provide other buildings on the block with CATV. Jean Loretto (P) purchased the building in 1971. Teleprompter (D) connected a direct, "noncrossover" cable line to the building two years later. Earlier, the State enacted Executive Law § 828, effective January 1, 1973, which provided that a landlord "may not interfere with the installation of cable facilities upon his property or premises." The State Commission on Cable Television said that a landlord is only entitled to a one-time $1 fee for installation. Loretto (P) was not aware of the cable until after she bought the building. Loretto (P) brought a class action against Teleprompter (D) on behalf of all owners of real property in the State on which Teleprompter (D) placed its components. She (P) claimed it was a trespass and, insofar as it relied on § 828, a taking without just compensation. The City of New York intervened. The trial court granted summary judgment for Teleprompter and the city. The Court of Appeals, over dissent, upheld the statute.

■ **ISSUE**

Does a permanent physical occupation of an owner's property, authorized by government, constitute a taking of property which requires just compensation?

■ **DECISION AND RATIONALE**

(Marshall, J.) Yes. A permanent physical occupation of an owner's property authorized by the government constitutes a taking of property which requires just compensation, regardless of the public interests it may serve. A permanent occupation has long been viewed as arguably the most serious invasion of an owner's property interests. A classic example of this is found in

---

cases where a person constructs a dam which permanently floods another person's property. A permanent physical occupation prevents the owner from both possessing the occupied space and excluding the occupier from possession and use of it. This power to exclude is one of the most important elements in an owner's "bundle of property rights." The owner is denied any control over the use of the property. Though an owner may still have the right to sell the property, that right is seriously devalued, as a purchaser would also be unable to use the occupied space. While the size of an occupation should be considered in determining compensation, it should make no difference in finding whether a taking has occurred. Teleprompter (D) argues § 828 only applies to rental property, and thus is a permissible regulation. An occupation of only one type of property, however, is nonetheless an occupation. This reasoning will not have adverse consequences on the state's ability to regulate housing conditions, because such regulation imposes duties on landlords and tenants, not on outside third parties. Landlords can still install fire extinguishers and smoke alarms, provided third parties are not involved. The State can still regulate an owner's use of property, but it cannot authorize a permanent physical occupation of the property. Judgment reversed. Case remanded on issue of compensation.

■ DISSENT

(Blackmun, J.) The permanent physical occupation formula is a very problematic standard. The exact meaning of "permanent" is unclear. Section 828 only requires that the cable equipment be allowed as long as the building "remains residential and the CATV company wishes to retain the installation." If this law results in a "permanent" occupation, other New York statutes that compel a landlord to make physical attachments (like smoke alarms) to his or her property must also constitute takings, "regardless of the public interests they may serve." The majority's "third party" problem would still exist even if Loretto (P) owned the cable herself (P). If Teleprompter (D) continued to transmit its signal through the cable, a host of conceptual arguments on whether such a signal is "physical" could result. The distinction between permanent occupation versus temporary invasion has no basis in Takings Clause precedent or economic logic. Takings claims should be evaluated under a multiple factor balancing test, and not by a set formula. Also, Loretto (P) would have had no other use for this space, and any determination of compensation should be made with this in mind. Moreover, the majority assumes that the tenants have no countervailing interest in allowing Teleprompter (D) to use the space. Finally, this decision suggests that the legislature cannot exercise its police power to grant Teleprompter (D) the rights to even one-eighth cubic foot of space.

Analysis:

The New York Court of Appeals heard the issue of just compensation on remand. The Court said the $1 sum was sufficient because cable service usually increases the value of a building, particularly in the eyes of potential renters. With this in mind, it would appear that Loretto brought this suit for nothing. Granted, Teleprompter's installments did constitute an occupation, but the Court of Appeals recognized it had increased the value of Loretto's property. The presence of cable television likely made the property more attractive to potential renters in a city where high-rise structures impaired television reception. It was also a taking that the tenants who desired cable service presumably wanted. In addition, Teleprompter could have argued that its cable television service, authorized by the City, equaled a public use. In California, at least, the courts have declared that the promotion of public recreation and education is a legitimate public purpose. The provision of cable television could arguably fit this purpose.

■ CASE VOCABULARY

METAPHYSICAL: Pertaining to theories and philosophies on the reality of something beyond mere sensory perception.

TAP: An intermediate point in an electrical circuit which can support additional connections.

Hadacheck v. Sebastian

(Brickyard Owner) v. (Chief of Police)

239 U.S. 394, 36 S.Ct. 143 (1915)

A BRICKYARD HAD TO BE SHUT DOWN ACCORDING TO A CITY ORDINANCE, EVEN THOUGH IT WAS BUILT LONG BEFORE THE CITY GREW; ITS OWNER WAS NOT ENTITLED TO COMPENSATION BECAUSE THE BRICKYARD WAS A NUISANCE

■ **INSTANT FACTS** Hadacheck built a brickyard outside city limits, but after the city grew and surrounded it, the city said Hadacheck violated an ordinance against brickyards.

■ **BLACK LETTER RULE** A regulation that deprives an owner of property for the purpose of prohibiting a nuisance is an exercise of the police power, and therefore does not result in a taking which requires compensation.

■ FACTS

Hadacheck (P) is the owner of a tract which is now within the limits of the City of Los Angeles. An ordinance is in effect in the city which makes it unlawful for any person to establish or operate a brick yard or any other facility for the manufacture or burning of brick within city limits. At the time Hadacheck (P) purchased the land, it was outside city limits. He did not expect the city to annex the surrounding area. On this tract, there is a very valuable bed of clay, which can be used to make fine quality bricks. The entire tract, if used for brick-making purposes, is worth about $800,000; if the tract were used for any other purpose, it would be worth no more than $60,000. Hadacheck (P) has already made significant excavations over much of the tract; it cannot be used for residential purposes. He (P) has also set up expensive machinery for the manufacturing of bricks. The city has since grown and annexed the land adjoining the brick yard. Hadacheck (P) argues, among many other things, that his tract contains particularly fine clay, so that if the ordinance is declared valid he will be deprived of the use of his property without just compensation. Also, he (P) argues the brickyard is not a nuisance, and does not pose a danger to public health and safety. He (P) claims that no one has registered a complaint about it during the seven years he (P) has operated it. Affidavits were provided which counter Hadacheck's (P) allegations that the brick yard was not offensive to public health, claiming that fumes and dust from the yard have caused discomfort to those living nearby. Hadacheck (P) was convicted of a misdemeanor for his violation of the city ordinance.

■ ISSUE

Can a person's property be taken in the prohibition of a nuisance without compensation?

■ DECISION AND RATIONALE

(McKenna, J.) Yes. A regulation that deprives an owner of property for the purpose of prohibiting a nuisance is an exercise of the police power, and therefore does not result in a taking which requires compensation. This is one of the most essential powers of government, and has few limitations. Though its particular use here may seem harsh, the general need for such power precludes any limitation, provided that the power is not used arbitrarily. A police power cannot be challenged by a person's interest in property because of conditions that were in effect when the property was obtained. To allow such opposition would hinder the growth and development of cities. To promote growth, private interests must yield to the good of the community. Granted, Hadacheck's (P's) business of brickmaking is lawful in and of itself. It is clearly, however, within the power of the State to regulate such a business and to declare that, in certain circumstances and certain areas, the business would constitute a nuisance. The affidavits provided, claiming the brickyard led to discomfort of nearby residents, further demonstrates that the adjoining area is now being used for residential purposes. Because of this situation, the brickyard does constitute a nuisance, and thus can be prohibited. Though Hadacheck (P) claims the enforcement of the ordinance will deprive him of the use of his (P's) property and his (P's) business, this is not entirely true. While Hadacheck (P) could not operate a brickyard on his (P's) tract, he (P) is not prohibited from removing the clay to be used at a brickyard outside the area bound by the ordinance. Though such operation of his business would be difficult from a financial standpoint, it is not impossible. Judgment affirmed.

Analysis:

The Court's categorical decision in Hadacheck has been heavily criticized. It appears that whenever a person engages in nuisance-like behavior on his or her property, the person must expect government regulation curbing his or her property rights if necessary. In Hadacheck's case, Hadacheck should have expected that Los Angeles would grow beyond its limits; that residents would move and build homes near his brickyard; that Los Angeles would annex the surrounding land; that the city would pass an ordinance against the business he would have been running for years up to that point; and that the city would have a valid claim to shut down his business, or possibly move it off his property after several years. But this chain of events seems to be a lot to hold Hadacheck responsible for. This categorical ruling is markedly different from the categorical ruling in *Loretto*. There, the Court said that a permanent physical occupation by the government is always considered a taking; here, a nuisance-control action by the government is never considered by the Court to be a taking.

■ CASE VOCABULARY

HABEAS CORPUS: Writ which brings a party before a court, mainly to release that party from unlawful imprisonment.

KILN: An oven or furnace used for the firing and drying of bricks during their manufacturing process.

TRAVERSE: Denial of an allegation.

Pennsylvania Coal Co. v. Mahon

(Mineral Rights Owner) v. (Surface Rights Owner)

260 U.S. 393, 43 S.Ct. 158 (1922)

UNITED STATES SUPREME COURT HOLDS THAT WHERE A COAL COMPANY DEEDED THE SURFACE RIGHTS TO PROPERTY BUT RETAINED THE RIGHT TO MINE UNDERNEATH, A STATUTE WHICH BARRED SUCH MINING COULD NOT BE SUSTAINED BECAUSE IT DESTROYED THE COAL COMPANY'S MINERAL RIGHTS

■ **INSTANT FACTS** A company sold surface rights to some land to Mahon, but retained the right to mine underneath, and such mining was prohibited by statute.

■ **BLACK LETTER RULE** While property may be regulated to a certain extent, if that regulation goes too far in diminishing the economic value of the property, it will be recognized as a taking.

[handwritten: economic discrimination, so rational basis standard of review]

[handwritten: so compensation is needed]

[handwritten: SHG p. 131 remedies for regulatory taking]

■ **PROCEDURAL BASIS**

Writ of error after decree for bill in equity for injunctive relief.

■ **FACTS**

In 1878, Pennsylvania Coal Company (D) executed a deed which conveyed property rights to the surface of some land to Mahon (P). The deed also states, however, in express terms, that the Coal Company (D) reserves the right to remove all the coal under that surface, and that Mahon (P) takes the premises with that risk. The deed also provides that Mahon (P) waives all claim for damages that may arise from mining out the coal. Mahon (P) claims that whatever rights the Coal Company (D) may have had, these rights were taken away by the Kohler Act, approved May 27, 1921. The Kohler Act forbids the mining of coal in such a way that would cause the sinking of, among other things, any structure used for human habitation. There are certain exceptions, including the mining of land where the surface is owned by the owner of the underlying coal and is more than 150 feet from anyone else's improved property. The Court of Common Pleas found that mining by the Coal Company would remove the supporting earth underneath the house and cause the house and surface to sink. Despite this finding, however, the Court denied Mahon's (P's) request for an injunction, holding that, if applied to this case, the Kohler Act would be unconstitutional. The Supreme Court of the State held the statute was a legitimate exercise of the police power and directed a decree for the plaintiffs. A writ of error was then granted.

[handwritten: diminution in value test]

[handwritten: reversed, so in favor of Pennsylvania Coal company]

[handwritten: Court held statute illegitimate]

■ **ISSUE**

Is a property regulation statute which eliminates a pre-existing property right the equivalent of a taking without compensation?

[handwritten: If a taking, then must be paid compensation for the taking]

■ **DECISION AND RATIONALE**

(Holmes, J.) Yes. While property may be regulated to a certain extent, if that regulation goes too far in diminishing the economic value of the property, it will be recognized as a taking. It has long been recognized that some property rights are enjoyed under an implied limitation and must yield to the government's police power. This implied limitation must also be limited, however, by the contract and due process clauses. At some point, eminent domain must be

---

exercised and compensation must be given for interfering with a person's property rights. Where that point lies depends on the facts of each case. Here, while there is undoubtedly a public interest in protecting the owner of a single home, the potential damage is not common or public. Indeed, the Kohler Act demonstrates the limited extent of this public interest, with its exception for people who own both the surface and the coal beneath. Further, the Kohler Act is not justified as a protection of personal safety, as the Coal Company (D) here has given notice of its intent to mine under the house. To enforce this Act would eliminate the Coal Company's (D's) interest in the coal, which is viewed as an estate in land in Pennsylvania, and go against a valid contract between the Coal Company (D) and Mahon (D). The Act does not offer a public interest sufficient to warrant the taking of the coal. The right to coal must include the right to mine it. To make it commercially impracticable to mine coal has basically the same effect as appropriating it or destroying it. Some cases have allowed a statute which required that a pillar of coal be left standing between two adjacent mines to protect against flooding. That requirement, however, provides an average reciprocity of advantage to the owners of the two properties. Here, Mahon (P) took the risk of obtaining only the surface rights to the land. The fact that the risk is likely to occur does not warrant giving Mahon (D) greater rights than he (P) paid for. Decree reversed.

■ DISSENT

(Brandeis, J.) While coal is still in place, it is still part of the land, and the right of an owner to use his land is never absolute. No landowner can use land in a way that creates a public nuisance or threatens the public welfare. A restriction that is imposed to protect the public health, safety, or morals is not a taking. Also, such restrictions do not cease to be public just because some private persons, like Mahon (P) here, receive particular benefit from them. A restriction is lawful if it is an appropriate means to the public end; here, keeping the coal in place is one of the only ways of preventing the surface from sinking, and thus is appropriate. While the majority expresses its concern over the diminution in value of one part of the land, that value should be compared to the value of the property as a whole. Further, the mere presence of notice against danger or a mere contract cannot prevail against the exercise of the police power when the public safety is threatened. While the majority argues that the public interest affected by this Act is limited, in reality the Act includes provisions dealing with mining under streets and roads, churches, hospitals, schools, railroad stations, and many other places where many members of the public gather. Such prohibitions are obviously for a public purpose. The majority states that an exercise of the police power requires an average reciprocity [mutual transfer or exchange] of advantage. Where the police power is exercised to protect the public from danger, however, there is no room for considering reciprocity of advantage.

Analysis:

Holmes's test of whether a regulation has gone "too far" seems less rigid than the other tests for permanent physical occupation and measures prohibiting nuisances. This rule basically says that when a regulation of a use of property that is not a nuisance imposes too great a burden on property owners, it cannot be enforced without compensation, through what Holmes called the average reciprocity of advantage. Persons who seem to be burdened by a government prohibition, say, against mining under certain structures, may not come away empty-handed, since these regulations are imposed for the benefit of the public, themselves included.

■ CASE VOCABULARY

ANTHRACITE: A hard natural coal which burns very cleanly; also called hard coal.

CONFLAGRATION: A very large and dangerous fire.

EXIGENCY: That which requires immediate action.

RECIPROCITY: A mutual transfer or exchange.

SUBSIDENCE: A state of falling, sinking, or collapse.

WRIT OF ERROR: A writ issued by an appellate court in order to compel the examination of errors alleged to have occurred.

Takeaway:
To know when a government regulation goes so far as to work an implicit/regulatory taking focus on the diminution in value to affected property owners. If the diminution in value to their investment-backed expectations is too great, a taking has occured for which just compensation is owed.

The diminution in value test is asking how much has been taken away from the property owners

Penn Central Transportation Co. v. City of New York

(Landmark Owner) v. (City)

438 U.S. 104, 98 S.Ct. 2646 (1978)

U. S. SUPREME COURT HOLDS THAT A NEW YORK LANDMARKS PRESERVATION LAW WHICH WAS THE BASIS FOR BARRING CONSTRUCTION OF AN OFFICE BUILDING OVER GRAND CENTRAL TERMINAL DID NOT EFFECT A TAKING BECAUSE IT DID NOT TRANSFER CONTROL OF THE PROPERTY, BUT ONLY RESTRICTED IT

■ **INSTANT FACTS** Penn Central made plans to construct an office building over Grand Central Terminal, but was blocked by a Landmarks Preservation Law.

■ **BLACK LETTER RULE** A law which does not interfere with an owner's primary expectation concerning the use of the property, and allows the owners to receive a reasonable return on his or her investment, does not effect a taking which demands just compensation.

■ **PROCEDURAL BASIS**

Appeal from judgment in action for declaratory and injunctive relief.

■ **FACTS**

In 1967, New York City's (D) Landmarks Preservation Commission (Commission) designated Grand Central Terminal a landmark under the city's (D) Landmarks Preservation Law. The Terminal, owned by Penn Central Transportation Co. (P) and its affiliates, has been described as "a magnificent example of the French beaux arts style." For at least 65 years, the property had been used as a railroad terminal with office space and concessions. The landmark law did not interfere with the Terminal's continued use in this capacity, but restricted any changes in the Terminal's exterior architectural features without the Commission's approval. In addition, landmark owners are allowed to transfer their development rights under zoning regulations to contiguous properties on the same block, or other properties they also own. At this time, Penn Central (P) owned several properties in downtown Manhattan. In 1968, in order to increase its income from the Terminal, Penn Central (P) entered into a long-term lease with UGP (P), a British corporation. UGP (P) was to build a 55-story office building above the Terminal, paying an annual rent of $1 million during construction and at least $3 million thereafter. Penn Central and UGP (P) submitted two plans to the Commission: one with a modern office tower over the French-style facade of the Terminal, and one with a completely redesigned Terminal. The Commission sternly rejected both plans, calling the first one "an aesthetic joke." It also said, however, that construction would be allowed depending on whether a proposed addition "would harmonize in scale, materials, and character" with the Terminal. Penn Central and UGP (P) brought suit in state court, alleging the landmarks law effected a taking of their (P) property. The trial court granted injunctive and declaratory relief, but the intermediate appellate court reversed. The New York Court of Appeals affirmed, finding no taking as the law only restricted, not transferred, control of the property.

■ **ISSUE**

Does the application of a law which restricts an owner's use of property, but does not interfere with the owner's primary use of the property or deny a reasonable economic return on it, constitute a taking?

■ DECISION AND RATIONALE

(Brennan, J.) No. A law which does not interfere with an owner's primary expectation concerning the use of the property, and allows the owners to receive a reasonable return on his or her investment, does not effect a taking which demands just compensation. There is no set formula for deciding these cases, and so this Court must look at the particular facts here. The extent to which the law has interfered with distinct, investment-backed expectations is particularly relevant. Penn Central and UGP (P) claim that the airspace above the Terminal is a valuable property interest that has been taken through the landmark law. This claim is rejected because the rights in the property as a whole, not those in individual estates, must be considered. Also, Penn Central and UGP (P) argue that the law effects a taking by significantly diminishing the economic value of an individual landmark site, the Terminal property, unlike other laws which impose restrictions on entire historic districts. This argument is rejected because this landmark law, like others throughout the country, is part of a comprehensive plan to preserve landmarks all over the city. The interference with Penn Central's (P) property rights is not severe enough to equal a taking. The law does not interfere with Penn Central's (P) primary expectation concerning the use of the Terminal for railroad service, office space, and concessions. Thus, Penn Central (P) is permitted to obtain a "reasonable return" on its investment in the Terminal. Moreover, Penn Central and UGP (P) have not been barred from any construction over the Terminal; only the two plans in question have been rejected. Because they (P) have not submitted plans for a smaller structure, it is not known whether they (P) will be denied permission to use any of the Terminal airspace. Finally, though Penn Central and UGP (P) claim their (P) airspace rights have been taken, they (P) have always had the right to transfer those rights to nearby properties. This situation may not be ideal for them (Ps), but those rights are still very valuable. Judgment affirmed.

■ DISSENT

(Rehnquist, J.) This landmark law is unlike typical zoning restrictions that usually provide benefits for, as well as impose burdens on, restricted properties. There is no reciprocity of advantage here. Only a few buildings are singled out with considerable burdens and no comparable benefits. Because there was no nuisance-control justification in restricting Penn Central's (P) airspace rights, the action resulted in a taking. Though the value of the transferable development rights may possibly be valuable enough to serve as just compensation, there is not enough evidence to prove this conclusively. The decision should be remanded to see if these transferable rights amount to "a full and perfect equivalent for the property taken."

Analysis:

The concept of "reasonable return on investment" is problematic. While prior to this decision, the New York Court of Appeals also relied on this idea, it noted that it was "an elusive concept, incapable of definition." The reasonableness of the return on the owner's investment must be based on the value of the property. However, the value of the property is inescapably dependent on the amount of return that is permitted or available. This circular reasoning is what makes the concept of reasonable return on investment a somewhat shaky one.

■ CASE VOCABULARY

ABROGATE: To end the effect of something through government action; to annul.

BEAUX ARTS: An artistic style which is known for its use of vivid decorative detail, historic elements, and a noticeable leaning toward grand, monumental forms in architecture.

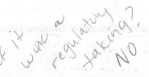

Lucas v. South Carolina Coastal Council

(Property Owner) v. *(Government Body)*

505 U.S. 1003, 112 S.Ct. 2886 (1992)

UNITED STATES SUPREME COURT HOLDS THAT THE ENFORCEMENT OF A SOUTH CAROLINA STATUTE WHICH RESTRICTED DEVELOPMENT IN COASTAL AREAS AMOUNTED TO A TAKING BECAUSE IT DEPRIVED AN OWNER OF ALL ECONOMICALLY PRODUCTIVE USE OF HIS PROPERTY

■ **INSTANT FACTS** Lucas claimed that a South Carolina statute which barred him from building on his barrier island property resulted in a taking without just compensation.

■ **BLACK LETTER RULE** A land-use regulation that deprives an owner of all economically valuable use of property by prohibiting uses that are permitted under background principles of property and nuisance law results in a taking, and thus requires compensation. ⊛

[handwritten: SHG P. 130 the categorical taking]

■ PROCEDURAL BASIS

[handwritten: If a taking, then requires compensation]

Writ of certiorari after bench trial in action for taking without just compensation.

[handwritten: nuisance law]

■ FACTS

In 1977, the South Carolina Legislature enacted a Coastal Zone Management Act, after the earlier passage of a similar law in Congress. The South Carolina Act imposed restrictions on owners of coastal zone land that qualified as a "critical area," defined in the Act to include beaches and adjacent sand dunes. Owners of such land had to obtain a permit from the newly formed South Carolina Coastal Council (D) before putting the land to a "use other than the use the critical area was devoted to on [September 28, 1977]." This Act marked the beginning of South Carolina's expressed interest in managing the development of coastal areas. In the late 1970's, Lucas and others started extensive residential development on the Isle of Palms, a barrier island [island parallel to shore which protects it from the effects of the ocean] off the coast of Charleston, South Carolina. In 1986, Lucas (P) bought two lots on this island for $975,000, planning to build single-family homes on them. These lots did not fall within the "critical area" described in the 1977 Act, and thus were unaffected by it. The land adjacent to Lucas' (P's) lots already contained similar structures. In 1988, the Legislature enacted the Beachfront Management Act. This Act directed the Council (D) to establish a 'baseline' connecting the landward-most "point[s] of erosion . . . during the past forty years" in the region of Isle of Palms where Lucas' lots were located. This 1988 Act prohibited the construction of occupiable improvements between the sea and a line drawn 20 feet landward of, and parallel to, this baseline. Lucas' (P's) land fell in this zone. Lucas (P) filed suit in the South Carolina Court of Common Appeals, contending this ban on construction effected a taking by completely extinguishing the value of his property. The trial court found that the 1988 Act "deprived Lucas of any reasonable economic use of his lots." Thus, the court concluded that Lucas' (P's) properties had been taken and ordered compensation in the amount of $1,232,387.50. The Supreme Court of South Carolina reversed, saying when a regulation on the use of property is meant to prevent serious public harm no compensation is required, regardless of its effect on the property's value.

[handwritten: U.S. supreme court says compensation is required]

■ ISSUE

Can the government enforce a land-use regulation regardless of its effects on the value of an owner's property?

■ DECISION AND RATIONALE

(Scalia, J.) No. A land-use regulation that deprives an owner of all economically valuable use of property by prohibiting uses that are permitted under background principles of property and nuisance law results in a taking, and thus requires compensation. In the past, this Court has recognized that if the regulation of property goes "too far," it will be recognized as a taking. Though "too far" has never been exactly defined, a taking has been found when a land-use regulation denies an owner the economically viable use of his or her land. Though this rule has never been formally justified, it has been accepted because such a loss, in the landowner's point of view, is the equivalent of a physical taking. Though the government has been allowed, in certain cases, to affect property values without paying compensation, this should not occur when a landowner has been deprived of all economic beneficial uses of his or her land. Here, the South Carolina Supreme Court felt the 1988 Act involved a valid exercise of the State's police powers to mitigate the harm to the public interest that Lucas' proposed development would cause. Lucas (P) essentially conceded that the State's beach areas were a valuable resource, that new construction contributed to the erosion of these areas, and that discouraging such construction was necessary to prevent a great public harm. The distinction, however, between an act which prevents public harm and one which confers a public benefit often lies in the eye of the beholder. Such a distinction is almost impossible to make objectively. Thus, this sort of harmful-use logic should not be used to separate regulatory takings which require compensation from regulatory deprivations that do not. To adopt the South Carolina Supreme Court's approach to this problem would essentially wipe out the limitation on regulation which goes "too far." Therefore, a State should only be allowed to deprive an owner of all economically beneficial use of property, without needing to pay compensation, when the interest in the regulated use was not part of the title to begin with. In other words, a property owner necessarily expects the uses of his or her property to be restricted, on occasion, by newly enacted legislation. That owner, however, should not have to expect that his or her property will be rendered economically worthless by similarly new legislation against certain uses of land. Such a limitation must inhere in the title itself, in the background principles of the State's property and nuisance law. The source of such a sweeping limitation, then, must not be the legislative designation of something as a nuisance, but rather the common-law doctrine. Judgment reversed and cause remanded.

■ CONCURRENCE

(Kennedy, J.) The majority opinion, though establishing a framework for remand, did not decide the question of whether a temporary taking had indeed occurred. Also, the determination that Lucas' (P's) property was deprived of all economic value by a mere development restriction is a "curious" one. In addition, the finding that a parcel of property is left with no value must be based under the Takings Clause on the owner's reasonable, investment-backed expectations. Though this definition of value may seem circular in some aspects, it is not entirely so. The Constitution protects expectations that are based on objective rules and customs that are generally accepted as reasonable ones. Finally, "reasonable expectations must be understood in light of the whole of our legal tradition." The common law doctrine of nuisance is too narrow to rely on when considering issues of a government's regulatory power, particularly in the context of today's complex, modern society.

■ DISSENT

(Blackmun, J.) With this decision, "the Court launches a missile to kill a mouse." First, if the state legislature is correct that the construction ban in the zone outlined in the Beachfront Management Act prevents serious harm, then the Act is constitutional. Earlier decisions have consistently upheld regulations meant to protect the common welfare. Here, Lucas (P) never challenged the legislative findings as to the importance of the construction ban, so the South Carolina Supreme Court correctly found that no taking had occurred. Second, the trial court's finding that Lucas' (P's) property had lost all its economic value is "almost certainly erroneous." This property can still be used for swimming, picnicking, and camping; Lucas also retains the right to sell this valuable land. Third, the Court has based many decisions on the idea that the State has the full power to restrict an owner's use of property if it is harmful to the public. It would be ridiculous to suggest that, under this new theory, an owner can have the right to harm the public if the right amount of economic loss can be shown. Fourth, the Court's reliance on a "background principles" standard is questionable, as well. Though the Court claims the harm versus benefit question cannot be objectively answered by a legislative decision, state courts make exactly the same kind of decision that the Court refuses to accept when made by the state legislature. There is no reason to think that modern interpretations of historic common-law doctrines will be any more objective than a legislative decision. Finally, there is no historic or common-law evidence of any kind of any limit on a State's ability to regulate a harmful use of property to the point of eliminating its economic value.

■ **DISSENT**

(Stevens, J.) This new categorical rule is an entirely arbitrary one. A court could define property very broadly so total takings would only be rarely found. Likewise, an investor could purchase the right to build an apartment building on a particular lot, and later argue that a zoning restriction against such a use would deprive the owner's interest of value. This rule cannot be justified merely by an owner's perception of the regulation; a regulation which diminishes a lot's value by even a fraction would almost always appear to the owner as a condemnation. The Court belief in the relative rareness of total takings does nothing to explain why some regulations should be categorized as takings and some should not. Also, a total taking does not necessarily mean that a property owner is being arbitrarily singled out, even though such an occurrence is possible. Furthermore, the exception for uses of property that are permissible under background principles basically freezes the State's common law. This action denies the legislature its traditional power to revise and develop law. Also, with this rule and exception, the Court neglects to consider the character of the regulatory action. This has traditionally been the most important element to consider in taking analysis, yet it is disregarded by the Court's decision.

Analysis:

The South Carolina Supreme Court decided, on remand from the Supreme Court's decision, whether the right for Lucas to build homes on his two lots inhered in his title. The Court found that no common law basis existed for ruling that such a right was not part of the inherent bundle of rights. Thus, the trial court was ordered to make findings of damages to compensate Lucas for the temporary taking. Damages were to be paid for the period beginning with the 1988 enactment of the Beachfront Management Act and ending with the date of the court's order.

■ **CASE VOCABULARY**

A FORTIORI: A term of logic which denotes that if one argument is held to be valid, another claim which is either part of that initial argument, or less improbable, or analogous to it must be a valid argument as well.

DISPOSITIVE: Persuasive; directed toward a certain point of view.

IPSE DIXIT: "He himself said it;" a positive statement that is based on an individual's authority.

SIC UTERE TUO UT ALIENUM NON LAEDAS: Common law principle that one should not use his or her property in a way that injures another.

Palazzolo v. Rhode Island

(Landowner) v. (State)

533 U.S. 606, 121 S.Ct. 2448 (2001)

THE SUPREME COURT REJECTS A BRIGHT LINE "NOTICE RULE" FOR REGULATORY TAKINGS

■ **INSTANT FACTS** Rhode Island (D) found that regulations designating most of Palazzolo's (P) land as protected "coastal wetlands" did not effect a taking partly because the regulations predated Palazzolo's (P) title to the land.

■ **BLACK LETTER RULE** The acquisition of title after the enactment of a regulation does not bar a challenge to that regulation under the Takings Clause.

■ **PROCEDURAL BASIS**

Certiorari granted after state supreme court rejected takings claim for damages.

■ **FACTS**

Palazzolo (P) owns waterfront land in Rhode Island (D). His corporation, Shore Gardens, Inc. (SGI) purchased the property in 1959. In the 1960s SGI submitted three proposals to state agencies seeking to fill the property for development, but all were denied, two citing adverse environmental impacts. In 1971 Rhode Island (D) created the Rhode Island Coastal Resources Management Council (Council) (D). The Council (D) promulgated regulations which designated salt marshes like SGI's property as protected "coastal wetlands" and greatly limited development on them. SGI lost its charter in 1978 and the property passed to Palazzolo (P) as its sole shareholder. Palazzolo (P) tried again to develop the property and submitted proposals to the Council (D) for filling the land, but the Council (D) denied them. After unsuccessfully appealing the Council's (D) last decision, Palazzolo (P) filed an inverse condemnation action claiming the Council's (D) regulations took his property without compensation. Palazzolo (P) alleged that the Council (D) deprived him of "all economically beneficial use" of his property, resulting in a total taking under *Lucas v. South Carolina Coastal Council* [regulation that deprives an owner of all economically valuable use of property results in a taking]. The Rhode Island Supreme Court ruled against Palazzolo (P) because the regulations predated his succession to legal ownership of the property, and because the regulations did not deprive him of all economic use of the land since an upland parcel still had development value. The court also held that Palazzolo (P) could not recover under *Penn Central Transportation Co. v. City of New York* [law does not effect a taking if it does not affect the owner's "reasonable investment-backed expectations"] because the regulations predated his ownership.

■ **ISSUE**

Does the acquisition of title after the enactment of a regulation bar a challenge to that regulation under the Takings Clause?

■ **DECISION AND RATIONALE**

(Kennedy, J.) No. Rhode Island's (D) position is essentially that purchasers and successive title holders are deemed to have notice of earlier-enacted restrictions and therefore cannot claim that those restrictions effect a taking. This position in effect allows a state to put an expiration date on the Takings Clause. Enactments which are so onerous or unreasonable as to effect a taking do not become less so through passage of time or title. Postenactment transfer of title does not absolve a state of its obligation to defend its actions restricting land use. Future generations too have a right to challenge unreasonable limitations on the use and value of their land, which is sometimes necessary since such challenges often take years to become ripe. Further, a rule that purchasers with notice have no compensation right would place different types of purchasers if different positions, depending, for example, on whether they wanted to hold onto their land or sell it. The Takings Clause is not so quixotic. The general rule in *Lucas* comes with an exception for limitations on land use that "inhere in the title itself" because the owner is constrained by restrictions that background principles of property law place on his land. Rhode Island (D) argues that *Lucas* stands for the proposition that a new regulation becomes one of those background principles, and those who acquire title after their enactment therefore cannot challenge them. Mere passage of title does not transform a regulation that would otherwise effect a taking into a background principle. A regulation cannot be a background principle for some owners and not for others, and it does not become a background principle for subsequent owners by enactment itself. Thus, the fact that Palazzolo (P) acquired title after the enactment of these regulations does not bar him from challenging them. However, these regulations did not deprive Palazzolo (P) of all economically beneficial use because he can still improve the uplands portion of his land. Palazzolo (P) admits that he retains some development value, but argues that the Council (D) cannot sidestep *Lucas* by leaving him "a few crumbs of value." While a state may not evade the duty to compensate by leaving an owner a token interest, this is not the case here. A regulation that permits an owner to build a substantial residence on an 18-acre parcel does not leave the property "economically idle." Even when a regulation does not eliminate all economically beneficial use, however, a taking may still occur under *Penn Central* based on factors including the regulation's economic effect on the landowner, the extent of its interference with reasonable investment-backed expectations, and the character of the government action. Since Palazzolo's (P) claim under *Penn Central* is not barred by the mere fact that he acquired title after these regulations became effective, we remand for consideration of the merits of that claim. Affirmed in part, reversed in part, and remanded.

Analysis:

In *Palazzolo* the Court explained that when the fact and extent of the taking are clear, compensation awards go only to the owner at the time of the taking and do not pass to subsequent purchasers. In regulatory takings cases, on the other hand, a landowner must wait for his claim to become ripe. This process, which may take years, may not culminate until after ownership has passed to another. Thus, the Court found that it would be illogical and unfair to bar postenactment owners from maintaining regulatory takings claims. The Court also relied on *Nollan v. California Coastal Commission*, the next case in this chapter. In *Nollan,* the dissent made the argument, similar to Rhode Island's (D) argument here, that since the Nollans purchased their home after the policy at issue went into effect, they were on notice of its restrictions. As the Court points out, the majority rejected this argument, reasoning that if the previous owners had a compensation right, they transferred it to the Nollans along with all their other property rights when they sold the property.

■ CASE VOCABULARY

QUIXOTIC: Capricious and impractical.

Tahoe-Sierra Preservation Council, Inc. v. Tahoe Regional Planning Agency

(Landowner Association) v. (Interstate Planning Board)

535 U.S. 302, 122 S.Ct. 1465 (2002)

A MORATORIUM ON DEVELOPMENT IS NOT A TAKING

■ **INSTANT FACTS** Property owners in the Lake Tahoe area were prohibited from undertaking any development of their property for thirty-two months in order to get a handle on the development needs of the area to preserve its natural beauty.

■ **BLACK LETTER RULE** A regulation that prohibits economic use of land for an extended but finite period of time does not constitute a taking requiring that the owner of the property be compensated.

■ PROCEDURAL BASIS

Certiorari to review a decision of the Ninth Circuit Court of Appeals applying *Penn Central Transportation Co. v. City of New York*, 438 U.S. 104 (1978), to determine the plaintiffs' damages.

■ FACTS

Due to a lack of adequate regional planning, the area around Lake Tahoe became overdeveloped. The clarity of the lake became threatened with algae fed by the run-off from paved areas. The Tahoe Regional Planning Agency (TRPA) (D) was established to study the problem and create goals to preserve the area. To help in the planning process, the TRPA (D) imposed a thirty-two-month moratorium on all development. An injunction was later granted that forestalled development for an additional three years. The Tahoe-Sierra Preservation Council (P) brought suit on behalf of interested property owners, alleging that the ban on development constituted an unconstitutional taking of the property. The district court agreed with the plaintiffs and held that the value of the property taken should be determined based on *Lucas v. South Carolina Coastal Council*, 505 U.S. 1003 (1992). On appeal, however, the Ninth Circuit Court of Appeals held that whether a taking occurred should be determined under *Penn Central Transportation Co. v. City of New York*, 438 U.S. 104 (1978).

■ ISSUE

Does a moratorium on all development during the process of devising a comprehensive land-use plan constitute an unconstitutional regulatory taking for which the landowners are entitled to compensation?

■ DECISION AND RATIONALE

(Stevens, J.) No. When the government physically takes possession of private property for public use, a taking has clearly occurred for which just compensation is due. Yet, a property owner can be equally deprived of his property when government regulations limit the purposes for which the property can be used. Treating all land-use regulations as Fifth Amendment takings, however, would undermine governmental objectives designed to further matters of public interest by demanding compensation to the objects of the regulations. Accordingly, the compensation due for a regulatory taking depends on the extent to which the government action deprives the landowner of the value in his property.

When the regulation amounts to a total taking of all economic value, as in *Lucas v. South Carolina Coastal Council*, just compensation is clearly required. In the absence of a total taking, however, *Penn Central* establishes the proper analysis for value taken. An estate in real property is determined by both its physical boundaries and the time dominion is extended over the parcel. A temporary restriction on use of property cannot logically render a parcel valueless. The ultimate question is whether the Takings Clause concepts of "fairness and justice" are served by hard and fast rules, or by a case-by-case inquiry as described in *Penn Central*. It cannot be stated enough that a delay in the use of property is not compensable. While a rule that allows compensation for deprivations of use for more than a year may be reasonable, this rule should be made by the legislatures. In a case where regulation only temporarily affects the development of land, the rationale set forth in *Penn Central* should be followed. Affirmed.

Analysis:

The plaintiffs in this case, unlike the property owner in *Lucas v. South Carolina Coastal Council*, had not been told they would never be permitted to build on their land again. They were asked to wait patiently while representatives from the surrounding area took the time to make a careful development plan—one that would hopefully slow development to the point that the property around Lake Tahoe would continue to be aesthetically pleasing. In that respect, the moratorium could be seen as adding value to the landowners' property.

■ CASE VOCABULARY

TAKINGS CLAUSE: The Fifth Amendment provision that prohibits the government from taking private property for public use without fairly compensating the owner.

Stop the Beach Renourishment, Inc. v. Florida Department of Environmental Protection

(Private Property Owners' Group) v. (State Agency)

560 U.S. 702 (2010)

COURTS CAN ENGAGE IN "TAKINGS" SUBJECT TO CONSTITUTIONAL LIMITATIONS

This beachfront property has been in our family for generations. Unfortunately, it won't be "beachfront" much longer.

■ **INSTANT FACTS** The state created an "erosion line" on the beach by adding dredged-up sand to the existing beach area and then claimed the land as public property, thereby decreasing the amount of beach owned by the littoral property owners.

■ **BLACK LETTER RULE** If an avulsion exposes land seaward of littoral property that had previously been submerged, that land belongs to the state even if it interrupts the littoral owner's contact with the water, and there is no exception when the state itself causes the avulsion.

■ **PROCEDURAL BASIS**

Supreme Court review of a trial court decision in the state's favor.

■ **FACTS**

Under Florida law, the state owns in trust for the public the land submerged beneath the navigable waters and the foreshore (the land between the low-tide line and the mean high-water line, which is the average reach of high tide over the preceding 19 years). Accordingly, the mean high-water line is the ordinary boundary between private beachfront property and state-owned land. The owners of beachfront properties, called the littoral owners, have special rights in addition to their public rights. These include the right to access the water, to use the water for certain purposes, and to an unobstructed view of the property, among others. Under older Florida common law, the littoral owner automatically takes title to dry land added to his property by accretion, which are additions to dry land that occur gradually and imperceptibly over time. When there is a sudden or perceptible loss of or addition to the land caused by a sudden change—called an avulsion—the property line does not change. Accordingly, when a new strip of land is added to the shore by avulsion, the littoral owner has no right to subsequent accretions to that land.

In 1961, Florida's Beach and Shore Preservation Act established procedures for beach restoration and nourishment projects, including setting an erosion control line. The fixed erosion control line replaced the common law fluctuating mean high-water line as the boundary between private and state property. Accretion does not change the property line under this law, but beachfront property owners continue to be entitled to all common law riparian rights other than the right to accretion.

In 2003, a city and county in Florida applied for permits to restore the beaches in their jurisdictions that had been eroded by hurricanes. The project envisioned depositing sand, which had been dredged from farther out in the ocean, along the shoreline to add about 75 feet of dry sand seaward of the mean high-water line. The new border would be called the erosion-control line. Stop the Beach Renourishment (P), a non-profit corporation formed by the beachfront property owners, brought legal action to stop the project. The state court concluded that the

---

doctrine of avulsion permitted the state to reclaim the restored beach on behalf of the public. The court also described the right to accretion as a future contingent interest, not a vested property right. The property owners sought rehearing on the ground that the Florida court's decision constituted a taking of their littoral rights contrary to the Fifth and Fourteenth Amendments. Rehearing in the state court was denied, but the Supreme Court granted certiorari to review the case.

■ ISSUE

Did the state court's decision constitute a "taking" of the beachfront owners' property without just compensation in violation of the Takings Clause?

■ DECISION AND RATIONALE

(Scalia, J.) No. If an avulsion exposes land seaward of littoral property that had previously been submerged, that land belongs to the state even if it interrupts the littoral owner's contact with the water, and there is no exception when the state itself causes the avulsion. Two core principles of Florida property law intersect here. First, the state, as owner of submerged land adjacent to littoral property, has the right to fill that land as long as it does not interfere with the rights of the public and the littoral landowners. Second, if an avulsion exposes land seaward of littoral property that had previously been submerged, that land belongs to the state even if it interrupts the littoral owner's contact with the water. The issue here is whether there is an exception when the state is the cause of the avulsion. State law precedent indicates that there is not. The state can fill in its own seabed, and the resulting exposure of previously submerged land is treated like an avulsion for purposes of property ownership. The right to accretions is therefore subordinate to the state's right to fill. The Florida Supreme Court's decision was in line with these principles. It did not abolish the members' right to future accretions, but merely held that the right was not implicated by the beach restoration project, because the doctrine of avulsion applied. Perhaps state-created avulsions should be treated differently insofar as the property right to accretion is concerned, but nothing in Florida precedent makes such a distinction. The Takings Clause protects property rights as they are established under state law, not as they might have been established or ought to have been established. We cannot say that the Florida Supreme Court's decision eliminated a right of accretion established under Florida law.

Justice Kennedy seems to think this is a due process case. The Due Process Clause cannot do the work of the Takings Clause. When a particular Amendment provides an explicit textual source of constitutional protection against a particular form of government behavior, that Amendment, not the more generalized notion of "substantive due process," must be the guide for analyzing claims arising thereunder. We cannot grasp the relevance of Justice Kennedy's speculation that the Framers did not envision the Takings Clause would apply to judicial action. What counts is that they envisioned what they wrote—that no private property can be taken for public use without compensating the private property owner. Justice Kennedy puts forth some vague notions of substantive due process but does not even say that they—whatever they are—will apply for sure. More importantly, Justice Kennedy places no constraints on the Court. The Takings Clause bars the state from taking private property without paying for it, no matter which branch of state government is doing the taking. Simply stated, a state may not transform private property into public property without compensation, but no taking occurred in this case. Affirmed.

■ CONCURRENCE

(Kennedy, J.) If a judicial decision, as opposed to an act of the executive or legislative branch, eliminates an established property right, the judgment can be set aside as a deprivation of property without due process of law. The Due Process Clause, in both its procedural and substantive aspects, is a central limitation on the exercise of judicial power. The Takings Clause also protects property rights. The idea that a judicial takings doctrine would constrain judges might actually have the opposite effect. It would give judges new power and provide assurance that changes in property rights are fair and proper because just compensation will be paid. But a judicial takings doctrine raises many complicated issues—issues that the Court need not reach today. It seems the better idea for the time being is to vest the takings power in the political branches subject to political control.

■ **CONCURRENCE**

(Breyer, J.) I agree that no unconstitutional taking of property occurred in this case, but the plurality unnecessarily addresses questions of constitutional law that are better left for another day.

Analysis:

The Court held that the Florida Supreme Court did not take property without just compensation in violation of the Fifth and Fourteenth Amendments. There was no taking unless the littoral property owners could show that they had rights to future exposed land and to contact with the water superior to Florida's right to fill in its submerged land. The Court's decision was based on the Florida-law principles that (1) the state, as owner of submerged land adjacent to beachfront property, has the right to fill that land; and (2) the exposure of land previously submerged belongs to the state even if it interrupts the beachfront property owners' contact with the water. Although all of the Justices agreed with the result, they did not agree with the portion of the opinion about judicial takings, *i.e.*, that if a court declares that what was once an established right of private property no longer exists, it has taken that property in violation of the Takings Clause.

■ **CASE VOCABULARY**

DUE PROCESS OF LAW: A flexible term for the fair and orderly administration of justice in the courts. Essential to the concept is the right a person has to be notified of legal proceedings against him, the opportunity to be heard and to defend himself in an orderly proceeding, and the right to have counsel represent him. Basically, due process is the fundamental fairness principle at the core of the Anglo-American system of jurisprudence. Due process also refers to the actual legal proceedings which serve to protect and enforce individual rights and liberties. The phrase is expressed in the Fifth Amendment to the U.S. Constitution: ". . . nor [shall any person] be deprived of life, liberty, or property, without due process of law," and also in the Fourteenth Amendment which applied the principle to the states.

PROCEDURAL DUE PROCESS: Constitutional guarantee that a person whose right to life, liberty or property is to be affected is entitled to reasonable notice and an opportunity to he heard and present a defense to the proposed action before a fair and impartial decision-maker.

SUBSTANTIVE DUE PROCESS: The essence of due process requires that no person be deprived of life, liberty, or property by unreasonable and arbitrary laws.

Nollan v. California Coastal Commission

(Beachhouse Builder) v. (State Commission)

483 U.S. 825, 107 S.Ct. 3141 (1987)

U. S. SUPREME COURT HOLDS THAT WHERE A DEVELOPMENT PERMIT WOULD NOT BE ISSUED UNLESS PROPERTY OWNER AGREED TO BUILD AN EASEMENT TO A PUBLIC BEACH, THE CONDITION CONSTITUTED A TAKING BECAUSE THERE WAS NO NEXUS BETWEEN THE CONDITION AND THE PURPOSE BEHIND WITHHOLDING THE PERMIT

■ **INSTANT FACTS** The Commission granted Nollan a building permit on the condition that Nollan allow the public to pass across his property to access a public beach.

■ **BLACK LETTER RULE** If a regulatory condition is imposed on a development permit, that condition must substantially advance the same governmental purpose that refusing the permit would serve or else the action will constitute a taking and require just compensation.

■ **PROCEDURAL BASIS**

Appeal from action to invalidate condition on development permit.

■ **FACTS**

The Nollans (P) own a beachfront lot located between two public beach areas. Faria County Park is located a quarter-mile north of the Nollans' (P) lot, while "the Cove" is located 1,800 feet south of it. An eight-foot high concrete seawall separates the Nollans' (P) beach portion of their property from the rest of the lot. The historic mean high tide line forms the lot's other boundary. The Nollans (P) originally leased the lot for several years with an option to buy, and this option was conditioned on their (P) promise to demolish the pre-existing bungalow and replace it. To do this, the Nollans (P) were required under California law to obtain a coastal development permit from the California Coastal Commission (D). On February 25, 1982, they (P) submitted a permit application to the Commission (D). The Nollans (P) proposed to replace the bungalow with a three-bedroom house like others in the neighborhood. The Commission staff (D) informed the Nollans (P) that it (D) had recommended that the permit be granted, but subject to the condition that they (P) allow the public an easement across the beach portion of their (P) property. This was to allow the public easier access to Faria County Park and the Cove. The Nollans (P) opposed this condition but the Commission (D) nonetheless granted the permit as recommended. In June 1982, the Nollans (P) went to the Ventura County Superior Court to invalidate the condition, claiming that it could not be imposed without evidence that their (P) development would affect public access to the beach. The court then remanded to the Commission (D), which subsequently reaffirmed the condition. The Nollans (P) petitioned the Superior Court again and claimed the condition effected a taking. The Court ruled in their (P) favor on other grounds, and the Commission appealed (D). The Court of Appeal reversed, saying the imposition of the condition was not a taking. The Nollans (P) appealed.

■ **ISSUE**

Can the State's requiring of an easement on an owner's property as a condition for issuing a development permit serve as the equivalent of a taking?

■ **DECISION AND RATIONALE**

(Scalia, J.) Yes. If the State imposes a condition on a development permit, that condition must substantially advance the same governmental purpose that refusing the permit would serve, or else the action will constitute a taking and require just compensation. The Commission (D) claims that the Nollans' (P) new house would interfere with the public's "visual access" to the beach, and thus create a "psychological barrier" to access. These burdens would supposedly be alleviated by requiring the Nollans (P) provide "lateral access" across their segment of the beach. Despite the Commission's (D) argument, it is impossible to understand how forcing the Nollans (P) to create an easement for people that are already on the public beaches reduces any visual obstacles that the new house creates in seeing the beach. In addition, it is impossible to understand how this requirement lowers any "psychological barrier" to using the public beaches. The use of the permit condition, thus, does not fulfill any of the stated "access" purposes. Justice Brennan argues that the easement should be granted because a person on the road would not be able to tell that a public beach is in the area unless the person can see people walking on the beach. This idea favoring the Commission's various access arguments is countered by the fact that a wall of houses would have completely blocked the view of the beach from the road, so no one there would see the beach at all. Property rights should only be abridged through the police power when such action results in a "substantial advanc[ing] of a legitimate state interest." This substantial requirement is needed due to the risk that the actual purpose of the use of police power may be to avoid compensation. Though the Commission (D) argues that the easement is part of a "comprehensive program" of public access to the beaches, if it (D) wishes to advance this purpose, it should use its power of eminent domain and pay for such an easement. Judgment reversed.

■ **DISSENT**

(Brennan, Blackmun, Stevens, JJ.) The majority has merely imposed a discredited standard in determining the validity of a state's exercise of police power. Despite this unwarranted, tight standard, the permit condition imposed against the Nollans (P) directly addressed the concerns over the burden on access that the Nollans' (P) new house would have caused.

Analysis:

The imposition of the lateral easement may seem like a valid means of achieving the average reciprocity of advantage Holmes' mentioned in *Mahon*. This may be particularly true for those who accept Justice Brennan's arguments that the condition answered the Commission's concerns over all the different types of access. Although granting the permit with the easement condition would appear to fulfill the public's need for access and the Nollans' desire to build, it would also impose a burden solely on the Nollans. If the public were given free access to a walkway across the Nollans' personal beach, it is likely that trash and debris would end up in the Nollans' backyard. There would also likely be a problem with crowd noise, particularly during the summer months and holidays when young people are out of school and families go to the beach. Furthermore, the likelihood of such inconveniences may force the Nollans, if they choose to sell their property, to accept a lower purchase price.

■ **CASE VOCABULARY**

NEXUS: A link or connection.

Dolan v. City of Tigard

(Business Owner) v. *(Municipality)*

512 U.S. 374, 114 S.Ct. 2309 (1994)

SUPREME COURT ADOPTS "ROUGHLY PROPORTIONAL" TEST FOR DETERMINING THE CONSTITUTIONALITY OF RULES REQUIRING DEVELOPERS TO DONATE LAND AS A CONDITION FOR OBTAINING A BUILDING PERMIT

■ **INSTANT FACTS** In exchange for the approval of a building permit, a city attempted to force a business owner to dedicate a portion of her property to the city for floodplain and recreational easements.

■ **BLACK LETTER RULE** Exactions are constitutional provided the benefits achieved are reasonably related and roughly proportional, both in nature and extent, to the impact of the proposed development.

■ **PROCEDURAL BASIS**

Writ of certiorari reviewing state court orders affirming decision of land use board and city planning commission permitting imposition of exactions in exchange for building permit.

■ **FACTS**

Florence Dolan (P) owned a plumbing and electric supply store in the Central Business District of the city of Tigard (D) in Oregon. Dolan (P) applied to the City (D) for a permit to redevelop the site. Dolan (P) desired to double the size of her store, build an additional structure on the property, and pave a parking lot. The City Planning Commission granted Dolan's (P) permit subject to certain conditions imposed by the City's (D) Community Development Code ("CDC"). The Commission required that Dolan (P) dedicate approximately 10% of her property for improvement of a storm drainage system and creation of a Greenway easement along Fanno Creek (which ran along a portion of Dolan's (P) property) and for a pedestrian/bicycle pathway. Dolan (P) requested variances from the CDC standards. She alleged that the Commission's exaction would cause an undue or unnecessary hardship. The Commission denied Dolan's (P) request. Dolan (P) appealed to the Land Use Board of Appeals ("LUBA") on the ground that the dedication requirements were not related to the proposed development as required by *Nollan v. California Coastal Comm'n* [an exaction is not a taking if it substantially advances the same governmental purpose that refusing the permit would serve]. LUBA concluded that there was a reasonable relationship between the proposed development and the requirement to dedicate land along the creek due to the increased amount of water runoff that the new development would create. LUBA also concluded that the pedestrian/bicycle pathway was reasonably related to the development, as the significantly larger retail sales building would attract more customers and employees who could use the pathway, thereby reducing motor vehicle traffic. The Oregon Court of Appeals and Oregon Supreme Court affirmed, rejecting Dolan's (P) contention that *Nollan* had abandoned the "reasonable relationship" test in favor of a stricter "essential nexus" test. The Court read *Nollan* to mean that an exaction is reasonably related to an impact if the exaction serves the same purpose that a denial of the permit would serve. The United States Supreme Court granted certiorari.

■ ISSUE

Must the benefits of an exaction be roughly proportional both in nature and extent to the impact of the proposed development?

■ DECISION AND RATIONALE

(Rehnquist, J.) Yes. The benefits of an exaction must be roughly proportional both in nature and extent to the impact of the proposed development. We adopt this "rough proportionality" test as a middle ground that is superior to the "reasonable relationship" test. Some states have required only very generalized conclusions as to the connection between the required dedication and the proposed development. Others have required a very exacting, specific and uniquely attributable connection. The majority of states have chosen an intermediate "reasonable relationship" test, but we find this confusing because of the similarity with the "rational basis" test under the Equal Protection Clause. Under the "rough proportionality" test, a city desiring to impose an exaction must make some sort of individualized determination that the required dedication is related both in nature and extent to the impact of the proposed development. If there is no "rough proportionality," then the conditioning of a permit on a forced dedication violates the Takings Clause of the Fifth Amendment. In the case at hand, it is difficult to see why recreational visitors trampling along Dolan's (P) floodplain easement is sufficiently related to the City's (D) legitimate interest in reducing flooding problems. Dedication of the Greenway easement to the City (D) would result in the loss of Dolan's (P) fundamental right to exclude others from her property. The City (D) has failed to make an individualized determination to support this part of its request. Likewise, with respect to the pedestrian/ bicycle pathway, the City (D) has not met its burden of demonstrating that the additional number of bicycle and vehicle trips generated by Dolan's (P) development reasonably relate to the city's requirement for a pedestrian/bicycle pathway. The City (D) merely found that the pathway could offset some traffic congestion, not that it was *likely* to do so. While the City's (D) goals of reducing flooding hazards and traffic congestion are laudable, they overly impose on Dolan's (P) constitutional rights. Reversed and remanded.

Analysis:

The Supreme Court, while purporting to establish a new "rough proportionality" test, essentially adopts the "reasonable relationship" test. In order for a city to condition a building permit on the dedication of land to the city, there must be a reasonable relationship between the dedication and the impact of the proposed development. The opinion clarifies the reasonable relationship test by requiring specific findings of fact; it thus supplements, rather than replaces, the *Nollan* rule. Some commentators argued that the *Nollan* and *Dolan* decisions would significantly limit the ability of localities to impose exactions. Others disagree, based on the practical reality that many land developers (especially those who do a lot of work in a particular city) would not risk their goodwill with city regulators by suing to challenge exactions that the regulators impose.

■ CASE VOCABULARY

EXACTION: A local government measure that requires a developer to provide goods or services or pay fees as a condition to getting project approval.

NEXUS: A close connection.

Koontz v. St. Johns River Water Management District

(Landowner) v. (Conservation District)

133 S.Ct. 2586 (2013)

LAND-USE PERMITTING DECISIONS MAY CONSTITUTE A TAKING

What happened?

Got mugged by the government. I want a takings analysis.

stus.com

■ **INSTANT FACTS** Koontz (P) applied for a permit to develop a small part of a parcel he owned that was classified as wetlands, but the Water Management District conditioned the permit on either reducing the size of the development to one acre or paying for improvements to other public lands; Koontz (P) argued that the district's actions constituted a taking.

■ **BLACK LETTER RULE** The government may not deny a benefit to a person because he exercises a constitutional right.

■ **PROCEDURAL BASIS**

Supreme Court review of a state court decision in the district's (D) favor.

■ **FACTS**

Koontz (P) purchased a 14.9-acre tract of land in Florida in 1972 that was largely classified as wetlands. In 1994, he decided to develop the northern section of his property and applied for the necessary permits. Koontz (P) wanted to build on 3.7 acres, and to offset the environmental effects of his proposal he offered to foreclose any possible future development of the other eleven acres by deeding to the conservation district (D) an easement on that part of his property. The district (D) considered the easement to be inadequate and informed Koontz (P) that it would approve his construction only if he reduced the size of his development to one acre and deeded to the district (D) a conservation easement on the remaining 13.9 acres. Alternatively, Koontz (P) could build on the 3.7 acres as he proposed if he also agreed to hire contractors to make improvements to district-owned land several miles away. Koontz (P) thought the demands for mitigation were excessive in light of the minimal environmental effects of his proposal, so he filed suit in state court. The trial court sided with Koontz (P). The Florida Supreme Court reversed, however, finding that its earlier decisions in *Nollan* and *Dolan* were distinguishable and therefore not controlling. The court held that unlike in those cases, the district (D) did not approve Koontz's (P) application on the condition that he accede to its demands; rather, the district (D) denied his application because he refused to make concessions. The United States Supreme Court granted certiorari.

■ **ISSUE**

Could the conservation district (D) properly deny Koontz's (P) permit based on his refusal to concede to its demands for a larger easement or to pay for improvements on other properties?

■ **DECISION AND RATIONALE**

(Alito, J.) No. The government may not deny a benefit to a person because he exercises a constitutional right. *Nollan* and *Dolan* involve a special application of this doctrine that protects the Fifth Amendment right to just compensation for property the government takes when owners apply for land-use permits. Permit applicants are especially vulnerable to coercion in cases where the government exercises its broad discretion to deny a permit. By conditioning a building

---

permit on the owner's deeding over a public right of way, for example, the government can pressure an owner into voluntarily giving up property for which the Fifth Amendment would otherwise require just compensation. On the other hand, insisting that landowners internalize the negative externalities of their conduct is a hallmark of responsible land-use policy. The *Nollan* and *Dolan* decisions accommodate both realities. They require that there be a nexus and "rough proportionality" between the property the government demands and the social costs of the applicant's proposal. The principles in those cases do not change depending on whether the government approves a permit on the condition that the applicant turn over property or denies a permit because the applicant refuses to do so.

We agree that if the permit applicant is offered one alternative that meets the requirements of *Nollan* and *Dolan* there has been no unconstitutional condition, but this is not an open and shut case. The offer to allow the applicant in this case to build on one acre when he sought to build on 3.7 acres implicates the need to determine whether *Nollan* and *Dolan* have been satisfied. The alternative proposal that the applicant expend money to improve other public lands does not eliminate the need for this analysis. Both scenarios implicate the concern that the government will use its substantial power in land-use permitting to pursue governmental ends that lack an essential nexus and rough proportionality to the effects of the proposed new use of the specific property at issue, thereby diminishing without justification the value of the property. We hold that the government's demand for property from a land use permit applicant must satisfy the requirements of *Nollan* and *Dolan* even when the government denies the permit, and even when its demand is for money. Reversed and remanded.

■ **DISSENT**

(Kagan, J.) The Court gets the first question right—*Nollan-Dolan* applies whether a permit is granted based on the owner's conveyance of a property interest or denied based on the owner's refusal to meet the condition. But the second question—whether *Nollan-Dolan* applies when the government conditions a permit on the payment or expenditure of money—causes concern. The *Nollan-Dolan* analysis applies only when the property the government demands during the permitting process is the kind that would be subject to a taking. That is, *Nollan* and *Dolan* apply only when the government makes a demand that a landowner turn over property in exchange for a permit. A requirement that a person expend money to repair public wetlands is not a taking.

Analysis:

The district (D) and the dissent argued that if monetary extractions were made subject to *Nollan* and *Dolan*, there would be no principled way to distinguish impermissible land-use extractions from property taxes. This could be important, because taxes and user fees are not takings. But, the majority notes, precedent has established that takings can occur when the government, by confiscating financial obligations, achieves a result that could have been obtained by imposing a tax. The majority opined that the need to distinguish taxes from takings may be more difficult in theory than it is in practice, and that in any event, the possibility of such a challenge did not alter the result in this case.

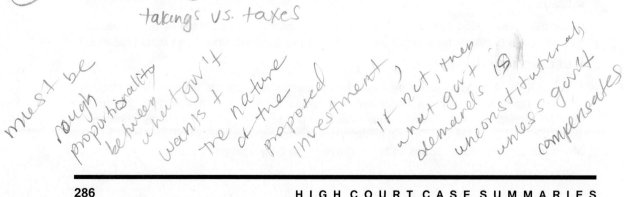